HEAD IN THE CLOUDS

The Best Stories From 50 Years of Free Flying

Edited by Andrew Craig and Hugh Miller

In the core, since 1988

Founded in 1988, Cross Country is a pilot-owned publishing company, serving pilots worldwide with an international free-flying magazine and specialist books.

First published in 2023 by
Cross Country International
Tollgate, Beddingham
Lewes
BN8 6JZ, UK
xcmag.com/publishing

Photographs and text are copyright Cross Country International Ltd. All rights reserved. No part of this book may be reproduced in any form or by any means without permission in writing from the publisher.

This book is sold subject to the condition that it shall not, by way of trade or otherwise, be lent, resold, hired out, or otherwise circulated without the publisher's prior consent in any form of binding or cover other than that in which it is published and without a similar condition, including this condition, being imposed on the subsequent purchaser.

A CIP catalogue record for this book is available from the British Library

Editors: Andrew Craig and Hugh Miller
Designer: Marcus King
Production: Marcus King, Charlie King and Ed Ewing
Proofing: Ed Ewing and Charlie King
Cover photo: Jérôme Maupoint
ISBN: 978-1-7393434-2-2

Typeset in Adobe Caslon Pro
Printed on Forest Stewardship Council (FSC®) certified paper and bound by Clays Ltd, Bungay, Suffolk

DEDICATION

For John Silvester

Contents

Introduction	11

1973: A leap of faith — 13
By Kaz de Lisse
A gripped Californian stands high on a slope, ready to take his first flight

Across India — 15
By Bob Drury
Bob Drury and John Silvester pioneer a 500km vol-bivouac route across the Himalaya in 1997

Dreamcatcher — 29
By Jim Mallinson
Jim Mallinson describes the elation of crossing five miles of sea to land in his own backyard

The Croatian survivor — 33
By Davor Jardas
Getting sucked into a towering thunder cloud is every pilot's worst nightmare

A hard day at the office — 43
By Haydon Gray
Life behind that selfie-stick grin, from an Interlaken tandem pilot

The longest day — 49
By Guy Delage
From Cape Verde to Brazil – the first transatlantic flight by weightshift microlight in 1991

Big Southern Butte   55
By John Dunham
In July 1974, using thermals to climb and travel was still just a fantasy for hang glider pilots

Between heaven & hell   61
By Felix Wölk
If you try and fly a 4,000m volcano in Central America, you'll likely get more than you bargained for

Wake up   65
By Hugh Miller
Hugh Miller describes rediscovering the raw adventure of paragliding's hike-and-fly roots

Ninth life   71
By Bob Drury
One sunny afternoon, Bob Drury finds himself locked out in a high-G spiral, unable to locate his reserve handle…

Blue sky blues   77
By Amy Anderson
There's one thing worse than bombing out on an epic day. Driving retrieve for someone else

Into the vortex   81
By James 'Kiwi' Johnston
Kiwi Johnston describes the ridiculousness of Quixadá. "You launch at 6:30am?" "Yes, because of the wind…"

On paragliding and certainty   103
By Allen Weynberg
Paragliding doesn't care about you and your disappointments. It's merciless

CONTENTS

Breaking three hundred miles   107
By Larry Tudor
Larry Tudor smashes the world record out of Hobbs, New Mexico – a feat he repeated several times in the 1980s and 1990s

The King's Trail   113
By Lenka Zďánská
Far north of the Arctic Circle, a land briefly wakes from its winter sleep

The ballad of Robb and Joe   119
By Matt George
As a boy, Matt George witnessed hang gliding's birth. As an adult, he finally embraced its freedom for himself

Stewart's story   125
By Hugh Miller
The story of Stewart Midwinter, one of Canada's best pilots, whose career was cut short by a life-changing injury

Dosti   135
By Jim Mallinson
Sometimes a seemingly disastrous mistake can turn into an unforgettable experience

Je suis un test pilote   149
By Andrew Court
On holiday in the 1990s, Andrew Court didn't expect test-passenger duties to figure in the itinerary

Chasing the dragon   153
By Craig Morgan
Tales from Brazil's arid Sertão region – a thermic nirvana with epic skies whipped by wicked winds

Dust devil
By Rick Brezina
Rick Brezina describes what it's like to be plucked from launch by a strong dust devil

161

Out of practice
By Matthew Whittall
There's often joy to be had in being rusty, out of practice — and even a little scared

167

Girl gone wild
By Kinga Masztalerz
Kinga Mastalerz finds new inner strength to complete her solo vol-biv trip in New Zealand

173

Kilimanjaro, 1978
By Ashley Doubtfire
The story of climbing Africa's highest mountain, and flying from its summit

181

Celebrate being alive
By Haydon Gray
The trauma of losing a friend brought this writer's reasons for flying into sharp focus

185

Goal fever
By Allen Weynberg
Who hasn't been seduced by the electronic sounds of success coming from our instruments?

189

In deep
By Guy Anderson
Guy Anderson's story of being lost and found has parallels to the mountaineering classic, Touching The Void

193

CONTENTS

The way of the Samurai — 205
By Bill Belcourt
Sooner or later, the risks involved in flying force us to make a choice: accept, or deny

One hundred miles — 209
By Chris Gibisch
Chris Gibisch describes how a wonderful community of competition pilots helped land him his personal best in Texas

Who's packing? — 217
By Christina Ammon
In Nepal, Christina Ammon digs deeper into the local flying economy, and starts to question her own perceptions

Storm over the Mediterranean — 223
By Andi Seibenhofer
An attempt at the world's longest paramotor flight becomes a life-threatening battle with hypoxia and hail

Lifting the veil — 229
By Nick Greece
During a thaw in US-Iran relations, pilots discover that paragliding trumps politics – every time

This is not a drill — 239
By Jorge Atramiz
When Jorge Atraniz hears the incoming missile sirens, he decides to check the weather forecast

The Monarca expedition — 243
By Ben Jordan
A five-month vol-bivouac across the USA, inspired by the migration of the monarch butterfly

Karakoram express   255
By Damien Lacaze
For Damien Lacaze, bivouac flying is paragliding in its most pure and committing form

Tumble in the Owens   263
By Bruce Goldsmith
Bruce Goldsmith describes the hang-gliding incident in Owens Valley that cemented his decision to take up paragliding

The Naked Mountain   269
By John Silvester
Paragliders make the impossible possible. John Silvester relives his dream day trip around Nanga Parbat

Finding Kiwi   273
By Andy Pag
The haunting story of the search for James 'Kiwi' Johnston in 'Nevadastan'

The greatest day   283
By Ed Ewing
Jonny Durand and Dustin Martin race wingtip to wingtip for 11 hours over Texas, in 2012

Harvest   295
By Hugh Miller
Two days of XC flying in an epic English season

The LA-X   303
By Logan Walters
Three adventurers head out for a vol-biv adventure around the Los Angeles Basin

Glossary   313

Introduction

It was a difficult summer for both of us, for different reasons. So the one day when we both found ourselves free, and finally circling up in a warm bubble of air under the only cloud in the sky, served as a stronger-than-usual reminder of what free flying gives us. The sense of freedom isn't palpable – it's actual. Earthly worries disappear 5,000ft beneath your toes, and open horizons stretch out in every direction.

The idea for Head in the Clouds came from this moment. After landing, we chatted about our different book ideas, and agreed to work together to gather the most beautifully told tales of the past fifty years of free flying, as told by the dreamers and the doers.

Many of the stories come from the pages of Cross Country magazine. Published since 1988, Cross Country has sought out tales of adventure from across the world, and aims to keep pilots' spirits up during the many down days. The book includes stories from some of the earliest gazettes of the 1970s.

We hope this collection will help you to understand the joy – and occasionally the fear – that it brings us. Most of us spend almost our whole lives on the ground, with the clouds far above us. Free flying offers the chance to reverse that normal order of things, so that for a few hours, we're up there among the clouds, with the ground spread out far below. This gives us the possibility of moments of delight, satisfaction and astonishment.

INTRODUCTION

We join buzzards, gulls and vultures in the play and joy that they've experienced for millions of years. We fly over landscapes that we'd never otherwise see from above, and we land in places that we'd never otherwise visit. The return journey from an unexpected landing field, and the people we meet on that journey, can themselves be part of the adventure.

It's not all joy, of course. As in any adventure sport, things can and do go wrong, and some of these stories don't shy away from the dark side of free flight. Many pilots who've been in the game for years have lost friends or have hurt themselves. But perhaps Head in the Clouds will help to explain why we do it, and why we love it.

Editing the book has kept our spirits up over a too-long winter. We hope it inspires you to enjoy a life full of play and adventure, whether you're in the privileged position to be able to fly, or not.

Hugh Miller and Andrew Craig

1973: A leap of faith

Kaz de Lisse

It was frightening, lifting up the kite and feeling the wind fill the sail. Trying to keep the kite into the wind on an even keel. People staring anxiously at me, waiting for me to take off. Nervously glancing over the edge of the slope. The people down on the beach look like ants.

My brain is saying: *should I do this crazy thing?* Glancing side to side to see if my wings are horizontal. Trying to think of some excuse to delay the flight… saying to myself: *what in the hell am I doing? I must be nuts. Why? Why?*

My heart is pounding, I can feel my blood racing through my veins. Trying to keep steady, I suck in my stomach, take a deep breath, it's now or never… Ready, set, go! Run, run! I feel the wind lift the kite, and my feet are off the ground.

Wow! Fantastic! I'm flying through the air! My heart beating even faster. I can't believe it!

Everything is happening so fast, the wind rushing into my face, my body tense, my mind straining. The sickly, scary feeling in the pit of my stomach. The ground is rushing up to me.

Push, push, not too much. Steady now, I tell myself.

The nose of the kite shoots up in the air, and I feel my feet touch the ground.

Wow! I had made my first hang gliding flight. It was one of the greatest thrills of my life (one of the others being when I landed on the island of Iwo Jima with the Fourth Marine Division in World War II).

I can remember as a little boy how I would climb up on the garage roof and jump off with an umbrella. There were many nights that I dreamt I was flying in the air. Now, here was the real thing! I was suspended in the air by nothing but a piece of cloth and a few pieces of aluminium and cable. I will always remember that first flight. Everything was happening so fast that I didn't have time to remember what I was instructed to do. The only way that I can describe it is that it was like an accident happening. I guess everyone will always remember their first flight.

I have been involved in this sport for only about a year now, and I just can't believe how rapidly it has grown. Would you believe that in a little less than two years we have over 3,600 members in the Southern California Hang Glider Association? One of the rewards of the hang glider movement to me was all of the new friends that I have made and all the good times I have had. I guess we all owe it to Dr Rogallo. Thanks, Doc!

Kaz de Lisse served in the US Marines in the Second World War, taking part in the fierce fighting on Iwo Jima in 1945. He went on to become flight director of the Southern California Hang Gliding Association, the forerunner of the US Hang Gliding Association.

Across India

Bob Drury

We planned, we dreamt, we argued, we guessed, we threw things in and out of mental bags till our heads hurt. We stripped down our harnesses, shedding every unnecessary buckle and tape to keep the weight down. By the last week we had thrown out the stove, the fuel, the GPSs, our books, even most of our clothes. As we would have to carry everything, weight was our enemy, and John in particular became obsessed with weighing every little item, even down to a tea bag! I chose not to weigh anything. If every item I took was considered essential, its weight was irrelevant. By the start of April we had two ridiculously huge bags packed with equipment; our final chosen items were almost identical. With 28kg each in special adapted glider bags, we set off for the adventure of our lives through the Indian Himalayas.

The night before you leave for a big trip, the air is always tense. My wife Claire was seven months pregnant and due to give birth three weeks after we returned. She knew the score; how remote and serious the situation could become should something go wrong. She knew the rules we would be playing by: if one of us went down, the other must follow. If that meant stalling into the jungle to help your partner who was bleeding to death, so be it. There are always the unspoken fears, the feeling of: is this the last time we ever see each other? We would be away for such a long time without any contact; this would be a harder trip for those at home than for us. I lay in bed that night with my arms around her, holding my child to be, hoping and praying I'd make it through the next two months and return to meet it. Tears of fear and anticipation rolled down our faces. Words were pointless. At 3 am I kissed her goodbye and slid out from the warm bed into the clothes I was going to wear for the next seven weeks. The dogs came to me to say goodbye. They knew, too. They'd seen the size of my bag and sensed the atmosphere. I stepped out into the crisp spring night of Snowdonia, quietly closing the door on one world to begin the long journey into another.

A faltering start

The next day brought a frontal system and cold rain, so we spent the day searching high and low for a better take-off spot. By the evening we had three: a possible low one from a military camp below McLeod Ganj, and two more brilliant-looking ones high above the village. It was here that the French pilots must have launched from: they were high, south-facing and really steep. The only drawback was the hour's slog up to reach them. Dozing off that night, we were still arguing the pros and cons of each, and by morning we had still reached no agreement.

Bionic John, with his broken and rebuilt ankles, didn't want to walk up high with our heavy bags and was adamant that we should go down to the military camp. I, on the other hand, was scared of blowing another day just for the sake of an hour's walk. Believing we would be doing quite a bit more walking this trip, I was keen to get on with it. Eventually John conceded and off we toiled in the hot sun.

An hour of sweating and panting later we were sat on a grassy knoll, our gliders laid out, waiting for the first thermic breezes of the day to blow up the hillside in front. We sat in silence, waiting and watching the clouds grow. Three Tibetan monks shuffled out of a stone building to sit and wait with us. Their gentle smiling nature calmed me further. Today was right, today was going to work, today the big adventure will begin.

At midday, three huge griffon vultures came trucking past us in the first strong thermal of the day. Five minutes later the next thermal came through, thrashing the bushes wildly in front of take-off. This time I was in it too. I tried desperately to keep the glider in the rising column of air but to no avail, the air rushed by me and then it was gone. I started fighting to stay up, flying backwards and forwards across the face looking for any little bubble of rising air to keep me aloft. Nothing. Down I sank. Halfway down the hill and I was screaming with frustration, I had to do something fast as there was nowhere to land below. Leaving the psychological safety of the steep slope, I glided out across the valley to a little pimple of a hill about a kilometre in front. The last chance, this has to work or I'm down. If one of you is down, you're both down and the day is over. Never leave your partner, that was the rule of the trip. I thought of John sat on the hill willing me not to ruin his day too, the pressure was immense. Suddenly, just as I had hoped it would, the little pimple worked releasing a beautiful thermal for me, blasting me skywards with three black kites and an eagle. I stood the glider on one wing tip and circled tightly till I was high at last and knew for sure that our mission had really begun.

The day was slow and patience was in order. Cloudbase was only at 2,500m, not the 4,000m we had hoped for, and the thermals rose slowly due to the dampness in the air, but we didn't care. We flew east along the ridge, the flat plains to our right and the first ridge of the Himalaya to our left. Jumping from spur to spur, we crossed massive valleys and ravines that led up to snow-clad peaks. Huge birds of prey joined us in each thermal and together we would circle our way back up to cloudbase, they didn't seem remotely interested in my blue glider but John's pink one had them all going.

The first I noticed was a fully grown Himalayan griffon vulture dropping from above and behind in full attack mode, straight for the top of John's wing. His talons were down and he was screaming his war cry; John had seen him and was screaming back. All I could do was settle in to watch the fight. Down came the huge bird to within inches of the sail, but just as it was about to make contact with the cloth, it hit the air flowing over the wing and seemed to bounce. As it got no reaction from the lifeless piece of nylon, it retracted its claws and settled in to surf the leading edge of the glider. I hollered with joy and shot off a couple of photos of John and his new mate. We'd passed their test, they'd accepted us. Phew!

By 4.30pm we had reached Billing, one of the few documented flying sites in India, but as expected it was deserted, just a solitary meadow like so many others; only the road to it distinguished it from anywhere else. 10km beyond it there was another clear meadow so we pressed on to recce it. It looked perfect, but the clouds were still sucking, and every time I lost height and glided in over our designated landing fields, I got blasted straight back up again by the thermic currents. It took a concerted effort to bring the glider in through the trees to make a dirt-raising skid across a terrace and land in a heap in front of a gaggle of giggling children. John crashed in seconds behind me. We unclipped, ripped off our helmets and danced for joy.

We'd done it, we'd started the big adventure and we were euphoric! It looked like the plan might just work. I started talking to the kids in Hindi and this blew them away even further. They obviously hadn't planned their day this way, but we had. After a quick chat the kids told us that there was some kind of government building just above us. Maybe we could stay there, they suggested?

The buildings above turned out to be a winch station built at the turn of the century by an English engineer to transport materials over the Pir Panjal mountain range for the first hydroelectric power station in India. Nowadays, despite road access to the power station, it's still often quicker and easier to transport things over the range by winch, and hence the station is still manned twelve months of the year by Mr Steech Kumar and his 'old man'. They were ecstatic at the thought of entertaining two 'Britishers'. Wine was brought out and food readied. We were shown to a room we could use for the night and taught which wires to pull out of the tangle of dodgy electrics to turn the lights on and off. At 8 o'clock food was served, and with it began the complicated process of Indian mealtime etiquette.

We sat cross-legged on Hessian sacks on the grubby kitchen floor, hungry, tired and confused as to how to deal with this next test of Indian culture. A small bowl of the most beautiful smelling dal was placed with great ceremony in front of us both. Our hosts had no food themselves yet, instead they sat down next to us to watch us eat. Was this some strange test of appreciation? Should we wait for our hosts to also fill their bowls?

Should we wolf down this wonderful food like the hungry men we were? Or were they in fact waiting for us to show our appreciation with some satisfied grunts before serving themselves? Hunger is a great motivator, and we opted for scoffing the dal with gusto whilst grunting appreciatively between mouthfuls. Our hosts loved this and studied us intently as we devoured their food, but still they wouldn't serve themselves. We finished our little bowls and everybody sat there smiling at each other. Should we ask for more? Should we ask for chapatis too? Should we wait for them to offer more? We sat there for a full ten minutes whilst the food cooled further, each party confused and trying to out-polite the other. Eventually our hosts relented and confessed.

"We would like you to feel at home, we want it to be like it is in England for you."

Ah, the penny dropped.

"Then please eat with us." I replied. "In England we would all eat together."

"All together?" The mere thought of it shocked them. How could it be possible to eat in front of guests, English guests at that? I insisted again and Steech Kumar reluctantly poured himself a bowl of dal. The old man, however, couldn't stomach this at all. He kept muttering and shaking his head as if still trying to come to terms with the idea. I could tell that John and I obviously didn't fit in with his childhood memories of the English Raj.

Epic flying, and long spells of bad weather

We were stuck in Rampur for three days as it stormed every day. We flew each day but were forced out of the sky not long after taking off by the growing storms, and each day we returned to our room at the Committee Rest House. Our celebrity status had grown as the news went round about the two English pilots, one of whom could speak Hindi. Wherever we went people called out our names and asked us our 'programme' for the day. It was hard to turn down the constant offers of tea and food from seemingly every shop and home we passed. By the third day we were tired of fame and my Hindi vocabulary was exhausted. We had to get away. We commissioned a taxi to the village of Dansa, high above Rampur on a huge south-facing slope where, from the air, we had seen a take-off near a road.

On hearing our destination, what seemed to be most of the town tried to cram itself into our little taxi. People clambered all over the car, trying to secure a place for the big show, and we literally had to drag them off before we could leave. It took an hour and a half to bump up the dirt road to Dansa, but once there we quickly found a sloping slab of rock which, with a little help, we could launch from.

The take-off was scary. The slab of rock was too steep to lay gliders on without people holding them up to prevent them sliding down over us. Below us the ground dropped away for five metres to the road and beyond that the power lines, but by getting the local villagers to hold our gliders up, we both managed to throw ourselves off the rock and get airborne again without injury.

Although the sky to our north was already littered with storm clouds the thermals were weak and scrappy and it took us nearly an hour and a half of patient flying to cross the first valley and climb up to cloudbase at 4,000m. From there we could finally see how dangerous the sky looked. Huge storm clouds rumbled over the big hills and we could see sheets of rain falling only 5km away. Directly above us the huge anvil tops of the storm clouds had hit the inversion and spread out like aprons, cutting off the sunshine from the ground. At least it might slow down the cloud development, we decided. We pushed on flying the smaller cumulus clouds that had formed under the storm clouds' aprons. It was 120km to Uttarkashi, the next large town. Tired of fame and people for a while, we decided to fly as far as we could and bivvy out the night on a hillside. It was a wild flight next to an awesome backdrop of monster clouds and Himalayan peaks. Bursts of rain and hail fell in every valley, and the occasional ray of sunshine painted rainbows across them.

By 5.30pm we had reached an impasse in the form of the Tons river valley. It was wide and heavily forested, and beyond it the jungle seemed to be thicker than before. Pushing on so late in the day seemed crazy, when below us was a potential landable clearing on the top of a spineback ridge. It appeared to have been cultivated to some degree, but there were only a few straw huts close by to indicate it might be inhabited. Provided we could land there, it would do for the night. The clearing was small and surrounded by old burnt pine trees, like spears ready to snag and impale us.

I came hurtling in through a gap between them, arriving over the small clearing far too high, and was forced to stall my glider down or face gliding straight in to the trees on the other side. I landed in a heap in front of twelve very startled Indians. They said nothing, they just stared at me, gobsmacked. The people of Rampur had never seen a glider before but these people looked like they'd never seen a white man before. I broke the ice in Hindi whilst John performed a proper landing for them to see.

We packed up and were wondering what to do next when we spotted a cave under a big rock above us. It had obviously been used for centuries as the floor was covered in straw and some blackened rocks placed in a circle for a fire. The locals offered to let us stay in their straw huts, but it was full moon tonight so we declined and made camp for the night. We got out our two pans and cooked noodles and soup for dinner with Complan for pudding. Throughout the evening people arrived to meet the 'strange men from the sky'. Some had walked for four hours from the valley floor to meet us and take the story back to their villages. The night was beautiful with a huge full moon lighting up our cave. I woke several times to find myself bathed in moonlight then suddenly it was sunshine and time to go again.

A forced interlude

Ghuttu is a beautiful old village set deep in a lush valley with stunning views of Thaley Sager peak and a friendly rural atmosphere. It needed to be as we were stuck there for ten days! Celebrity status was once again ours, and I spent many a wet afternoon sitting in woodsmoke-filled chai shops, struggling to explain the principles of glider flight in Hindi, whilst John drew diagrams on the backs of cigarette packets for our amazed audiences. They were fascinated by us and flying, and if we ever return I wouldn't be surprised if they'd fashioned some sort of flying machine from goat skins and string! We learned from the locals that when we had first come into view, high in the sky, huge arguments had broken out in the village as to what exactly we were. The older folk were convinced we were huge colourful birds, whilst the younger people had us down as balloons or new aeroplanes.

Front after front, storm after storm; April turned to May and the winds blew from the east. After a week it began to get difficult to imagine ever leaving Ghuttu.

"You know you've been somewhere too long, when you're teaching the hotel cook to make egg and chips!" said John one morning. It was no joke: time was running out for me, as I had an appointment with Claire and our first child, and couldn't be late.

Finally on May 9th, the early morning sky didn't have quite so many cumulus clouds forming, so we ordered a donkey for a 10 o'clock start. By the time it arrived there were big clouds as usual, but the most alarming thing was the high cirrus cloud that was charging across the sky at about 300km/h. Normally we wouldn't even consider flying with a wind like that up high, but it was at 7,000m. The cumulus at 4,000m weren't going anywhere near that speed, and besides, we'd been there far too long. We decided to go for it and loaded the donkey up for the hour-and-a-half walk to take-off.

We quickly got kitted up and were in the air for midday. It was still quite early and it took us a while to soar up the hill and climb in to the better air above the valleys, but as soon as we were above the ridge tops, the thermals starting ripping up towards the clouds. My radio had stopped working, so I resigned myself to a day without communication with John.

At cloudbase we had to make the first decision. To cross the valley now at its widest point, which would mean a long glide and getting up from low on the other side; or continuing up the valley in the lee of the main westerly wind, to where the valley was much narrower. I wanted to cross straight away, but John, being higher, had already left to take the other route. With no means of communication, I had to follow him.

We glided along only a couple of hundred metres apart, sinking lower and lower back down below the ridge, and ended up stuck on a remote wooded spur. Now we were caught in the turbulent lee side of the main westerly wind and the strengthening southerly valley wind. The thermals were throwing us around like rag dolls. It was all I could do to keep the glider mostly inflated, and steering was almost impossible. John managed to hold on to a rough punchy thermal long enough to gain 400 metres and throw himself out of the turbulence on to the other side of the valley. That just left me, fighting for survival. The glider was in front, then behind, then below, sometimes out of sight as it took the full force of Himalayan lee-side thermals. Each time a thermal hit me I'd try spinning the glider round hoping to stay in the lift, but instead I'd just fall like a stone with a deflated glider towards the trees, missing them by only a couple of metres. Landing would mean crashing. There was nowhere to run to and nowhere to hide; I just had to hang on in and hope I got a ride out before I crashed.

I always think back to moments like this when people say how serene and peaceful paragliding looks. I was stuck there for twenty minutes until I finally hung on to one of the passing rockets of air long enough to jump across the valley to safety.

Once up above the top of the mountains again things calmed down. The climbs were strong but much smoother than below, and a real pleasure to fly, and with the strong westerly wind we made quick progress. There were storms about as usual, but in between them we caught glimpses of huge snow-covered Himalayan mountains towering though the clouds. That's where we wanted to be, right in the heart of the big ones, but the weather was still refusing to let us in close, so on we flew. We crossed the Alaknanda river, got low on the other side and spent an hour soaring slowly up a huge jungle face with a gaggle of vultures.

We reached ridge level again and followed it south, away from the storm, until we found a little col and the ridge dropped below us for a moment. As we passed over the col, only four metres above the forest, a gang of langur monkeys went bananas, leaping about, thrashing the trees and screaming incomprehensible threats at us. They obviously thought we were two huge hungry predators looking for dinner, but preferring vegetable curry to monkey, we glided on.

I'd got so absorbed in the beautiful views that I'd forgotten to keep an eye on John and now he was nowhere to be seen. It was a long tight valley with only one dusty jeep track halfway up one side. I knew he must have landed somewhere in it, and common sense would make him land close to the track, so I flew along above it scanning the ground for him and his bright pink glider. I got to where I'd last seen him low over the road but I still couldn't spot him.

"How can I not see 25 square metres of pink nylon from only 300m up?" I wondered. With my radio still not working I couldn't call him so I glided on until I sank down to road level and landed next to the track.

The usual quantity of happy excited people came bounding up to meet me. I packed up and started questioning them, but none had seen another glider in the valley. Luckily a jeep came bouncing around the corner, packed with locals on its way up the valley. I climbed on top and off we trundled. I started trying to formulate some kind of a plan, but with no pre-arranged rendezvous I was stuck. I just had to hope that, as I spoke Hindi, John would know it would be easier for me to find him then the other way round, and he'd sit somewhere and wait. The sky darkened and it began to rain.

We stopped at a police check and I got hassled. The cops were interested in my 'balloon' and wanted to check it out. I got nervous of them finding my radio and giving me even more hassle, so I frantically babbled out my quandary to them in Hindi. This gave them something else to do and took the heat off my glider bag. They talked to each other in their local language for a few minutes before turning to me and announcing triumphantly, "You will not have a problem sir. The other balloon is just around the corner in the next village."

I think their helping me satisfied the urge to be policemen, so they let me continue and just a kilometre further I met John coming down in another jeep.

John was just as amazed that I hadn't spotted him from the air as I was. I had passed straight over him only 300m above him. He had shouted and waved but to no avail, so he'd packed up and started walking. So how could I have possibly missed him? Easy. John's glider is pink on top but white on the underside, with 'Wings of Change' written in big letters across it. With the glider lying on its top surface the writing disrupts the white enough to camouflage it, and the pink top surface is hidden from view. To cap it all, I stupidly had been scanning the ground for the colour pink and although my eyes must have passed right over it, I never picked it out from the browns and greens of the valley floor. We made a pact to always lay them top surface up if we needed to be seen.

Frustration forgotten

Okhimath is a beautiful little hill station which looks out on to the huge 7,000-metre massif of Badrinath and Kedarnath peaks. The mountains shone brilliant white against a deep blue sky with that crystal-clear high-altitude look, that always lets you know you're in big high mountains. We knew straightaway today was going to be good, very good! We found a perfect grassy take-off ten minutes' walk from town and, for the first time, we kitted up without a crowd of curious faces watching our every move. We had learned by now that it was much less hassle for us if no one knew about the aircraft in our bags. Having arrived by bus after dark the night before, we'd enjoyed a stress-free time in Okhimath and had left town that morning like innocent trekkers.

We launched into a good wind and soared up the side of the steep valley, laughing at the crowds now frantically sprinting up the hillside below us. The first hour after take-off was hard work. It always seemed to be slow going until we got above 3,000m, but once there, it usually took a storm or a big mistake to bring us down. We kept moving deeper and deeper into the mountains, away from the security of civilisation, searching for the thermal that would carry us up to the beautiful cumulus clouds that were forming high above us. We had to soar along jungle-covered ridges for almost 15km before we finally hit a huge wide thermal and got blasted up to the waiting clouds.

From 4,000m the view was mind-blowing. The panorama to our north was a jumble of snow-covered monsters, whilst to our south the jungles of the Himalayan foothills stretched as far as the eye could see, into the hot hazy plains. Nanda Devi, to our east, stood proud at 7,817m, dominating our field of vision. Like moths to the flame we charged off towards it.

We jumped from cloud to cloud for another 15km till we reached the first big valley crossing of the day. The view was too much for us to believe;

we gabbled down the radio at each other shouting out the names of the peaks we recognised from our climbing days. We shot off photo after photo, wandering around like headless chickens under a huge dark cloud. This is what we had come here for!

It took us almost an hour to compose ourselves and decide what to do next. We had imagined we would fly to Joshimath, 20km to our north, but now it was obvious that today was not a day to waste. 100km was easily attainable, and for the first time on the trip the sky showed no signs of storming. To the south of Nanda Devi the mountains dropped down to below the snow line before rising up again, into the snow, to over 5,000m. That had to be the route for us; stunning scenery over wild terrain, but no roads for at least 80km. There were to be no mistakes today!

We set off across the valley to the big sunny bowl opposite and climbed straight out of it back up to 4,200m. We said goodbye to roads and civilisation and headed off into the wilderness together. Flying slowly and cautiously over two huge deserted river valleys, we stayed as high as we could, but inevitably we lost height and sank in to a remote wooded valley. At the top of the valley was a glacier and the huge south face of Nanda Devi. From our aerial vantage point we could see the base camp for teams attempting the mountain, and I chuckled to myself as I thought of the climbers and trekkers who must trek eight days to reach there, whilst we could just nip in and out in a matter of hours. We joined forces with two huge vultures and soared up the south-facing side of the valley, back up to the snow line. John spotted what looked to be two people stood on the top of the ridge in the snow and shouted me to follow him over.

We glided over together and discovered two human-sized monoliths of rock standing proud of the snow. They had perhaps been erected as custodians of this beautiful remote valley. Standing alone like soldiers on the top of a snow-covered ridge at over 4,000m, they testified to the magic of this inaccessible kingdom.

We crossed the valley on to its shadowy north face and arrived a long way below the top. We had to find a climb out of here, or we were in for a night out and a week's walk if the weather broke. We flew like birds, no mistakes, we were going to get out. We scratched about on a slope covered with old burnt trees, hunting madly for the elusive thermal. Senses honed, our eyes and ears took in everything; the bush that rustled below us, the piece of straw that wafted past, the birds around us, the whoosh and silence of every gust of air and the biggest indicator of all, the other glider. I don't know who found it first; what mattered was that we were both in it. Stuck together like glue, wing tip to wing tip, we banked the gliders up at a crazy angle and screwed the tiny thermal for every ounce of lift it had. It hesitantly carried us back up to ridge level, then breaking free of the mountain, it catapulted us back up to 4,700m.

From there the view was even more breath-taking than before. We could now see into the Nanda Devi Sanctuary only 10km away. The Sanctuary remained untouched and unseen by mankind until explored by Shipton and Tilman in the 1930s. In the late 70s the Indian government closed it to foreigners for ecological reasons, and has only reopened it again in the last few years. I knew few western eyes had seen inside this hidden world of vertical granite spires and ice-clad peaks, and certainly never from our privileged position. The situation was so fantastic I found it hard to concentrate on flying, and I had to force myself to turn away and continue on.

We turned east again and set off gliding downwind, covering ground easily in the buoyant late afternoon air. Below us the terrain was inhospitable, steep-sided valleys and gorges, shadowed by the sinking sun, with few landing places should we be unfortunate to get low in one. But we were high and intended to stay high! It turned in to probably the longest glide I'd ever done. We only climbed once in 40km. Instead we cruised along, eventually finding the single-track road and the little town of Kapkot. The thermals had finished for the day and the sun was sinking fast, so we spiralled down to the river bed and landed.

It was after 6 o'clock and we'd been in the air, without food or water, for more than six hours. I landed and collapsed in a heap. My legs were like jelly, so I just lay in my harness as the crowds came charging towards us. People gathered round me and the questions started, but I had nothing to say today. I was dumbstruck, with tears in my eyes. This was what I learned to paraglide for; this day, this flight and this feeling. No one could take this day from us now. We'd done what we came here for, to fly where no one had ever flown before and where few will dare to follow. John came staggering up to me, pushing his way through the mass of people circling me.

"That", he announced, "is the best day's flying I've ever had, and I don't know how I could ever better it!"

When someone like John Silvester, who has flown paragliders for more than ten years in every continent on the planet, says something like that to you, you know you've touched something very special. We started giggling like naughty kids and the moment was gone, filed away in our memories, for us to pull out and sample whenever we needed it.

A former editor of Cross Country *magazine, Bob Drury has made several pioneering expeditions in the Himalaya. He lives with his family at the foot of Mt Blanc, France.*

Dreamcatcher

Jim Mallinson

As a child, I spent my summer holidays at our family's house by the sea on the Isle of Wight, a large diamond-shaped island to the south of the British mainland. I've done many things for the first time down there, paragliding being among the more wholesome. I learned to fly on the island in 1995, and once the mania for cross-country flying had taken hold, it didn't take long for me to think of crossing the Solent, the strip of sea between the mainland and the island.

Several hang glider pilots and one or two intrepid paragliders had done it in the 80s and 90s, getting enough height over the New Forest and gliding across the Solent's narrowest part, a channel just over a kilometre wide between Hurst Castle and Yarmouth. But in 1996 new airspace around Bournemouth airport put a stop to that. One or two pilots, including my instructor Innes Powell, have managed to cross from the island to the mainland, landing under the airspace's 2,000ft floor, but a flight to the island via that route would have to stay below it for 15km, so is effectively impossible.

Now the only feasible way to do it is via the eastern part of the Solent. But it's much wider there, 5km at the narrowest point, and from my local sites getting into position over the city of Portsmouth, the starting point for the glide, would require flying a wide 75-kilometre-long arc around Southampton airport. A good northerly tailwind would be nice for the crossing, but too much wind would make it impossible to keep out of Southampton airspace.

I toyed with the idea for years, and did have a go in 2013, but when I got to the coast I was at 3,000ft (910m) and sinking. There was a growing cumulus cloud a kilometre out to sea, but good sense kicked in and I landed in a park in Portsmouth.

The forecasts for Friday 22 June looked perfect from four days out: a lightish northerly, strong thermals and not much of a sea breeze. I mentioned it, as I had done many times before, to my regular flying mucker Eddie Colfox. But on the day he had logistical trouble and, reluctant to go for it on my own, I thought I'd join the XC fiends making plans on Telegram and go somewhere with potential for a longer flight. Then I had logistical problems of my own – car trouble – and called Andrew Craig to see if I could get a lift from him. He was going to Combe Gibbet, once southern England's premier north-facing site, now somewhat neglected by the XC hardcore as it's only 80km from the coast. But it's from there that I've always thought I'd try the island flight.

When we reached the top of Combe in Andrew's camper van, there were a handful of hang glider pilots there – always a good sign – including XC maestro Nev Almond. He was planning a 180km triangle on his Atos, with his first turnpoint near my route. On take-off there were plenty of paraglider pilots too, and someone asked me my plan for the day. I didn't want to say, thinking that it was ludicrous and to announce it would make it even more unlikely. But I did, a little sheepishly, and I set a goal on my Flymaster of our family house on the eastern tip of the island. I had the house keys in my pocket.

The day was as good as they get. Nev was nearly at base as I climbed out with Xiaoting Jones. Two red kites had a stronger core downwind. They were at only 1,000ft or so, but I committed myself by joining them and was soon corkscrewing up in one of the best climbs of the day to a cloudbase that was already 4,000ft at 12 noon. The wind was a little to the east of north, so I had a lot of crosswinding to do, but there were good clouds in the right places, and it was easy if slow progress getting around Southampton airspace.

All the way I kept looking towards the island, hoping that there would still be cumulus clouds above it if I got to Portsmouth, showing that the sea breeze was yet to kick in. Near Petersfield I spotted Nev heading north having bagged his first turnpoint.

I'd done the hard work so could stop crosswinding and use even weak lift, letting the drift take me towards Portsmouth. Just before the city I got a good climb to 5,000ft. There were fewer clouds over the island than earlier, but there were still one or two forming. I noticed some wispies above the coast at Portsmouth and glided under them, but they were dissipating, leaving weak, broken lift. Hanging on to zeroes I checked the numbers. My GPS said it was 10km and a 10:1 glide to my house in Bembridge, but that route was over water all the way. I knew from years of poring over maps late at night that the beach at Ryde, the nearest part of the island, was 7km away. I was at 3,400ft. A rough mental calculation told me that was about a 7:1 glide. I could have turned slightly westwards and flown 3km along the coast to Havant, from where it was 5km to Ryde, but there hadn't been any clouds in that direction for some time, so it would probably put me in a worse position than I was now.

A tailwind of 10km/h or so and a 7:1 glide needed over 7km of water. I was flying an Ozone Zeno and reckoned I'd make it with plenty of height, and perhaps find a climb on the other side that would enable me to land by our house in Bembridge. With that aim in mind, I pointed a little to the left of the shortest route and committed myself. Any thought of numbers vanished; now I was flying by feel. And it felt good. I looked down at the container ships, ferries and cruise liners heading in and out of Southampton. I could see the whole island: our house on the eastern end, Freshwater where I learned to fly to the west and the wild coast of the southern tip.

After two or three kilometres, shaky air woke me from my reverie. My sink alarm came on and I checked my Flymaster, returning to the world of numbers: my groundspeed – OK, waterspeed – had fallen to below 30km/h. I'd dropped into the sea breeze. My easy glide wasn't feeling so easy any more. Subconsciously I turned towards the nearest bit of the coast, the beach at Ryde, and pushed out the speed bar. The tide was out and I could see the golden sands extending out a kilometre or two under very shallow water. I wondered what would happen if I had to land there.

I never consciously thought that I wouldn't make it, but I surprised myself when, after a couple of kilometres with the speed bar on and the sink alarm wailing, I sat up in my harness, let my body relax, punched my fists in the air and shouted: "I've done it!" I vainly turned towards Bembridge once again, but I arrived over land with just 600ft of altitude in a steady 10km/h headwind of smooth, lift-free sea air. After a quick S-turn, I landed with my back to the sea in a field next to a crescent of holiday homes just the other side of the beach. A family of tourists took no notice of me as I succumbed to the mixture of elation and wistfulness that achieving a long-held aim brings about. I need a new dream.

Jim Mallinson is an academic and an expert on the history of yoga. Fluent in Hindi, he has also worked as a paragliding guide in India. He lives in Wiltshire, and captains the South in the annual North–South Cup, a light-hearted flying contest between the northern and southern halves of Britain.

The Croatian survivor

Davor Jardas

Saturday, 26 July. I had a feeling I shouldn't fly that day. My friend Matko and I woke up at six o'clock, packed in a rush, took a shower and headed for Buzet, the site for the competition. The weather didn't look good. We drove through showers, and the car thermometer gave an outside temperature of 16°C – very low for the time of year.

This was the first official Croatian paragliding competition. The crew was already there when we pulled up; Boris, Kruno, Karlo, Danko, Bozo, Radovan, Srecko, Leo, Zlatibor, Joza and Sandi. We hardly get together, so we had a cup of coffee and a natter. I was on the organisation committee. Sometime before noon we set off to Raspadalica launch.

This was my first time there. The place faces south, 560m ASL, wide enough to allow for four wings in parallel, but relatively short and steep with a railway line just 100m below. It was hot, about 27°C, and 2/8 of the sky was covered by nice cumulus. We agreed on the task and briefed the pilots. Air start was at 14.30; the first turnpoint was at Crnica church, west of the start, then the church of St Thomas to the ast, then the big crossing south to Buzet, then again to Crnica. The goal field was just north-west of Buzet. I moved a little away from the crowd to concentrate and relax, calming myself by imagining an ideal take-off and great flight conditions. If I had been alone, I surely would not have flown that day. Some intuitive alarm within myself turned on. But I was the president of the biggest and most active Croatian club, and my ego would have fallen apart if I refused to fly with no reason.

Leo was first off, then Danko. I dressed myself in shorts, a fresh T-shirt, a white cotton shirt and a thin windstopper jacket. I mounted my Aircotec Top Navigator on my left leg, and adjusted and checked the radio frequency. I also checked my reserve, just in case I might need it. I launched at 14.05 straight into a good one. After the first climb, I read my Top Navigator's wind information: WSW, 16km/h. We were flying along the ridge, with some thermals as well as wind. Although it was hot, I took my gloves from the side pocket and put them on. To the east we could see the beautiful mountain of Ucka, near which lay a big cu-nim, pouring rain. That shouldn't bother us, I thought, as it was over 20km downwind.

Ten minutes before the air start, I gained some decent altitude. Nice, constant thermals, from 0.5 to 3m/s. At 14.25, Danko, my instructor, had a radio briefing with the ground support crew, and after a short conversation the decision was made to cancel the task. The reason was overdevelopment a few kilometres north of our position, over Mt Zbevnica (1,014m). A radio message followed: the competition is cancelled, please aim towards landing. It sounded calm – no rush, no panic – so I took my time, and headed off to the south towards the sun and white puffy clouds, unconcerned about the black monster that was looming from the north. A big mistake.

Leo was about 150m SW of me and 50m above. I noticed Danko and Karlo to the W and above, maintaining big ears. Others were somewhere behind, to the N and NE. I was at 1,300m and decided on my first B-stall at 14.30. I was descending at -7m/s until I reached 1,000m. Then the B-stall deformed into a rosette, like with a frontal, tips forward. I didn't like it – it looked scary. So I released the B-stall, re-inflating and stabilising the wing, and then repeated the B-stall. After a few minutes, I looked at my vario and saw to my amazement that I was ascending at 2m/s. I looked up to see Leo get sucked into the cloud, where cloudbase had lowered to 1,300m. Before he entered, he took a picture of me. A couple of seconds later, holding the B-stall and ascending at 5m/s, I pierced the cloud's base and my world went white.

At this point I'm perfectly calm. I'm very close to the edge of the cloud and I have my Top Navigator with its GPS compass function. Aiming towards the south and getting out of the cloud shouldn't be a big deal, but I start losing valuable time, pissing about with my compass and speed bar. Navigating by the compass alone is not easy. Because of the compass's delay I find myself steering south and actually going north. I can't believe my eyes. Then the vario needle goes crazy. It's fluttering at 10m/s.

With no fear I pull a full frontal collapse for the first time in my life, as the dark fiend's grip on me tightens. But even with the whole leading edge folded, my ascent rate remains unchanged. My mind spells it out: Davor, you've entered a cumulonimbus. I'd read many accident reports before, but now can't remember a single one where the outcome was survival. It gets cold, very cold. Moisture condenses on my clothes, and then it's raining, and the water freezes over my summer clothes.

The radio is sheer panic, calling out: "Davor, where are you? Radovan, please reply." A desperate voice shouts advice: "Davor, avoid throwing your reserve at all costs!" It's ten minutes since I entered this monster and my altitude is almost 2,600m.

I am in a strange state of mind: calm, and relaxed. I don't care about the radio panic nor advice which seems irrelevant. Instead, my mind is fully occupied with a single thought: I have to warm up. I have to protect myself from the wind and rain and ice, wrap myself up in something, or else I will freeze.

I release the frontal collapse and decide to deploy my reserve so I can pull in my paraglider and wrap it around me for some shelter. As I release, the vario goes crazy, peaking at 18m/s. I tug my left A riser, the lines go slack, and I enter a spiral. I wrench at my reserve handle on my right side, lobbing it away into the dark gloom.

Then horror, pure fear: the reserve hangs limp, undeployed at the end of its lines, and my main canopy is out of control, cravatted on the left side. I'm still climbing at a horrendous speed, and so it takes ages for the reserve to deploy. Seconds later I hear a muffled crack and see it open and overtake my glider. Thank God! With a burst of adrenaline-induced energy, I haul in the main canopy arm over fist and wrap its damp nylon around my shivering bare legs.

I radio to say I am alive, at 4,500m, under reserve parachute and still going up at 10m/s. That was my last radio call. Boris told me later he was horrified with the unrelenting scream of the vario, contrasting with my voice, which was gentle.

The radio yells back: "Where is Davor. Davor, call us back!" My dear friends, I think, I cannot call you now, because I need to preserve every particle of energy, which could make the difference between life and death.

I remember an accident report about a twisted parachute during a longer descent. But looking up, my Czech-made Sky Systems 32-metre reserve is stable and tense. In a few seconds I establish a relationship of trust with it. Hailstones batter me, hitting from all directions, drumming on my helmet, harness and wing. The vario is wailing out an impossible tone, but I cannot look at it in case the numbers make me faint. I am now being thrashed in all possible directions.

Lightning flashes surround me, bursting the dull greyness to the left, right, below and above. Every few seconds a dimmed flash of light is closely followed by a thunderous explosion. How far away was that one? If hit by a bolt, I'd be fried in a second. Davor, chances that you will survive this are zero, pure zero, accept it as a fact. In my foetal position I desperately pray to God to save my life. Would there be many people at the funeral? The easiest death would be to faint from hypoxia, then fall into my reserve and fall, smashing hard into the ground. My father, who lives close by Rijeka, does he know that I am here, above him, his only son, and that these are my last moments?

Then something else crosses my mind: Davor, what kind of thoughts are these, you must not give up, you are still alive, have you done everything you can to protect yourself? A quick look at the vario tells me that I am at 6,000m! At that altitude, I will either faint due to the lack of oxygen, or freeze. I consciously start to breathe faster, to hyperventilate, in order to avoid fainting without oxygen. The air starts to get terribly cold. I'm in shorts at nearly 20,000ft, with the wind blowing fiercely. I'm freezing. No, I can't afford to feel cold! I remember my friend Kalman. He was caught in an avalanche in the Himalayas, at Pisang peak, and he survived with an open leg fracture. He had an enormous desire to live: he could not afford freezing, especially not giving up! Davor, I forbid you the luxury of feeling cold, you can't afford it now!

How high will I go? For how long? Where am I? When and where will I fall from the cloud? I calm down again. I think, right, now it is all about those tiny little things that can mean the difference between life and death. While you are still conscious and OK, what can you do for yourself? Are you well wrapped in the canopy? I free my right hand, pulling the canopy from my back, trying to wrap it around me as well, using my last molecules of energy: I feel weak. If I pass out, it is important not to suffocate. I shift my head to hang down on my chest so I should be able to breathe even if I'm unconscious. Then, it would be important that I don't freeze, so I check that the canopy is well wrapped and secured around me. I pretended I fainted for a moment, letting my hands loose, and it seemed OK. Would the paraglider canopy entangle with the spare?

The cu-nim pulls me higher, to 6,500m, at a speed of 20m/s. The cold is unbearable. The worst of it is the icy wind blowing between my back and the harness, where I'm not protected. My leg straps cut into my groin, sending stabs of pain through me, but it is nothing compared to everything else. The reserve is rotating and jerking all around me. I don't know if it's above or below me. Frankly, I don't care.

Then I start to descend, from -3 to -17m/s, until I reach 3,300m, then I lift up again, up to 5,500m, then down again. Suddenly I see something. Earth. I cannot believe my eyes. My hopes rise, maybe I'll survive. Earth, Mother Earth, it exists, it is here, I am looking at her, I am travelling towards her. A beautiful lake, forests, nature. Hail falls almost horizontally, melting, warming up and transforming into big raindrops. But the reserve is bucking and spinning out of control.

It's a whole new situation. I'm now fully focused on the next trauma: landing. I try to get rid of the main canopy wrapped around me, to release it partially so that it'll lend some resistance to slow my descent, but I am too wrapped up. The scene worsens: I am flying towards power lines and a burnt forest with sharp, naked branches pointing to all directions. Oh, no! After all I went through, would I end up finished on power lines or nailed to a spear-like branch?

Davor, don't be unthankful for the miracle that allowed you to exit the cumulonimbus without injuries! In my mind, I think about landing and PLF-ing. I'm really shifting over the ground, like I'm driving on a highway. I stretched, trying to put my legs together, preparing to roll on landing. I pass a few metres above the power lines and hit a tree with my air bag, which absorbs the smash. I stand on my feet, frozen, wet, scared, shocked, but still, alive, completely uninjured! It seems impossible! I am shaking from the cold. It's raining cats and dogs. I look at the figures on my Top Nav instrument, and see that I've travelled 21km from where I entered the cloud.

I hike out to the road, and stand in the middle, trying to stop cars with my thumb, but the cars just circle around me. Shaking, I continue to walk, thinking 'Davor, you look like a forest goblin, completely soaked, with a rucksack on your head, covered in leaves and with a bunch of nylon in your hands. Who would be crazy enough to let you in their car?'

I'm relaxed. It's not a matter of life or death anymore. Soon I come across the village of Säusönjevica. Civilisation, people! I pass the nearby graveyard, approaching a new house. There are signs of life: a kid's bike, a car, tools and stuff around. I haul my lazy body up the stairs to the first floor, ring the bell and knock on the door. A man appears. I can't stop my flood of emotion: "Please excuse me, I was flying with my paraglider and got sucked into a storm cloud, I am cold and in shock, can I call my friends from here, please help me…"

Branko Rabar welcomes me into his home. A great man. I give him the organisation's number. His wife wraps me up in a blanket to get warm. I tell them: "It's a real miracle I am here talking to you…." I take a shower and the warm water soaks away all the dirt, sweat, fear and shock. We drink tea on the balcony, where the sun is shining, the sky is crystal blue and there's no trace of the thunder cloud which I had battled with all afternoon. By 4pm, only an hour and a half since I entered the cu-nimb, a totally new day had begun.

The others

My instructor Danko went through a couple of negative spins resolved by a full-stall, after which he landed in a meadow. Karlo entered a negative near the ground, and threw his reserve at about 30m. It barely opened, but he landed uninjured as his canopy hit a power distribution pylon and ripped, taking his weight. Srecko pulled all the risers on one side, a new manoeuvre in paragliding. The wing entered a steep spiral, which he held for about 20 minutes, keeping just below cloudbase. He could not feel his arms for days later. Radovan pulled big ears, leaving only a few cells open. He still went up at 10m/s but was eventually spat out by the cumulonimbus. Seriously disorientated, he couldn't recover his glider in time and hit the ground hard, suffering serious bruising and a twisted ankle but incredibly nothing worse.

Kruno did a full stall, but when he released his glider surged and cravatted, so he threw his reserve. He was spared by the thunder cloud. But he couldn't pull in his main canopy, and he hit the ground hard, crushing his vertebrae, but with no severe consequences. Leo was given the same horrific treatment by the thunder cloud as I. He didn't throw his reserve (he was dressed in a skiing jacket), but maintained a full frontal deflation by inserting his legs in his A-risers and pulling down. He was thrashed into a forest near Ucka.

Altogether, seven candles could have burned, but all of us survived. During the evening, we settled in at the private hotel, and I invited everyone for dinner to celebrate our new life. We went to a restaurant with a symbolic name: Fortuna. After dinner I went to bed. I thanked God for saving my life and fell asleep, completely exhausted.

Davor Jardas had a break from flying while having young children. He now works as an IT security officer at the European Commission in Brussels. He also practises and shares the Vipassana system of meditation and is back flying.

North and light

Ed Ewing

One day in winter, the wind turned north and light, and I set up to topland in the small car park on top of the sea cliffs. I floated in like a butterfly and touched down. I stepped forward and launched again. In that moment I rediscovered the magic. That first note of the orchestra, the distant roll of thunder from a storm, the sunset as it flares into an ocean. I stepped down onto the earth and I took off again, like a bird. It was almost miraculous: it does exist, after all, I wasn't making this stuff up. I was happy.

Ed on recovering from a flying accident

A hard day at the office

Haydon Gray

If you've ever stood on take-off at one of the popular tandem sites such as Annecy, Interlaken or Ölüdeniz and wondered what it's like to be a tandem pilot, let me help paint the picture for you. The following three scenarios are snapshots of life as a tandem pilot – not necessarily the worst or the best, just some of my reflections.

Scenario One

It's -10°C and I'm lying face down in deep powder snow at the front of the take-off. A mousy little yelp from my Korean passenger squashed underneath me reminds me that I'm not the only one stuck here, although she must have a lot more questions going through her head than me. The risers are twisted between us, making movement difficult and the karabiners are frozen shut.

I twist and turn, flailing in the snow trying to free my passenger from our weird, kama sutra-inspired contortion of limbs. We awkwardly untangle and get to our feet while other pilots fly over our heads.

I push my passenger up towards the take-off as I pull my wing together. The leading edge fills with snow, making it even more of a struggle to carry, and I swear loudly as sweat trickles down my back under my thick winter layers. We will take off again, but this time I will start further back, I will wait for less backwind and my passenger will run faster and hopefully, we will fly.

Scenario Two

Sheltering from the rain under the old hut on take-off are pilots from three different companies. It's the last flight of the day. The take-off is a muddy, slippery, grassy mess. We've been flying all day, taking off into holes in the clouds hoping they won't close; hoping it won't rain on us in the air or on the landing; and hoping it will get better.

We watch the lake for any telltale signs of outflow gusts from the storms hanging around, but so far we're lucky. There's not much light to make good pictures, but we all work the angles, hoping that after the flight the passenger will still buy them. Eventually we take off, fly, land and pack our muddy, wet, previously new-looking gliders into our quick-pack bags. It was a short flight but better than nothing.

Scenario Three

It's a bluebird day in the Alps and the temperature is over 30°C. The paragliding bus is packed full with passengers and pilots, and I'm squished between a mountain guide and a former snowboard Olympian. The air in the bus is a zesty mix of body odour and perfume until someone opens the sliding door and sweet cool air rushes in.

We drive the last mountain curves, passing cows wearing big bells around their necks. The pilot doing the instruction talk tells the passengers a joke we've all heard a thousand times: the white cows make white chocolate and the brown cows make dark chocolate. I roll my eyes and zone out again. As we arrive at the take-off, we roll out of the bus, and in almost one fluid movement we harness the passengers and spread the wings. The warm rush of thermals up the front of take-off rustles our colourful carpets of nylon. We take some cheesy GoPro photos then count one, two, three and gently nudge our passengers to start running. After a few steps our feet leave the ground and we're flying towards the column of climbing wings.

The thermal is strong and I bank in hard, watching the ground disappear as we rush towards cloudbase. I tell my passenger to smell the air that carries the scent of the spruce forests and dairy cows below us. We watch a butterfly flutter by as we approach the limit of airspace and the cloud starts to wisp around us. I fly away from the lift and we gently float over the shimmering aqua blue lake below us and finally turn back on final glide towards Interlaken. Five minutes after landing the glider is packed again and my passenger leaves with a huge smile and a USB stick of memories. What a life!

As a young solo pilot, I looked up to tandem pilots as gods. I was envious of their wing control; their confidence with the passengers; the authority they commanded on the take-off; and their skills in demanding conditions. Now I'm one of them. I'm a tandem pilot in Interlaken, Switzerland. Skygod? No. Flying taxi driver? Closer.

Interlaken is one of the busiest tandem sites in the world. I don't know numbers from other sites, but with almost 50,000 flights last year in Interlaken, the airspace is busy, to say the least. As tandem pilots we each do a maximum of nine flights a day in summer and seven in winter. Almost all of the flights leave from the same mountain, with a couple of different take-offs facing different directions.

Our higher take-off is preferred by pilots, because we can drive directly to it and it means a longer flight for the passenger. The downside is that it isn't very steep and it's not suitable with backwind. Not that we don't do it. We do; we just don't want to be there with a heavy, non-running passenger with the wrong wind.

Our main take-off is about 300m lower, and is a seven-minute walk from the parking. It doesn't sound like much, but when you do it nine times a day it gets old. The take-off here is smaller but steeper, so it's easier to assist with older, heavier or disabled passengers, all of whom we seem to fly more and more often. Although our company has a policy of no passengers over 80kg after the 4pm flight (because the wind turns katabatic), a few still manage to slip into the bus.

The tourism landscape of Interlaken has changed a lot in the short time that I've been there. The yearly photos taken since 1980 at the oldest hostel in town, Balmers Herberge, show that it's been a popular haunt for young Americans, Canadians, Kiwis, Australians and Europeans — the kind of crowd that you used to associate with the party, travel and adventure lifestyle. Nowadays there's an increasing proportion of young Koreans, Indians, Chinese and Middle Eastern travellers, who come for the same experiences.

The biggest challenge for us as pilots is to overcome the language barrier and respect any cultural differences. Out of experience we tend to stereotype our passengers and customise our briefings and flights depending on nationality. We expect Indians to sit down on take-off; Middle Eastern guests to want to use Snapchat; and the Koreans to scream when we do "bingle bingle" (Korean for rollercoaster). Although sometimes it can be a real challenge, we're also lucky to interact with such a diverse tourism group.

We fly in a big mountain valley with two blue lakes either side. On the south side the Bernese Alps (famous for the Jungfrau, Mönch and Eiger) separate us from the Valais/Wallis, and on the north side the Güggisgrat divides us from the Emmental and, further north, the Jura regions. The mountain landscape influences the flying conditions dramatically, but we're lucky to have very good weather-forecasting and a profusion of weather stations.

Conditions change a lot from day to day and season to season. We tend to fly until we can't, or shouldn't. The line is grey. Sometimes we drive up the hill against good information just to "check it out". It's all part of learning. We commonly experience strong valley winds and outflow from storms, and we're affected by föhn, bise and low cloud. High demand and tight turnaround times mean we don't always have the luxury to wait for the best conditions, and often we fly when you wouldn't bother as a solo pilot.

The two lakes either side of Interlaken are sometimes our greatest defence against strong winds, especially the notorious föhn, famous in the

Alps for strong, gusty and unpredictable winds. The cold, dense air that sits above the lakes often acts like an invisible force shield protecting us. We've flown days when weather stations less than 20km away are showing föhn wind gusting over 100km/h.

Often there can be backwind at take-off, either from katabatic airflow or north/north-west wind. Interlaken tandem pilots are accustomed to launching with backwind, but it requires a passenger who can run. In difficult cases other pilots will give start assistance, which basically means running down the take-off holding the passenger and launching them off the hill. Mostly it works but sometimes it doesn't, in which case pilot and passenger become closely acquainted with the front of the take-off. Depending on the time of the year it might be covered with snow, cow dung, mud, grass or a mixture of them all.

Landing in Interlaken with grass and mud stains or only one shoe is generally pretty funny, unlike when a passenger empties their breakfast, lunch or the remnants of their big night out during the flight. If passengers warn the pilots they're feeling sick, the pilot can fly straight, avoid the thermals and pass them a spew bag if they have time. Otherwise it means washing the paragliding gear in the fountain or, worst case, running home for a shower. The more conservatively you fly as a pilot, the less likely it is to happen, but even a straight-line flight from the take-off to the landing can still evoke a puking from the wrong customer.

If conditions permit and our passengers want to thermal, soar or do some basic acro, we love to oblige. On a thermic summer day the sky is dotted with gliders exploring the air. On a busy day it can feel like a choreographed routine of dancing tandems all spinning, diving, looping and pirouetting towards the landing.

Like with any job, some days it can be frustrating, but generally it's fabulous. The summer days are long and the winter days are short and cold. Working outside all day can be both a joy and a curse. But whatever the conditions, you're working with good mates.

Working as a self-employed pilot allows the flexibility to chase other passions. Our pilot team includes engineers, a software developer, mountain guides, professional athletes, paraglider acro/XC champions, family fathers, photographers and even a music DJ.

What a desk is to an office worker, a chair suspended from a plastic bag flying over the Swiss Alps with someone sitting in our lap is to us. While not all our customers may be suited to this sort of adventure, it's always a privilege to be able to give people the experience of paragliding.

Haydon Gray is from Canberra, Australia. He has a degree in environmental science, and has lived in England, Ireland and Papua New Guinea. Haydon continues to fly in Interlaken.

The longest day

Guy Delage

I reached Prahia, the capital of the Cape Verde Islands, eight days ago. I've slept by day in a soundproof room at the residence of the French Ambassador, and woken up late each afternoon to continue my preparations.

The French mission allows me to use its fax machine and receive phone calls from France. My sleep schedule has fully shifted, and my trike is waiting and fully fuelled in the huge hangar of the airport. I'm as ready as I'll ever be. I have dispatched my letters — possibly my last words to beloved ones.

A meteo fax arrives at 18.45 local time. The Inter Tropical Front (ITF) seems reasonably calm, but the forecasted winds are not too encouraging: a weak NE trade wind followed by a south trade wind beyond the ITF. However, there are few clouds over the island and the wind has dropped below 20 km/h. It's promising.

At 21.45, Meteo France provides me with weather updates from two ships in this part of the Atlantic. They indicate more favourable winds. Intuition tells me to go at once. Besides, with Christmas Eve approaching there will be all kinds of problems connected with seasonal festivities. The dice are thrown.

The departure check list begins: inform Meteo France that the 'longest day' has just begun, tell Radio France that the mission is on, get to the airfield and run the engine on three tanks to get rid of any trace of water, purge my bowels, fight with a controller who asks me to file a flight plan that was given 10 days earlier, dress myself and connect the urine disposal system, top up the tanks, load the food and flasks of hot coffee. Step into the machine, verify all systems OK, program the watches, verify the GPS program, set the radio frequencies, check the safety equipment, strap myself in, taxi up the runway and align the trike for take-off!

The Rotax 912 obeys and delivers its powerful blast. I have the feeling of rolling endlessly, then the tarmac lit by the headlight slips away. I'm airborne. Local time is 00.20. I climb above the runway and turn carefully: I have a very heavy load. Above the water I turn onto a 220-degree heading and slowly climb above the light stratus layer to 2,500ft.

I can count my number of night flights (around a familiar airfield and by full moon) on one hand. I'd attempted a night VFR qualification course at Nantes, but the club was unable to provide this form of training regularly. As a result, I was up in the sky with the best IFR instrument there is: the moon. I had SAL on the radio, and set my course on a nice bright star. I forced myself to pilot without looking outside, dealing only with my three available instruments: an electric ball/slip indicator, a compass on the control bar, and the Transpak, the formidable GPS without which I would not be here to tell the story.

Gradually, the stratus layer changes into a carpet of cumulus, forcing me to climb. As a result my speed reduces, so I descend through the layer to get into a more favourable wind. Below, it is pitch dark and bumpy. Concentrating on the instruments, I try to stay on top.

My speed is close to 100km/h with a 12-15 knot tailwind as predicted by the ship observer. My altimeter shows 800ft. I look overboard and try and spot the surface of the ocean, to no avail. It's too dark.

My adventure slowly turns into a nightmare. I manage to contact two Air France flights who relay my position to SA and Dakkar, and give me a Met report.

In the morning, a few gaps appear in the cumulus layer. I climb to 5,000ft. My speed has dropped a bit to 90km/h. I feel better, less tossed about. I drink a lot and force down some bananas and dried figs. Gradually the cumulus clouds grow taller and taller, and I have to dodge them. I maintain a 220-degree heading.

Ten hours into the flight, hell awaits me. A huge column of rain spreads across the horizon. I know I should try to pass behind or after the rain. It grows into an enormous black wall with white forerunner alto-cumulus clouds, barring my route. I am in clear blue sky, but am already getting tossed about in violent turbulence. I dodge eastwards 150 degrees, then 120, then 100.

The surrounding clouds are just enormous. Their tops are boiling. A gap opens to the east, but as I start flying towards it, another cumulonimbus quickly develops, blocking me. Doing a half turn, I catch sight of another cumulonimbus developing where I've just come from. I'm closed in. I continue along the black wall searching for a crack.

Under the clouds, I descend to 300ft above the ocean, really afraid, and totally aware that the slightest mechanical failure would be deadly. If forced to make a water landing, there wouldn't even be enough time to open my canopy and get myself out. It's 11.45. The cloud layer is so thick and black that it obstructs my entire field of view.

Suddenly, there's a heavy downpour, and a great flash of lightning right in front of me, and then my shortwave radio starts smoking. The display is dead. Three useless kilograms on my lap. Throw it overboard! I'm thrown into a vicious turn. The instruments indicate 190ft! There's no escape from the omnipresent storm. I bounce around the cockpit and hit the wing with my headset. Suddenly I'm glued to the wing with the vario blocked at ten down. Even full throttle makes no difference. I'm certain I'll crash, the water is just metres below my wheels. Two flying fish hit the windscreen. I just manage to climb again, trying to turn to escape the clutches of the monster. I'm in a terrible gloomy struggle, with no visual landmarks, concentrating on my instruments alone.

Is this a nightmare or am I hallucinating? One and a half hours later a ray of light appears. Dawn. I emerge into a succession of black walls and curtains of rain. I'm on another planet, a magnificent and terrible vision. My hearing and sight are blurred, my mouth is dry. I feel faint. I force myself to swallow some chocolate and drink water. I think of my two sons and all those who believe in me. Try to relax, remember the plan, eat, drink, urinate, hang onto the vital functions, that's all there is left — that and the instruments.

Again I find myself engulfed by the storm, convinced this time I am going to die. This insane struggle takes three full hours. It grows lighter, then gaps appear in the cumulus, the wind has suddenly veered to the south. I look behind me to see a monster cumulonimbus that bars the entire horizon and covers me with its anvil. I decide to risk climbing. At 8,000ft my speed increases from 30km/h to 60km/h. I am still alive.

I'm totally exhausted, my limits are long exceeded, yet I must hang on another 12 hours at least: there's 1,000km left to go. My stomach, kidneys and bowels are as tight as a knot. Weeing is the only way to relax for a few moments.

Forget the damned GPS, the compass, try to extract myself from this abyss, try to rest, write a few words on the distress beacon.

At 7,000ft, beyond the cumulus, below the sea is white, the cross wind strong, and my groundspeed is 70-75km/h. My subconscious does the piloting while I struggle to interpret my instruments. Can I hang on? Loss of consciousness is a constant menace. I have nothing left to eat.

500km short of landfall at the Brazilian island of Fernando De Noronha, a voice calls me. It's an Air France flight en route to Paris. I break down in tears. Suddenly life exists somewhere else – it's not only an illusion. They inform Radio France of my progress and give me a met report from San Fernando. Seven hours of flight left… hold on, rest a bit, relax.

Night falls quickly and the moon rises, illuminating cumulus clouds 3,000ft below. I ignore how long I can still hold on… Doubt invades my mind. 150km remain. I hear the voice of Christopher the photographer at Fernando De Noronha, trying to contact me. The GPS has been inactive for an hour, unable to pick up a signal. Will I find the island? Wait: there's a gathering of clouds that look a bit different to the right. Do they indicate islands at sea? I descend below the cloud layer and see the beacon. It is there!

I confirm visual contact on the radio and descend. The runway is lit. Then suddenly the lights go off. A cliff jumps past my face. A last turn with my last bits of energy remaining, full throttle, and the runway reappears to my right. Death retreats once more… I line up once again, maintain the glide on the engine, then the runway is underneath, and my wheels touch. A dozen people are standing there with the photographer, along my taxi way. I park the trike in the shade, anchor it, undress myself and lie down until my body stops trembling. I am suffering from severe shock.

It takes another 12 hours to recover from shock, during which I have to eat sugar and avoid sleeping. We had noted this problem during real 44-hour simulations. After 12 hours, my abdomen stopped its convulsions and my cardiac rhythm returned to normal. Christmas is spent in total calm, trying to forget my memories of that infernal journey on another planet.

Guy Delage was born in 1952 in the Aisne department, in north-eastern France. He has had many adventures in sailing and wild water swimming. As well as flying across the Atlantic, he's swum across, sleeping each night on a raft that he towed.

Big Southern Butte

John Dunham

A cross-country flight in July 1974 was still a dream for most pilots. I believe that my flight was the longest in the world at that time. The flight was done on a home-built Windlord standard wing, with an Albatross sail. It might not seem such a great accomplishment today, but consider this: I was flying a 5:1 glide ratio wing that weighed only 17kg. I had no variometer. I had no parachute. There were no other cross-country pilots to learn from, and the most important thing: I was too young and too dumb to be afraid!

Telluride, Colorado, site of the Rocky Mountains Hang Gliding Championships, July 1974. It's one of those places you hate to leave because you're firmly convinced that this must be paradise. After the most enjoyable, relaxing nine days of flying I'd ever experienced, it was time to say goodbye and head for parts unknown. There I was in my hammock slung between two aspen trees, catching some sleep before our last morning in the Rockies. Reggie Jones and I were tentatively planning to leave the next day to scope out some new flying spots in Arizona's White Mountains, before heading home to San Diego.

2.30 am: I slowly awoke from my dreams to find myself deeply involved in a conversation with Bob Dart and Lloyd Short, winner of that day's contest. "Come with us to the Butte, John. It's paradise! The most outrageous place you will ever fly! It will be a great place to take your Windlord for some cross-country flying! The only direction the air goes out there is up! Everywhere you fly there's lift. Thermals! Ridge lift! Soaring! It's unreal! There is so much lift you could drive to the base of the mountain and fly up! Without your kite!"

Well, half asleep or not, I wasn't going to let all this exciting talk keep me from making a rational decision. So, finally I gave Bob and Lloyd a definite answer: "I'll think about it". And I promptly fell back to sleep, wondering where in hell the "Butte" was.

By the time I fully realized what I was doing, we were in Salt Lake City headed for Idaho Falls in Lloyd's truck – with Mike Mitchell, Curt Stahl and friends tagging along behind chanting "goin' to da Butte" in four-part harmony.

Arriving in Idaho Falls on Wednesday, we met with the local crazy kite flyers from Soaring Sports and spent the night in town as their guests. It seems they were planning a get-together at the Butte that weekend, and were happy to share their secret mountain with us. Bright and early Thursday afternoon, we had a barrage of kite flyers "headin' to da Butte" through fifty miles of flat, desolate desert.

The first time I saw that mountain I was truly amazed. Picture a flat desert as far as you can see, with nothing but sagebrush and dark lava beds dotted here and there, generating heat into the sky. On an average afternoon you can see dust devils as large as white tornadoes being sucked up seemingly into fluffy white marshmallow clouds lined up in streets as far as the eye can see. Out of this ocean of nothingness jolt three volcano-like mountains spread out fifteen miles across the desert. The largest and farthest west of these hills, better known as Big Southern Butte, juts up 2,500ft from base to top and has a passable dirt road which will take you in any direction. A southwest wind prevails here this time of year (July), which is perfect for a take-off at the 1,900 feet level that's as easy and clean as you could hope for. For almost a mile you have a smooth, soarable face on the mountain, dropping off into a desert which looks like an ocean from the top. Your landing area is anywhere: no obstructions, fences, power lines, trees, nothing.

Our first flight Thursday wasn't much. It was not quite soarable, and there was no thermal activity to speak of. But after an incredibly smooth sunset flight off the north slope, we were ready to stick around another couple of days.

"You should have been here last week!" said one of the local flyers. Where have I heard that before?

That night we camped at Frenchman's cabin in the landing area, four miles from the usual flying spot on the mountain. There's an old airstrip with a windsock next to the cabin. It couldn't have been more perfectly situated. Nobody minds people camping there, as long as they leave things as clean or cleaner than they find them.

Friday was marked by three decent flights and a rolled-over kite truck. Apart from the setback of having to spend the afternoon and half the next day pulling Lloyd's truck out of the gully that it ended upside down in, everyone was having a good time, and Lloyd's truck was still running like new – minus a front windshield. Still, nothing spectacular had happened in the air.

Saturday: feeling burnt out and ready to call it quits after two mediocre flights, we were sitting at the cabin contemplating our travels when all of a sudden small, white, fluffy thermal clouds began to billow out everywhere we could see. Also, the wind seemed to be picking up in a decent direction. Rushing up the mountain in Lloyd's truck at sixty mph with no front windshield was an exciting experience. What was even more exciting was to see the wind blowing up the face in a perfect direction at 20mph, more or less.

Throwing our kites together, we were ready to go... but who's first? Having been wind dummy the last two days, I proceeded to the end of the line and watched the circus start. Keith Nichols of San Diego decided to be the dummy in his Seagull. Two light steps and he was off. Keith looked tense as if he was expecting to get thrown around, but we were all surprised. It looked like a smooth day at Torrey Pines, with five times the lift. Keith went up and out for a quarter mile before turning, and was still going up. Mike and Curt, then me and then Bob. It was now 5.30pm and there was plenty of time before sunset, which was not until about 9.00 at that time of year.

Here we all were, driving around in the sky above the Butte, having a grand ol' time in air smooth as silk. Not having paid any attention to my altimeter earlier, I was surprised to realize that Mike and I were now about 1,000ft above take-off, even though we were way out in front of everyone else soaring the ridge below us. Mike was doing his fancy 360s in front of me as I sat hovering and conserving my energy. After about fifteen minutes of soaring, Mike and I had 1,200ft over the take-off.

It now seemed as if we had worked ourselves into the horizontal flow of air and were having problems penetrating away from the ridge. No problem. Almost as if someone blew a horn, everyone started crabbing out away from the mountain to the north and headed for our landing area four miles away. Leaving the mountain, my altimeter now read 3,200ft above the desert floor. Everyone else headed for the cabin, more or less in a straight line, playing around for a long time until they landed on the airstrip. Meanwhile, with my eye on a sunny patch of ground and a developing cumulus, I headed downwind of everyone else and was surprised to see the needle of my altimeter creep up to 3,500 as I headed out over the flat desert.

There I was, 3,500ft up and wondering where to go next. There was no need for a variometer, because the lift seemed to be everywhere. After flying around sort of pointlessly, I turned around and headed back to the landing area and found the headwinds too strong to penetrate. Then and there I made up my mind not to fight it. Turning downwind, I headed for the cumulus cloud, which was looking darker and larger all the time.

For as far as I could see there was nothing but desert spotted here and there with Atomic Energy Commission installations and a few dirt access roads. Ten miles to the north of the Butte, the main highway cut through the desert. I figured my best bet would be to head for the highway and follow it downwind, but for now, I wanted to play around with that cloud. Making a few long passes underneath it, I was surprised to see the needle of my altimeter climbing at a very fast rate, and getting faster all the time. Nearing the base of the cloud, I was beginning to worry.

The wind was getting interesting, to say the least. At one moment it would feel like there was a strong headwind, then cross, tail and every which direction. There was nothing violent as far as turbulence goes. At my highest point my meter read 5,500ft over the desert floor. At that time I was looking at the base of the cloud perhaps 500ft above me, and getting heavy rain in my face. Due to the fact that I had no shirt on and that I was getting sucked up at a faster and faster rate, I pointed my "point-nose parachute" for clear sky. Breaking out from under the cloud, my sail inverted violently and I was thrown around a bit, but things smoothed out quickly. There was a surprising temperature change now, and the warm air felt good for a while.

Seeing that my altitude was dropping at a sickening rate, and because the cloud was now between me and the highway to the north, I decided to go for another swim. Wham! Through the turbulence, back under the cloud; it was elevator time again. Getting cold and wet didn't seem to matter anymore. You never saw a happier, more free-spirited pilot than I was under that cloud. There's something about being in the air more than a mile up and not worrying where or even when to land. If only there had been other clouds like this one downwind, I could have gone until sunset. With confidence in my machine and in my ability to cope with the situation at hand, the shackles were off. I was defying gravity. So it seemed for a while. This had to be the most refreshing, exhilarating experience I had ever encountered in my life.

After regaining my altitude of 5,500ft, I decided to fly out of the cloud, setting up max glide to the main highway. I almost turned around to head back to the cloud to play some more, but flying prone for almost an hour sometimes puts a strain on one's body, and it was time to go for distance.

After a five-mile final glide I crossed Highway 26, turned upwind and settled down gently next to the camper of an older couple who were headed west on their summer vacation. With a grin from ear to ear, I walked up to their camper and said "Hi!"

When they asked where I had come from, I pointed and said, "see that mountain way over there?"

"Yeah".

"Well, I took off from the other side of it, flew up to that cloud, and finally ended up here!"

The couple looked at each other and broke out laughing. They asked if I needed any help.

"No thanks," I replied. "My friends should be along any time to pick me up. Thanks anyway!"

After they drove away, I sat down and looked at the cloud I had just passed up and the mountain from which I had come. Ten minutes after I sat down, the cloud picked up its skirts and threw 30mph winds and the heaviest rain squall I'd ever seen at me. With a thunderous voice, it seemed to say: "Take that!" and headed slowly off to parts unknown. There I was sitting on the ground, wishing I was going with it.

As it turned out, I had gained approximately 3,600ft and travelled 11 miles downwind of the mountain. One of these days, hopefully next summer, I will encounter similar conditions. I hope I'm a little more prepared than I was last July. It's my dream to become as knowledgeable as the birds we're trying to imitate in this sport, and to be free to go where they go. I feel like a guest in their ocean of air, and I'll jump at any opportunity to learn firsthand what comes to them naturally. My thanks go out to the late Lloyd Short and my good friend Bob Dart for initiating this experience in the ultimate.

John Dunham had his first flight with his father in a J2 Cub in 1958. As well as hang gliders, he's flown ultralights and motor gliders, and has done aerial photography for wildlife films. He spent many years inventing and marketing ballistic parachutes for light aircraft.

Between heaven & hell

Felix Wölk

The sound of the erupting Volcán de Fuego shook the thin fabric of our tent. Each thunderous bang frightened me just as much as the last.

I opened the tent to take another look. Just a mile away, lava and glowing rocks rained down, lighting up the volcano's flanks with an eerie blood red. Far below the lights of civilisation twinkled. I forced myself to close my eyes, but the thin air troubled me, as did the cold, and the unease at our intended adventure. But the forecast promised a weather window. This would be our third attempt to fly from Acatenango, and our last chance…

At 4am, after a sleepless night, my companion Pablo and I trudged into the night. Only movement could warm me up. With every step, lava dust swirled in the beam of our helmet lamps. The stationary dust raised our hopes: there was not a breath of wind.

Our climb the previous day to our base camp had taken us from the heat of the valley. We'd passed through dripping rainforest. Ferns, climbing plants and huge trees with giant roots were like something from a fairy tale. Above that, we entered a zone of dead trees, victims of raining ash.

Up here at 3,700m the thick dust meant slow progress. One step up meant two sliding back, and our lungs complained about the lack of oxygen.

Dawn slowly turned the eastern horizon a shade of grey as we reached the crater rim. We felt light wafts of wind coming gently from the east.

Meanwhile, in a regular rhythm, every few minutes the Fuego spat ash into the morning sky.

Below us lay an unbroken layer of cloud, and beneath that, Guatemala. To the south, towards the Pacific, the cloud cover was breaking up. Then suddenly, a bright light beamed from the horizon and the equatorial sun rushed into our day, flooding us with colour and detail.

Pablo and I tried to read the air based on the look of the clouds. We estimated the wind in the valley to be 20km/h. We hurried, because twice already we'd experienced a change in the weather within minutes, which had meant we'd had to abort our intended flight. On those occasions, clouds had overdeveloped from below, rushing up to envelop us.

Even now there were worrying signs of change. The cloud layer started breaking parallel lines, but our paragliders were ready for take-off.

After five steps I lifted off from the crater. It was 6.45am, and a beautiful morning. Pablo followed me into the uncertainty.

At first, the flight was absolutely celestial. Far below us a pure white duvet of cloud stretched out all the way to the horizon to the north. And in front of the rising sun, the cone of the Volcán de Agua threw a gravestone-shaped shadow onto the sea of cloud below. Above us, an eternal endless blue.

But the clouds below were changing by the minute, shape-shifting into a wave-induced mountain-and-valley scene. To the south, the cloud was quickly dissipating as it descended into warmer air below. After 15 minutes flying through still air we reached the top of the cloud layer. Below it would either be a dream or a nightmare.

Down we go, like planes descending through the clouds on final approach. White, grey, white, wispy – and clear. Seconds after emerging, we had zero groundspeed facing into wind. I pushed my speed bar and crept desperately forwards for a few moments, then an invisible giant hand pushed me back, towards the south. I radioed Pablo, who was behind me, fighting the headwind.

"My instrument's showing 70km/h of wind from the north!" he said.

The wind was clearly getting squeezed and compressed around the volcano. We turned tail and ran towards the plains. With 110km/h groundspeed we rushed towards the Pacific, the frozen lava stream of

Fuego racing past underneath me. When the valley opened up, I started to look for a clear space to land. A few kilometres upwind of a likely spot I turned my wing into wind and steered by looking over my shoulder, as I flew backwards over the ground.

The air got rough. I began to climb, so pushed speedbar. Then the first collapse hit me. I recovered. Straight after that my vario wailed hysterically. What is happening? I thought.

Well, the föhn wind descending from the north was being compressed under the cloud, creating lots of lee-side turbulence already. And rushing in from the south was a strong sea breeze pushing in from the Pacific coast. And in the middle of it all, a 3,800m volcano. As the winds smashed into each other, it created a confusing cauldron of different air masses, all furiously bubbling away under the lid of a strong inversion. This was serious. Pablo had literally been blown away – I looked and saw him swinging wildly 400m higher, far to the south – then there was a bang. I looked up: my canopy looked like a sausage. OK… wait… let it inflate, let it fly. The heavy hit had knocked me far to the south and threatened to blow me past the landing field. Behind it the ground surface was completely unpredictable.

A brushfire on the ground gave me a flicker of hope. The smoke from it was switching around in different directions, but showed light winds at the surface. Barely 300m above the ground I was still fighting non-stop to keep my position. Again and again I climbed like a rocket, again and again the glider cells were knocked empty of air. My nerves were stretched to the limit. I tried to take deep breaths to steady myself.

About 100m above the ground, I was downwind of my landing area, and still struggling to penetrate towards safety. Below me were trees, cables and broken-up riverbeds. I stepped on the bar and just managed to get back above my field, stood still facing into a gust of east wind and, moments later, touched down. With two brake wraps one side and a tug on the opposite A-riser the other, I killed the wing, and tumbled over backwards.

Exhausted, I radioed Pablo. He answered. Relieved, I collapsed into the grass and breathed again.

Pablo and I roughed it back to Antigua in the public "chicken bus". Pablo read from his instrument: "Take-off 06:45. Max climb 11.4m/s. Max wind 72km/h."

"Nice morning flight," he added in ironic summary.

I mulled over what had been the most difficult paraglider flight of my 28-year career. I felt like a total novice, a naïve European fool. Really, the only thing that had saved us both had been reliable wings and luck.

Days later we learnt from locals that high pressure with a northerly flow gives rise to a special kind of meteorology in Guatemala. The inversion marks the split between two worlds: above, it's all calm and peaceful, but below, the wind flows are far more exaggerated than the met charges would suggest.

We made our way to a fiesta in Antigua, a town at the foot of the Guatemalan volcanic giants. A new mayor had been elected and there were massive celebrations with military pyrotechnics rocketing into the sky. Marimba bands kept everyone jumping.

In the Antiguan streets "space cookies", hashish biscuits, were much in demand. In the Café No Se, barmaid Katrin flashed her eyes and kept her victims topped up. Then, after closing time, we surrendered to our fates and were driven to a dark, graffitied cellar bar. This place had style! Beer and Latino beats kept us up till the early hours. Following our flight through heaven and hell, these bare-wall catacombs were the last stop in our adventure. But there was still a monstrous, magical presence in the air. A being that glows, smokes and thunders non-stop, high above, but too close for comfort – and always in charge.

Felix Wölk is a photographer, skier and instructor in both hang gliding and paragliding. He's represented Germany in hang gliding, and has set a tandem paraglider world record for speed on a 100km out-and-return flight.

Wake up

Hugh Miller

We turn right and leave the neat fields and hay bales behind. Winding our way up the mountain track, I catch a glimpse of Obiou's summit through the pine trees. A white monolithic head, she stands proud against the wind and clouds that rush onwards before being whipped into confusion in her rear.

We drive high above the tree line to an exposed col, where a shepherd is herding his flock down to safety. A tree stands black and leafless in the cold wind – a solitary victim of a lightning strike.

"We stay here", says Jérôme.

Part of me wants to rush back down to the cosy home comforts of Café Sports, to television and warmth and safety, but another part wants to stay put, to see what will happen next. It's the first evening in my introductory week to para-alpinism. After training for a triathlon over the summer, I'd felt fit enough to accept Jérôme's invitation to taste out this new hybrid sport… hiking with a rucksack that weighs less than 8kg and flying unflown peaks. What could be so daunting about that?

As night falls and the storm envelops us, we huddle around candlelight in the mountain hut listening to the wind and rain batter and spit. Dawn: a dense, freezing fog. At 6am, led by Jérôme's optimism, we're packing bags and spitting out toothpaste ready for the climb. Within an hour the Obiou appears like a vision through the fog.

After an hour's hike up the grassy shoulder, the climb gets technical as the route cuts into the side of the rock face. I have to focus on my immediate vicinity: the next handhold, looking for the next arrow. Below: vertigo. To the sides: vertigo. Above: impossibly steep. I feel like an ant on the surface of the moon that's been tipped on its side.

Another three hours' solid effort and we summit. Three black vultures drift above us, visitors from another world, effortless as weightless astronauts. My boots slip on the loose shale as I shake the skinny lines out. The wind tugs and grabs at the light cloth. It's gossamer thin.

I pick up the harness. It weighs nothing. It looks like nothing. It is nothing. I've just completed my first serious alpine scramble, it's midday in August, the thermals are pumping, I'm about to fly a tiny mountain glider I've never flown before, and the harness – also new to me – looks like it'll offer about as much comfort as walking down the high street naked but for a G-String. I'm sure Jérôme can smell my fear.

I tighten the tiny harness maillons. I'm so on edge, I don't know what I want to do. I'm nailed right to the spot: either it's a four-hour fairly intense scramble down with no water, or a midday flight. Laziness wins. I pull the glider up and it bumps into the air, I turn, and suddenly everything is familiar; I'm running, the glider's pulling, and we're off, the shallow slope suddenly dropping away to a 300m cliff, fingers of rock pointing up accusingly at me.

I hear the clatter and crack of rockfall, and look down to see three boulders chasing each other down a gully. I punch out into the strengthening wind to descend to our car parked on the col. I touch down, and everything falls quiet and still, but for the tinkling bells of the alpine cows. I don't think I've had so much adrenaline in my system since flying the World Championships in Castejon de Sos ten years ago.

"Hey Jérôme," I say after we land. "I take you to the English flatlands, and you bring me here!"

5am, three days later. Jérôme, his friend Olivier and I slurp down coffee and hike off up the road to le Trélod, our head torches showing the way. I want it to stay dark and cold forever; under starlight; the mountains silhouetted; the expanse above us. Gradually blacks become greys as the hues of first light arrive.

We trudge up a steep, sodden slope through woods, trying to push our feet against the tree roots rather than the soft mud. Then we contour along the grassy upper slope, past a waterfall, and see a chamois erect on the peak above us. The talk is easy – Paris, the flatlands, children, life. When we get to the top, the world is utterly still. It's 8.30am and we lay out on the dew.

The sun is now bright. The day has started. Moments never last. I run down the slope, the glider bursts into life behind me, and I'm flying faster than I think I ever have before, swooping around the slopes, diving over the edge of a cliff, then pushing out over the valley's villages and church spires 1,000m beneath me. I hang forward in my harness, look straight down at the world moving below.

As I dangle, life suspended, I realise I'm back where it all began in the 1980s, experiencing something of what the pioneers of paragliding must have felt. Physical challenge, new mountains, a fresh perspective. Hike and fly is to paragliding what ski touring is to skiing on piste. Getting away from the crowds into the wild silence. No back protection, no windsock on launch. Just myself, my wing, and the elements, ever-shifting. And with so little to go on, I realise that even after sixteen years of flying I'm still very much a beginner.

We land in a thick wet meadow next to Olivier's family holiday house. Breakfast time, but we've already lived a day. Whatever else now happens, I feel complete.

Hugh started flying in 1992, and continues to have his head very much in the clouds

MINI STORY

Your record is broken, son

Dora Göksal

At 6.32pm, I landed at 312km.

Kids arrived quickly, and an older man asked me where I had come from.

"Kahramanmaras," I replied.

He didn't seem impressed.

I told him I'd just set a new Turkish national record.

He raised his eyebrows, then looked over my shoulder.

My flying budy Umut was about to cruise over us.

"Your record is broken, son," he said, shaking his head.

Then something else caught his eye.

He pointed his finger at a speck. It was a little behind Umut, but much higher.

"Don't worry son, his record is broken too."

Dora on the humbling end of a big day in Turkey

Ninth life

Bob Drury

To the question "Have you ever thrown your reserve?" I had always answered, "not yet!"

But the kind of places I fly, and the style of flying I like, has always meant that it was inevitable that sooner or later the shit would hit the fan. In other words, parts of the story I'm about to tell you were always going to happen: it was just a matter of time, and an unavoidable part of me being me that led me into the situation. It was what followed after that I really could have done without.

It was a warm, sunny Saturday afternoon in spring and the sky above Col de Bleine, France was rapidly filling with pilots keen to blast away the working week from their hair. The sky was clean and organised with cu's popping over the peaks in the distance, and the local XC pilots were heading off towards St André in abundant lift.

As I climbed away from launch I felt excited. I knew that these days were always brilliant, as we were here just to practise aerobatics and wring the living daylights out of our wings.

Over the past year, I've been slowly working my way into aerobatics, trying not to rush things and trying to perfect each manoeuvre before moving on. I already had SATs and big reversals dialled and, more recently, I'd been trying to perfect my helicopter spins. Although I still couldn't get a smooth, clean rotation every time, I felt comfortable with the manoeuvre so I went straight into it, even though it's one of the harder tricks to master.

My first attempt rotated fine for a few revolutions before starting to get a bit messy. I was deliberately spinning it quite fast, faster than I normally do; playing with the rotation and trying to get more familiar with the different sensations I received. Once the 'chopper' got messy I tried to resettle it, but ended up exiting badly with a small cravat that took a stall recovery to sort out.

Back at cloudbase I got straight back down to business again and sent the glider into another 'chopper.' Again I let the glider spin quite quickly, watching to see if the extra speed of rotation would clear the one wing tip I often seemed to have tucked in when helicoptering. After a few rotations things started to get messy again. The rotation was flicking me around and the wing was beginning to surge about too much. Normally this is a sign to exit the manoeuvre and start again, but with so much height and keen to understand more I tried to work at it again, making tiny adjustments to the controls to see if I could settle it down.

I must have released slightly too much at some point because suddenly the glider snapped out of the rotation, flung itself violently sideways and flicked me towards it. Unweighting the lines, I fell back under the wing, side-slipping it, and in an instant 70% of the wing had rolled in and cravated. As I saw the wing rolling in I knew what would happen next, so my hands were already forcing the brakes down into a full stall.

The glider stalled and I held on to it, studying it, to see if there were any signs of recovery – there weren't. I was holding on to a screwed-up ball of cloth that looked more like a wedding dress than a paraglider. I held the stall for a few more seconds watching it thrash about, looking to see if the wing was untangling, and then began to ease up on the brakes slightly to give the glider more of a chance to inflate and recover from the situation. Instead the glider rotated, and in a split second I'd twisted up my risers, locked up the controls and accelerated into a violent spiral.

Once you've lost use of the controls there seems little point holding on to them but, perhaps for comfort more than purpose, I put them both in my left hand and kept as tight a rein on the glider as I could in the vague hope that it might slow down the rotation whilst I tried to reach above the twists to get to the lines.

But the glider was already locked in to the deepest of spirals with the wing showing no signs of recovering. Fighting against the building G-forces, I tried desperately to pull myself forward and grasp upwards towards the lines; but it was useless, I was totally pinned by the G-force and couldn't even move.

Reaching this moment in my life was so inevitable, almost unavoidable through where my flying had taken me, that I was completely unsurprised to realise that I finally needed to throw my reserve. After nine years of flying, and having watched so many fall out the sky before me, I was neither shocked nor worried by the prospect of my parachute ride down. I went for the handle.

Out of the corner of my eye I caught the red glow of the handle sitting snugly on my right shoulder so I threw my hand towards it. Grabbing and holding tight, I pulled hard, and then stared at an empty hand.

Shit, I've missed!

I went back again, this time twisting my head more to get a closer look, and began feeling around with my hand, but nothing, it had gone! No more comforting red glow waiting to end the dizzy blur.

The spiral continued, even deepening, or was it the massive G's I was pulling that were getting to my head? I went back to work, groping and pulling at anything I could find, but nothing.

I couldn't believe it! I'd even placed the handle carefully on my shoulder on take-off that day to ensure I'd be able to reach it just in case today was going to be 'the day'. I began to get pissed off.

"Where the fuck is it?" I shouted out loud in frustration.

I decided to lose my gloves, and with immense effort I brought my hands up close to my face and used my teeth to rip them off and throw them away. Something caught my eye. I stopped for a moment and felt slightly amused to see one of my gloves pinned against the under-surface of the wing waving back at me.

Now, back to work. Where is it?

I could get a better feel now and went back to raking the back of the harness where the second handle should be; bits of material snagged on my fingertips but still nothing would pull. For the first time I started to worry that I might not be able to deploy.

Once, in the Himalayas a few years ago I'd had cause to go for my reserve and that time too I'd failed to deploy. I had extended the back of my harness and made it deeper to carry more gear for vol-bivouacing which had resulted in the handle being much further around the back than before. It would have been a low throw that time except I'd missed the handle – I should have cratered but miraculously the glider recovered and I managed to hook turn away from the hillside in the nick of time, missing it by barely a metre. I never flew that harness again!

The optimism that had kept the panic away up till now began to dissolve and I stole a glance downwards to see how low I was. I was gutted to see a blur of green trees, and lifting my head up I realised I was below ridge height. Col de Bleine isn't very high, 300 metres at the most and I'd lost control over 1,000 metres above the ridge!

I must have been locked in the spiral for 30 seconds or more by now, although it felt like a lifetime longer, and strangely enough the situation had become almost familiar. Whirling round so fast, hurtling downwards, locked in my harness by the immense G force, with just the blur of green and flashes of blue to distract me from the cocoon of my own little world, it seemed almost futile to try and resist. These are my last few seconds I realised. I'm not getting out of this, there is no 'extra man' this time. GAME OVER. I relaxed.

"It's pointless," I thought. "I'm only three or four seconds from impact and going so fast that it won't even hurt".

Death is such a let-down. You know you can't escape it – it's inevitable. Yet few of us are really ready to go when the Reaper's card lands on the doormat. Even the seasoned optimist within me, hardened by years of luck, was now failing to find a way out – depressingly there appeared to be no happy ending.

Realising that I was finally going to die, after all the years of risk I'd somehow survived, brought forth a weird mix of emotions. I was bitterly disappointed rather than scared by my impending death. Even though I had already dodged far too many bullets in my life to really have any cause for complaint, the circumstances surrounding my tragedy were too avoidable to just lie back and take it.

How long I relaxed for, and whether or not life truly flashes before your eyes in your last seconds before the screen goes blank, I can't say. However it can only have been milliseconds and I know I did a lot of thinking. Somewhere in the myriad of pretty images, sounds and smells of life an idea popped into my head. I think it almost tried to pass me, sneaking quietly by on tiptoes hoping that the crushing G force would keep me still for the last few seconds. I almost let it. The inescapability of my situation brought comfort now and it seemed foolish to fight it. But being sometimes excessively optimistic I saw it, and as I had nothing else to do at the time, I grabbed it from the melee.

I realised that the vaguest chance of survival still existed. If I could somehow get to the back of the harness I might yet be able to pull the second handle. But that meant getting out of the harness! Pulling my shoulders in I slipped my arms free of the shoulder straps, and grabbing at the risers in front of me, I physically dragged myself forwards against the pressure of the spiral. Once free of the harness's shoulder straps I twisted my body around to face backwards and, throwing my arms around the back, I committed myself to the move.

I was fully aware that without the shoulder straps that had locked me in so well I might just be ejected from the harness and flung in to free fall. As a climber I'd always wondered what it would be like to fall to my death, and I began to imagine how it would feel like once I shot free of all the webbing and was ejected into clear air. I decided that once that happened I'd relax and try to enjoy the end of the ride.

I was surprised to find that I stayed stuck in my harness so I began to rake away at the back of the harness again. My vision was lost in a blurred sea of greenery and my body was tensing slightly in anticipation of my impending impact.

Then something happened. Something changed: a slight drop in pressure and a distant noise. I was upside down, facing backwards and half out of my harness when I saw the ribbon of black bridling streaming away from me, upwards, between my legs towards the sky. It took another moment to understand what had happened and what could happen next, and then I instinctively threw my legs wide hoping they might jam on my leg loops and keep me in as I decelerated, grabbing at the risers till the forces ebbed away and I swung gently under my parachute. Only 100 metres below me the only clearing in the forest for miles around waited for my arrival.

Walking back into my garden later that day, the kids were still playing in the garden and the dogs were still sleeping under the bushes. Lifting her eyes from her book, my wife Claire watched me as I sheepishly pulled the edge of my parachute out from the top of my glider bag for her to see.

"Strange, I had a weird feeling that you'd throw your reserve today!" she said, sounding unsurprised, before turning back to her book.

I guess living around my flying for so long has desensitised her to the risks. So far I had always made it home. I sloped off to play with the kids in the pool. It took me a couple of days to summon up the courage to tell her what had really happened.

So what should I draw from this encounter with the Reaper? Not to do aerobatics over ground? Not to do aerobatics at all? That I need a new harness? Well, all of these factors would have helped me, so I'll take them all on board. But no, what really sticks in my mind is that you can never beat a will to survive and phenomenal amounts of luck – because I never knowingly reached and pulled that handle.

A former editor of Cross Country magazine, Bob Drury has made several pioneering expeditions in the Himalaya. He lives with his family at the foot of Mt Blanc, France.

Blue sky blues

Amy Anderson

We set off for Mid Wales on the weekend of 1 August, 1994 with my little brother for his summer camping holiday. At the time, flying seemed not to be the priority, so I readily agreed to kid-sit just in case it was flyable. Little did I know that this one weekend was to see the British record broken not once, not twice, but three times, and there I was in the car with Tom saying: "Is he ever coming down, Amy!"

We spent Friday night with the sound of rain spattering rather unpromisingly on the tent. But, to Bruce's delight and my gathering doom, the morning dawned bright and windless. Bruce rang Mike Campbell-Jones at Paramania, who gave us directions to what turned out to be a fantastic north-westerly site. Neither of us had ever heard of the site near Builth Wells (I still don't know its name). It's one of Mike's private finds, and we would like to thank him very much for letting us use it.

We found a steep but decent track to the top. Having got a little lost on the way up and then dithering about, going down dead ends and avoiding cows, we were rather late arriving at the top. By this time the sky was looking good, and Bruce leapt out of the car in a frenzy. He had his glider out and was in the air before I even had time to get the sandwiches out. So much for a relaxing weekend!

At first the thermals were pretty weak, and things didn't look too good. After half an hour Bruce was still on the hill. Now being rather desperate, he left the hill with all of about 800ft. To my amazement, he started to climb quite convincingly out of what looked like certain doom in that all too familiar dead hole that seems to haunt potential XC sites.

Well, that was the last Tom and I saw of him for the rest of the day. Several ice creams, drinks and "Can we go home soons?"s later we managed to contact him on the radio as he approached Gloucester. Tom's new-found toy significantly helped Bruce as he was struggling in a zero at 500ft with Tom shouting: "All right Bruce, we can see you!" repeatedly in his ear.

The gruesome journey finally came to an end in a pub garden on the outskirts of Gloucester. Bruce had flown 80km, and I needed a stiff drink.

To Tom's and my delight, the next morning looked grey and dull as we looked out of the tent at the campsite we'd found only two miles from the pub. But by the time we'd cooked breakfast and packed up, the sun was out. Our hearts fell as Bruce suggested that we take a quick look at Frocester, which was only about four miles from the campsite.

On first attempt he went straight down. It seemed that our luck was in; lunch, an ice cream and then home. After a pleasant picnic at the bottom of Frocester, I had a sudden guilt complex and offered to drive Bruce to the top again for another go. Tom looked daggers at me. This time the sky looked even worse, but he took off and went literally straight to cloudbase in a few minutes. Such is the irrational nature of flying.

At the small town of Malmesbury only 20km from Frocester, Bruce was so low that Tom was shouting at him out of the sun-roof. We were happy that he was down. But to our horror, he started climbing, very slowly at first, but definitely climbing. Tom had started to twig on to the fact that if Bruce was going round in circles, it meant no more ice creams for a while longer.

A mere five hours and 90km later, Tom and I really started to get just a little bit annoyed as, for the zillionth time, Bruce was slowly and painfully circling out from a possible landing height. He'd promised to land before Winchester because he was certain that he wouldn't get the height at 6pm to clear the airspace. Well, he did. By this time, Tom and I were so saturated with lost hope that we drove on aimlessly following the dot in the sky. We stood licking the third ice cream of the day in Winchester, looking up at the sky and saying: "Will he ever come down?"

People looked at us as if we were mad. I was seriously starting to wonder if they were right as Bruce's cheery little voice came over the radio saying: "I've just passed Winchester and I'm on my way to Petersfield."

I had visions of Brighton, Dover… even France wasn't totally out of the question.

To our amazement however as we approached Petersfield, we saw the dot get bigger and bigger. Expecting it to disappear again, we were taken by surprise by Bruce's hurried message that he was going down in a place called Warnford, just west of Petersfield.

We found him standing by the road with a huge grin on his face. He'd flown 117km. I didn't know who deserved more congratulations, him, or me and Tom?

The celebrations for Bruce's new British record included a McDonald's in Portsmouth, champagne at home, and total elation on Bruce's part all the way until Monday morning, when we stepped into the Airwave office to find that Richard Carter had flown 163km on Saturday.

What more can I say other than: c'est la vie!

Amy Anderson lives in Portugal and continues to fly, kitesurf and paddleboard. In the 1990s Amy lived and worked in Annecy, France, as part of the Airwave research and development team. She is currently writing her first novel.

Into the vortex

James 'Kiwi' Johnston

Come on man! Are you ready to join the four-hundred club?

I had been hearing about the flying in Ceará since the early 2000s. An old Paragliding World Cup buddy, Philippe Karam of Mexico, had told me stories of the XC competitions where they had legendarily retrieved competitors from long flights by aeroplane. Often as I had struggled towards my first 100-mile flight, experienced pilots told me that a quick trip to Brazil in October or November would put me out of my misery.

"Just go to Ceará," they had said. "It's easy to fly 100 miles there." But the logistics had always seemed uncertain and daunting. Along with the stories of how wild and windy the launch was, that had kept me from turning that dream into a reality.

The opportunity to actually go to northern Brazil had arisen rather unexpectedly, when a couple of weeks earlier I had found out that three of the United States' most experienced cross-country pilots – Josh Cohn, Nick Greece, and Jon Hunt – were going to Quixadá in early November. Since all three are long-time friends of mine, for around US$100 a day for the hotel and retrieve, I was welcome to tag along.

Everything seemed to be going smoothly enough as I got off the plane in Rio, until my glider bag turned up in the baggage claim, but not my smaller secondary backpack. I groggily realised that it contained my clothes, my size-13 flying boots and most of my instruments, including my essential Delorme tracker, which I usually carry in my hand luggage. The American Airlines staff assured me that my bag would be transported to my hotel in Quixadá, and I had nothing to worry about.

The next day I arrived in Fortaleza several hours before the rest of the group, and Paulo Rocha, our retrieve operator, had arranged a ride for me with a group of Brazilian pilots, one of whom I already knew from competitions around the world. As the excited group rented a pair of cars, I pumped the locals for information about the flying conditions.

"The best place in the world to fly!" one of the Brazilians answered emphatically. "On my first flight there last year" he explained with a smile on his face, "I flew 375km. Ten hours and 375km on my first flight! This year I think I will I fly over 400km for sure! There is nowhere else in the world like Quixadá."

These glowing recommendations were exciting, but I still couldn't wrap my head around the mechanics of the place. There was much talk about Leandro Padua's record-breaking flight the day before, and how after launching at 6.30am he had soared for over two hours before catching his first thermal on his way to 486km.

"You launch at 6.30 in the morning?"

"Yes, because of the wind. The wind is so strong even then that three people will hold your glider down."

"And then we all soar around for two or three hours? How many pilots?"

"Many pilots. The beginning is not easy."

The beginning is not easy. That could mean a lot of different things, especially in Brazil. Three people holding my glider down in the wind, so that I could launch at 6.30am to ridge-soar for hours with a bunch of other crazed XC pilots, anxiously waiting for the first thermal to arrive, sounded like one of the seven layers of Dante's paragliding hell.

My anxious feeling only intensified after the American group arrived at the hotel in Quixadá that evening, and we were briefed by Paulo, an amiable Brazilian full of irrepressible Latin enthusiasm. The group had decided that we would not fly the next day so as to recover from the travel and get our gear together. But Paulo – knowing that we had just missed two of the best days in Quixadá history, and probably not wanting to tell us that conditions were deteriorating – quickly browbeat Nick Greece and Josh Cohn into agreeing to a 5am start for the group the next day instead.

It was during this briefing that I realised from their serious demeanour that this was no mere holiday XC jaunt for Nick and Josh. They were here on brand new Ozone Zenos as training for the 2018 spring in Texas (and the chance of an open distance world record), and intended to set a declared goal record while here in Brazil. That suddenly made the tone of the mission rather more intense, for I had seen Josh and Nick with their race-faces on many times before. When I mentioned that due to my missing bag I had no tracking device, radio, or shoes, Paulo insisted that this was not a problem, and that I should fly too. "Come on man!' he practically shouted in the hotel lobby, "Are you ready to join the 400 club? Let's go!"

I pondered his question. Despite Paulo's hearty enthusiasm, 400km seemed like a goal far beyond my personal reach. While Josh Cohn and Nick Greece are both former US champions with multiple Texas towing campaigns on their XC resumes, and while Nick and Jon Hunt had put up the first 200 mile flight in the Rockies in 2013, my own XC achievements were far more limited. After twenty-five years of paragliding, I had only managed to fly my long-time goal of 100 miles (a measly 160km), the previous year in 2015. I knew I was still the low man on the XC totem pole.

My personal journey as a pilot has had many ups and downs, from its origins in the late 1980s in New Zealand, to being an active competitor in the USA and internationally in the 1990s. I set the site record in Valle de Bravo in 1996, flew 85 miles in the USA that summer, and the 100-mile barrier felt like it would fall any day. Then I moved to a city far from any decent paragliding, and was relegated to intermediate status for the next decade-and-a-half. The combination of a divorce and being allowed to travel internationally again after years of wrangling with the American immigration system suddenly brought paragliding back into prominence, and with it the enduring desire to fly 100 miles.

As it turned out, all it took was a January in the uber-consistent conditions of Colombia to get my flying back on track, and after my first flight over 100 miles in 2015 (from Sun Valley, Idaho), I most surprisingly flew over 100 miles again on my very next flight two days later, resoundingly shaking that monkey off my back. Another winter in Colombia, and I really enjoyed getting back into competition flying again after an absence of fifteen years. In July 2016, I completed the longest task in competition paragliding history – 224km in the US Paragliding Nationals – on a day that, after a late start and spiralling down to goal at 5pm, I felt I could have flown 200 miles.

As we logged a handful of standard routes into our various instruments during Paulo's briefing (Nick Greece kindly lending me his spare 6030 for the following day, while I downloaded XC Track onto my smartphone), I noticed that there was a waypoint on the 'standard route' right at 318km, very close to 200 miles, at a town called Piripiri. Since the name itself looked Maori (the native tongue of New Zealand), I took this as a sure sign. The other three could chase 400km (248 miles) and their records, while Piripiri and Two Hundred Miles – a far more manageable distance in my mind – would be my personal goal.

"So a 5am start tomorrow! Make sure you are ready!" Paulo positively beamed with excitement at the idea.

"Five am? It really needs to be that early?"

"Yes, you must launch early because of the wind, six, six-thirty. You shall see, and then tomorrow you will know! Quixadá is the greatest place in the world to fly!"

The village idiot

The pioneering group that developed the flying in Quixadá (led by the tandem world-record holders André Fleury and Marcelo Prieto) made a paradigm shift in XC flying when they recognised that paragliders could use the adiabatic gradient of the bone-dry sertão, and so could launch at 7am instead of 10.30am. By flying as a team through the difficult barely-thermic conditions of these early morning hours, the Brazilian trio of Prieto, Frank Brown, and Rafael Saladini smashed the open distance paragliding world record with their flights of 461km in 2007, and first brought Quixadá into international free-flying prominence. Hence the required 5am wake up call, which arrived mighty quick, and an hour later we had driven up the paved road to the launch on a rocky spine below a monastery on one of the distinctive granite, tree-flanked monoliths that surround the town of Quixadá.

Having always heard Ceará described as flatland flying, I was unprepared for the raw beauty of the landscape. The monoliths reminded me of parts of the south-west United States, or of the Linzhou region in China, one of those strange alien landscapes straight out of a spaghetti western movie. Paulo explained to me that Quixadá meant 'corral' in Brazilian Portuguese, with the ring of monolithic mountains that surround the town believed by Brazilian New Agers to create a powerful vortex. UFO sightings were also apparently common – one of the drivers had a fine tale of a UFO interrupting a soccer game when he was a child.

"They took one guy from town, you know, the aliens," Paulo explained to me, punctuating the sentence with his wild explosive laugh, "and when he came back, he was not the same. He was like, how do you say… the village idiot! Hahahahaha!"

The village idiot. Someone I found myself sincerely hoping that I wasn't going to resemble in a few minutes while attempting to fly. The launch – which generally only one glider at a time occupies because of the wind – is a steep swathe less than 100m wide cleared off the side of the mountain, with a few pieces of carpet nailed to the ground down low in the centre. After you waddle down to this carpet ramp, three Brazilian helpers pull your glider out in the wind – which at 6.30am was already whipping stronger than anything I could remember ever launching in – and hold it down as you take the position below.

The crucial spotter stands above you on the ridge, bent over at the waist and staring down the mountain with his hand shading his eyes (watching the movement of the scrubby trees in front of launch that act to slow the wind, we decided). When he sees a lull approaching, he shouts "Now!" Praying that he's correct, you pull the glider up and go. It's the most exciting launch in paragliding that I've ever experienced; get it right, it's relatively clean, and once off the ground you can penetrate away from the mountain easily enough on speed bar, but if you get it wrong, things can get ugly quickly. It's made more nerve-wracking by the presence of 30 or so of the world's most die-hard cross-country pilots sitting watching you.

We had watched a couple of pilots get plucked and dragged upon arrival, but they were clearly Brazilian intermediates, we decided. Then in his typically determined manner, Josh Cohn took the slot, with Nick Greece right behind him. Since my pre-flight plan was simple – if Josh thought it was doable then I would go – that put me up next. And while I was green with envy that Josh and Nick were having their first flights on their brand new Ozone Zenos (not yet then available in my large size), when my helpers pulled my glider out in the whipping wind, I was suddenly glad to be on my trusty Ozone LM6, and not launching an unknown high-aspect glider for the first time. I was also instinctively happy to see that Paulo was my spotter, while I tried to ignore the fact that I was about to launch in as much wind as I had ever attempted, in a pair of sandals.

"Go!" Paulo shouted! Seriously? was my first thought as I looked at the windsock on the ridge, where the wind's velocity seemed unabated, but I took a deep breath and quickly brought the glider up. My first attempt was close but saw me jerked into the air and then aborted – my launch helpers quick as lightning on the glider as it came back to the ground. On the next attempt I ran up the hill at the glider as fast as I could, and the resulting launch was smooth and professional. A couple of seconds later I felt as if I had been ripped into the air by a bungee cord, the feeling almost indescribable as you really hit the wind and get boosted. Then, once on your speed bar and flying away from the mountain, things get surprisingly calm, the 6.30am air buoyantly smooth and laminar.   Lesson One for Quixadá: rip up the rule-book and throw it away – normal does not apply here. For example, the 'ridge-soaring' that I had been so dreading turned out to be entirely different to any that I had ever experienced. The lapse rate of the adiabatic gradient means you can fly straight away from the mountain and slowly climb on some mornings, and you often 'soar' as far as a kilometre out in front. And while the monolith we launched from is in itself a fairly large mountain, the sky seems unlimited with such a giant envelope of early lift, an area in which 30 or 40 pilots can quickly get spread far apart.

Which as it turns out, is not what you want, for in Quixadá, and especially for the first 140km, it's ideal to all fly together if possible. But unlike in a competition, where you have a defined start gate and a known start time, you now have a free-flying situation where you are jostling to be in the right position to be with the first gaggle that decides it's high enough to go (the first gaggle generally containing the best pilots). This is not as easy as it might sound in such a large search space, and if you are low or out of position when the first gaggle goes, then it's best to wait for the second, more-cautious gaggle to venture out, since trying to go alone at the start is an almost guaranteed bomb-out.

Of course, I didn't know any of this on my first flight. I was just trying to keep my eyes on Josh and Nick as we soared around in the wind at seven in the morning seemingly half a mile from the hill, as I tried to figure out how that was even possible. The thermals started around 8am, smooth and easily defined, and when I saw Josh and Nick head out over the back with Brett Zaenlinger, a rare American pilot who's been coming to Quixadá for over a decade and was acting as our de facto local guide, I headed off with them.

By 9am we were high and with a stunning view of the area. We flew slowly down a small valley to the town of Madalena, where a number of pilots then converged.

Transitioning into a blue and windy area of small ridges and mountains, Brett and I found ourselves flying together north of the small town of Fazenda Caiçara. After three hours of flying, so far little of what I had flown over seemed anything like flatland flying to me; other than the scorched fields out in the valleys, the area had been full of rocky features and undulating terrain.

It had also been far from easy, more like a sustained, disciplined fight to stay in the air, and as we drifted low in the increasing wind towards a rising tree-covered no-man's-land in which I could see no landings, it became obvious that you needed to gain altitude to get up on the first of a series of plateaus that ran like giant steps to the west.

Unsure of what lay ahead, I considered that I had no radio, and that Paulo had not found me a tracking device, but instead had handed me a piece of paper with phone numbers on it on launch, and told me I should have someone call him when I landed. A retrieval plan that had seemed dodgy at the time now seemed like optimistic lunacy as I surveyed the vast area of harsh and desolate Brazilian wilderness.

As I zeroed along in the strengthening wind and considered my options, I saw a glider landing a small distance from a hamlet of small houses – the only habitation I could see for miles. I decided to play it safe and also land near there, figuring a driver had to be coming for this pilot. Setting up on the windward side of a sun-baked clay field, I let the considerable wind bring me backwards behind the trees and then applied a little bar to move forward again and land in the wind shadow, moving quickly to control the glider on the ground as it tried to drag me back towards the wire fences.

Once on the ground, the heat hit me in a solid wave. Bundling up the glider as fast as I could, I moved towards the shade of a convenient tree. I was around 130km from launch and it wasn't even yet noon. I watched Brett drift low into the same area that I had just bailed out from and then keep drifting out of sight. A pair of young lads from the nearby village appeared, and as I pulled off my full-face helmet and harness, I wondered if they had ever seen a stranger-looking alien. My missing bag had forced me to fly in not only sandals, but also a pair of psychedelic purple-striped trousers that I had bought at a Trance Festival in Holland.

"Telefono?" I asked hopefully as I finished packing my glider, and the boys led me back to their house. Once in the cool inside, I met several members of the family and handed one of them Paulo's piece of paper, doing my best to explain that I wanted them to call the number and tell Paulo where I was. (I imagined making that request if I had landed on some random ranch in the United States and was speaking Brazilian Portuguese.)

Three of the women led me into the kitchen and sat me down at a long table, where they brought me plates of food and poured glasses of a very tasty cold juice, while one of them called on an old-style telephone connected to the wall. As poor as my Portuguese is, I could tell there was a lot of explaining going on; the area I had landed in was clearly away from any paved road and apparently not easy to describe. Then as luck would have it, I noticed that one of the women was on her cellphone. "Tienes cellular aquí?" I asked in my shaky Spanish, my Portuguese alternative. "Não, internet. Una antenna."

No freaking way – this little ranch house in the middle of nowhere had wifi! I couldn't believe my luck. Busting out my smartphone, I quickly located myself on Google Maps, dropped a pin, and then via Facebook and email sent the coordinates to Paulo. Too easy. I pulled up the tracking page to see how the others were doing, and realised that Jon Hunt had also landed close by. I hadn't even finished my lunch before he and our Via Sertão driver turned up looking for me, and I was sad that I had to leave the shady little house so soon. This first interaction with the local people in this vast country we were flying over impressed me greatly with their genuine hospitality, and by the time I left I came to believe that the people of the sertão were some of the kindest and friendliest I had met anywhere; perhaps a requirement for surviving in one of the harshest environments on earth.

Having Jon Hunt turn up in the retrieve vehicle took some of the sting out of landing 'early' – in few places does misery love company more than among grounded XC pilots, and we half-joked that this must be the only place where a four-hour, 120km flight felt like a bomb-out. JH and I have been flying together since 1990, and throughout that decade when I lived in Jackson Hole we went paragliding together most flyable days. Jon is a legend in the Rockies, both as a paraglider pilot and as a skier, but he rarely leaves home in Jackson Hole in the summer.

After all the years I had flown with him in the United States, I had jumped at the chance to go fly with him in a foreign country, and the fact that he was on the trip was the main reason I had tagged along. But like virtually all Jackson Hole natives, Jon is often unconsciously pretty competitive, and I could tell he was chafing at the fact that we were on the ground while Nick and Josh were still in the air out ahead of us, all the talk of the 400km club clearly affecting him.

"Relax!" I chided him with a grin over our ritual safety debriefing. "It's the first day, and we are just getting the feel of the place. Neither of us have been in the air in months, and we just flew XC for four hours. Most places we would be stoked.

"I know I can't keep up with Nick and Josh on those Zenos, so I'm not going to try, I'm just stoked that these nice people here had wi-fi, and that you and Paulo's guy managed to find me. Tomorrow is another day, and today was a good start – we still have nine more days. For now let's just head back to the pool and chill."

I maintained this heady optimism as we bounced along the dirt-track back to Fazenda Caiçara, and then became puzzled as we were shuttled into another vehicle that started heading west on the road, even though I was sure that Quixadá was to the east. Figuring that we were off to pick up another pilot before turning around, I observed that our driver, a heavy-set lad with thick glasses, seemed to employ the same strange fifth-gear technique as my driver from Fortaleza, often shifting from second straight into fifth, and letting the engine get painfully close to dying on any kind of an incline.

As someone who was raised in a motorcycle- and car-racing family, it was painful to behold, and Jon laughed from the back seat when he saw me shake my head in astonishment at another one of our driver's low-rev gear changes. "This is the guy that drove us from the airport," Jon told me. "He drove 45mph the whole way and never changed gears once, so we nicknamed him Fifth-Gear."

As I had presumed, we were picking up another passenger, a Swedish pilot at least a decade older than Hunt and me who had landed past Monsenhor Tabosa. I gave him the front seat, figuring that we hadn't gone too far, and that once we turned around we would soon be back in Quixadá. But for some unknown reason, Fifth-Gear headed off north, and then east, and then finally south – and after a seven-and-a-half hour painfully slow loop back to the hotel, I exited the cramped back seat of the rental car vowing I would never go down near Monsenhor Tabosa again.

Josh Cohn – who, in what would become a pattern during the days ahead, had gone down at midday while leading – had flown 225km and somehow arrived back at the hotel shortly after us, while Nick Greece, on his first flight on the Zeno, flew 380km in nine hours and didn't arrive back at the hotel until close to 4am, not long before the rest of us were rising to fly again.

Listening sleepily to Nick's rendition of his flight and the arduous retrieve over the hotel breakfast that next morning before he headed off to bed, one thing seemed abundantly clear: the following nine days in

Quixadá were going to be a marathon. However, little did I really know just what a test they were really about to become.

The second day you launch at Quixadá must generally be better than the first, if only because you have the comfort of knowing what's coming. Still, it seemed even windier on the mountain than the day before, and the crew of pilots assembled for the day showed no sign of wanting to launch. Undaunted, Josh Cohn broke out his equipment and opened the launch window before 7am in what would become a pattern for the days ahead. Bound to my plan that if Josh went, I would go also, I soon followed suit, the wind jerking me off my feet and into the air even before I had a chance to get under the glider.

Better understanding the mechanics of the area, I searched well out in front of the monolith for lift, afraid that if I came in too close I might get blown over the back. With the increase in wind speed, the lift felt lighter and more broken, and it took a while before I got high enough to get on course. Flying with a small group of pilots, slowly, one by one, we went down, and when I landed around the 50km mark I could see no gliders in the sky ahead of me.

A motorcycle gave me a ride to the edge of town, dropping me off at a gas station with a pay-by-kilo restaurant attached that turned out to be the standard meeting place for downed pilots in the area. To my surprise Josh was already there, and I joined him and another pilot at their table. "Have you read the book Thermal Flying?" Josh asked, and I nodded, expecting some diagnosis of the shifting conditions we were experiencing. But instead Josh introduced me to "Burki", Burkhard Martens, the other pilot at the table – and author of the aforementioned book – who had flown 411km on a Skywalk Chili 4 (EN B) a few days before.

As the three of us sat silently eating our barbecue, I marvelled that I was dining with two of the most knowledgeable paraglider pilots in the world, and yet couldn't think of a single question to ask them!

Arriving back at the hotel, I walked into the lobby and found Nick Greece lecturing a silent Paulo from Via Sertaõ, our guide-and-retrieval service. Paulo looked less than amused and left shortly afterwards without his characteristic cheery farewell. Nick, an intelligent and compassionate pilot who has lived in the Rockies for over a decade, is also originally from

New York – and sometimes the blunt, no-nonsense New Yorker in Nick tends to come out.

In this particular case, despite having his longest foot-launch flight, Nick was unimpressed that it had taken Paulo's driver so long to find him some 385km away. Considering that Paulo was responsible for all of our retrieves, I tried to point out to Nick that he had just had one of the best flights of his life and made it back to the hotel for breakfast, but he seemed unimpressed. He was clearly focused on the idea of him and Josh setting a declared goal record.

This professionalism carried over into our own private group meeting, where despite my protestations he and Josh decided a 4.30am start was required. After my objections were overruled and Nick and Josh returned to their maps and route planning for their proposed 420km flight, I began to seriously wonder what I was doing there – for while I enjoy competition paragliding, this trip was not turning out to be my idea of a fun XC holiday with my friends, and I began to worry that if Nick and Josh didn't lighten up, it could be a long week.

The alarm went off at 4am the next morning and Jon Hunt and I sleepily made our way down to the hotel restaurant – only to discover that it hadn't even opened. Nick and Josh were already there sitting outside on a bench. After five minutes of sitting silently in the dark, Josh diplomatically suggested that we could probably start half an hour later the next day.

Back in our room after a hearty breakfast and coffee, I headed to the bathroom. Meanwhile, Jon Hunt had stepped out on the balcony and noticed that Josh and Nick were in a car and already leaving – clearly I was not behaving professionally enough for the pair. Flustered, Jon told me to hurry and said he would help by loading my glider bag into the next car, and less than five minutes later I joined him for the ride up the mountain, annoyed that Nick and Josh had ditched us without warning. My annoyance turned into full-blown Kiwi pissed off when I arrived on launch and realised that my Velcro flight deck – which had gotten wet from my Camelbak the day before and had been drying on top of my glider bag overnight – had been left behind in the rush.

As the others readied their equipment, I commandeered the fastest of the Via Sertaõ drivers and returned to the hotel at top speed. Quickly locating the missing flight deck, we then raced back up to launch. By the time I had my glider out and was in my harness ready to go, it was 7.45am, I was the last one on launch, and the wind was straight-out howling.

"It is right on the edge," Paulo told me, "but if we wait for a thermal to block the wind, then you can go. You must be quick though!"

Following Paulo's instructions I waddled down to the launch carpet, the anger at being in this situation overcoming any nervousness. I was determined to get in the air. A noticeable lull was followed by Paulo's command to go, and I pulled my glider up in as much wind as I had ever launched in before, lifting cleanly off the ground as my feet jerked around and I went straight for the speed bar. Moments later I flew into the same thermal that had blocked the wind enough for me to launch, and after a few hectic moments keeping the glider inflated, I found myself high above the ridge and drifting downwind.

Knowing that there were 30 or more pilots out ahead, all my competitive juices were now flowing along with the residual anger from being knocked out of my routine that morning. If there is one thing I've learned after more than 25 years of flying, it's that consistency is the hardest skill to acquire, and some days I fly much better than others for any number of reasons.

On this particular day, I began flying like the world class pilot I occasionally am, climbing quickly, pushing bar, and wasting no time as I reeled in pilot after pilot marking the lift out ahead for me. Past Magdalena, I spied what looked like the main gaggle heading into the torturous rising plateau between Fazenda Caiçara and Monsenhor Tabosa that had foiled me on my first flight. As I sat in a decent climb preparing to follow them, I noticed a faded-red Gin Boomerang 10 taking a very different line south. At first I wondered what this pilot was doing out there by himself, but then I saw that he was connecting with a good cloud street, so I elected to try this more southern line also.

Chasing the Boomerang as hard as I dared, I managed to get low for the first time that day in an area covered in scrubby trees with no LZs just south-east of Fazenda Caiçara. After a moment of wondering if my day was going to end badly, I hooked a fast-drifting bubble of lift a few hundred feet above the trees and took it out of there, managing to connect lower in the same thermal as the Boom 10 (who turned out to be a Polish PWC pilot) just as he was leaving.

For the next hour and a half I hung desperately half a thermal behind this faded pink Boomerang as we took a wide-sweeping route that carried us easily up and on to the first plateau before the small city of Monsenhor Tabosa. It was now about 11am (and the 130km mark), and we had just caught and passed the gaggle to the north of us, when I got my first real sight of the textbook cloud streets that were already well formed on the flats out ahead of us. This was the kind of legendary Ceará flying I had come for.

The wind strength had been steadily rising as the day lengthened, with each thermal drifting us across great swathes of terrain and pushing bar giving us groundspeeds well over 80km/h. I was flying at my limit, hanging on to the Boom 10, which was clearly being piloted by an excellent pilot who seemed to know his way around. The line he took us on was genius; we had flowed up on to the first plateau as smooth as water rolling over a flat rock, and then followed a steadily more impressive cloud street slightly across the wind north of Monsenhor Tabosa and through a passage between two granite monoliths. (The amount of wind you are flying in can make going around something more attractive than going over it.)

The view ahead of us as we came through the gap and the ground dropped away again was truly breath-taking, with perfectly spaced cloud streets more than a mile above the increasingly flat terrain. Then, as we were passing close to the small gaggle that I had been watching to our north, my radio crackled for the first time that day: "Hey Kiwi, is that you on the LM6?"

It was Brett Zaenlinger, the American pilot who'd been providing us with excellent info and support since we'd arrived, and who I had now caught up with, even though he had launched an hour ahead of me. An Alaskan fisherman, Brett has been coming down to Quixadá for over a decade, and had told us stories of the pre-Spot tracker days, when getting back from a big flight could in itself be a big adventure. It was Brett who had suggested we bring lightweight hammocks to stuff in our harnesses in case of long waits in remote areas, and it was Brett who had provided us with the three "standard routes" of around 400km for our instruments, one of which we were now one-third of the way along.

Pretty much everything about Brett thus far had been likeable, and when he told me that we wanted to cut to the south a few miles and follow the road, I took his advice without really thinking about it. It was only after we were climbing up together under the next cloud that I remembered the Boomerang. "Hey where did that pink glider go?" "The Boomerang? Oh, he just kept going straight along that street we were on and jumped the corner … the big boys like to do that. I figured we would play it safe and stick to the road."

Silently I cursed myself for not paying better attention, since I had been enjoying the challenge of flying with the other anonymous pilot. But at least now Brett and I could talk with each other, and since he was on a new Ozone Zeno, I now had a chance to see one in action up close.

But in a classic case of two pilots trying to adjust their speed to fly with each other – one flying red-hot on a glider he knew well, the other flying slower while learning a new wing – we almost went down after our first thermal together. Then, as we slowly ground our way back up in light broken lift and wind, with the Zeno seemingly performing much better than my wing in the slow and difficult climb, I noticed it was 11.45am. "Uh oh," I told myself, "better watch out, here comes The Pause."

The Noon Pause. A phenomenon I had become fascinated with over the past two seasons in Colombia, and the burning question that I had forgotten to ask Burkhard Martens and Josh about. It is a significant reduction in thermal strength and activity that routinely happens between approximately 11.30am and 12.30pm. It is most noticeable in the tropics, and I had become quickly aware of it when learning the basic mechanics of flying in Roldanillo, Colombia, where you often jump from a long chain of mountains on the western side of the valley in the morning to the better convergence conditions on the other side of the valley.

The more I flew in Colombia and the more I witnessed and tested this pause in effect, the more curious I became about the causes. I then came across an article by Cross Country's own Bruce Goldsmith that explained the phenomenon quite simply. It's all about the sun angle: at noon, when the sun is directly overhead, it's heating all the ground under it equally. Which means in simple physics terms, as the sun moves from 11.45am to 12.15pm, you no longer have a hot side and a cold side of a trigger point, (or a high pressure/low pressure differential). Everything is lying there baking in the direct sun, waiting for the sun angle to change enough that one side becomes hotter than the other and start triggering again (which also explains why that first thermal after the pause is often such a boomer: the ground has been acting as a heat trap).

In a generally low-wind place like Colombia, that explanation made complete sense to me, and now in the much windier flatlands of Brazil, I found out that it was just as true, as suddenly my weak and broken thermal gave out on me while Brett climbed out on the Zeno above. Searching back upwind I found nothing and then, without hesitation, I went on a long glide downwind to 250m AGL exactly at noon.

With my day nearly over at around 160km just before the city of Nova Russas, I made a desperate 90-degree turn in heavy sink, flew at the nearest good-looking trigger (a farm barn), and then zeroed for a while in a scrappy bubble until it joined a column of lift and I began to climb again. By 12.15 I was back at 1,800m (1,500m AGL) and at 12.45 I caught a climb to nearly 2,500m, one of my highest points of the day.

Brett had been chasing me and been just as low as I had, and when we were back at base he asked why I hadn't stayed in the climb that he was in. The fact was that in the lighter broken lift my heavily-loaded LM6 couldn't climb with Brett on the Zeno, and in some cases couldn't climb at all. But once we got past 12.30pm and were at cloudbase, I wasn't too worried about sinking out and was leaving lift on three-quarter bar, leading out and going downwind.

After my 227km flight in the US Nationals in Chelan, I had wondered when I would ever get that chance again. And now unbelievably here I was – seven flights later – sitting over a mile off the ground, past the 100-mile mark before 1pm, and with the wind strengthening and cloud streets stretching out in front of me as far as the eye could see. With the lessons of the Chelan flight still fresh in my mind, at this point I had no doubt that 200 miles was on the cards.

But there was still a long way to go. While the writer in me sits here struggling for adequate words to describe the sensation of being under those monster cloud streets high above the Ceará flatlands, the photographs I took over the next four hours tell the real tale of what seemed like textbook conditions at the time.

For the next 70km or so I had Brett acting as my guide. He provided the crucial advice that I should try and get as much altitude as possible before transitioning on to the next high plateau before Serra da Pedra Rachada, the highest point the ground would reach all day. However, Brett was also committed to staying with the road, which was cursed with large patches of shade, while I kept seeing pilots to the north of us clearly enjoying more sun and more stable cloud streets.

The result was I kept diving out into the desert to the north chasing better climbs and then coming back to Brett on his line along the road, and I ended up getting low again at around 1.45pm in the rotor of the long north-south ridge that he had been warning me about, committing to a line with minimal landings and a long walk out. Thankfully, it worked. An hour later and we were 10km from the town of Pedro II and down again to under 400m AGL from cloudbase at 2,600m. After this last low save, Brett told me he was going to switch radio channels to try and contact our retrieve driver, and although I fiddled with the knobs of my radio, I never heard from him that day again. Flying by sight, we were soon separated in the vastness of the area.

A couple of kilometres before Pedro II a strong climb took me to cloudbase at 2,500m again, and with my radio silent, the next hour and a half was like flying in a dream as I followed the road towards my stated goal of Piripiri. Catching my last big climb at 3.45pm, the road turned north and I went on a cross-wind glide for the last 45 minutes with Piripiri in sight.

Thinking only of making the 200-mile mark, 195, 196, 197 – surely I would make it, I kept telling myself – as I reached the edge of the city I realised that 200 miles would put me right in the middle of downtown! Now only 200m off the ground, I was forced to turn west again and skidded along the outskirts of the city, hoping for one more bump of a thermal which never came. Finally I turned into the wind and landed at 4.30 in a field beside some lads playing soccer 198.5 miles (318km) from where I had launched some eight and a half hours earlier.

Ironically my obsession at making it to the city of Piripiri actually did me in – for if I had been studying my instruments more closely, I could have turned west a mile earlier (or more) and probably broken the 200-mile mark just by using a better angle with the wind. (If I had stuck to the more northern route like the Polish pilot had, I might have made it another 25km or so, since the longest flights of the day came from that line. On XContest I had the fourth longest flight of the day and the fastest average speed; XContest scored the flight at 327km – 203 miles). And while I was slightly annoyed with myself for this mistake, I can't really say I was disappointed since I knew that this was a new New Zealand open distance record, and that after nearly 30 years of paragliding, I had now flown further than any of my countrymen!

Once out of my gear I handed out stickers, candy bars and high-fives. After snapping a couple of selfies and my usual safety debriefing, I walked less than half a kilometre down a dirt road to a sealed road. As I was heading into the city in search of a bar with an internet connection, I was astonished to see Brett and our driver, Fifth-Gear, driving towards me in a Via Sertaõ car! Not only was this the longest flight of my life, it was probably the quickest I have ever seen a retrieve vehicle arrive outside of goal.

Fifth-Gear dropped us off at a local barbecue restaurant while he went off to find other pilots. The Polish PWC pilot on the Boom 10 turned up in another vehicle, and then Fifth-Gear came back with a Swedish pilot who had just broken the Nordic record. As we sat drinking beer and discussing our flights, the Polish pilot commented that it hadn't been a very good day, and I laughed.

"No, I am serious," he said. "This was a slow day. The clouds were not so high, there was too much shade… today was difficult, definitely below-average for here." At first I thought he was joking, but then Brett and the Swedish pilot – who had both flown multiple seasons in Quixadá – agreed.

"Below average!" I had to silently concur that yes, this had not been as good a day as the task we had flown in Chelan. But still, if this was a below-average day here, then what was a good day like? On the record-setting days in early November, pilots were getting 500m higher than we had that day. With a week's worth of flying still ahead, suddenly 400km seemed very possible, even probable, if I could get a day better than this one, combined with what I had now learned about the route.

But we had to get back to Quixadá first. As we all piled into the car, Fifth-Gear looked across and realised that I was sitting in the front seat beside him, and after a moment of staring at me, indicated that I should drive. "Seriously?" When he nodded, undoubtedly afraid of my commentary if he drove, I didn't wait for him to change his mind and was soon behind the wheel, a position Fifth-Gear let me occupy for most of the speedy eight-hour drive home. I was beginning to really like the lad, who I found out was a local student Paulo had hired for the season; in fact I had liked every local I had met since I had arrived in Northern Brazil.

A couple of hours into the drive, when we crossed back into Ceará and I realised that I had flown clean out of the state, the enormity of my flight really struck me, and I felt humbled by both the terrain and the people I had passed over. After nearly 30 years of paragliding, this flight felt like an incredible reward for persevering, if nothing else, and further proof that free-flying is the greatest sport in the world.

Trumped

At breakfast the next morning, Nick Greece told me that Donald Trump had won the US elections the night before as I had been driving back from my epic flight, and it took the table some time to convince me that he wasn't having me on. We should have taken that as a sign for the week that was to come, for after a promising beginning, conditions worsened considerably, with the wind rising each day.

Undaunted, Josh Cohn opened the window on launch each day as he and Nick Greece continued their quest for a Distance-to-Goal record, often joined in the air by the relentlessly mile-hungry Swiss pilot Kevin Phillip on his six-week quest to break the Swiss record, and Juan Sebastian Ospina, the rising Colombian/British star who had just arrived. Flying together, these four pilots formed as talented an XC gaggle as you could ever hope for, and their struggles over the week highlighted how difficult conditions had become. The increase in wind in the mornings shredded the light lift to the point of no return and made it difficult for groups to fly together.

Josh Cohn continued to lead out in full race mode, and kept getting caught in the noon pause that he and Nick had been sceptical about when I had first brought it up; they became true believers as the week wore on. They admitted they had gone down during the pause just north of me on the day of my record flight, meaning not only had I claimed a national record, I had also outflown Josh, Nick, and Jon Hunt on the same day – something that had definitely never happened before!

As the days wore on, a sense of desperation on launch began to appear, the mental toll of bombing each day just as debilitating as the relentless heat and long silent retrieves. Talk of records became replaced with prayers for a single decent flight, as the locals all said they had never seen a week as windy as this one – even Paulo's cheery optimism noticeably waned.

Ever conscious of his sponsors, Nick confessed to me that he had had 400km on glide the first day, and had flown crosswind to a hotel and road (at 385km) for the easy retrieve, figuring he had plenty of days ahead of him. Heavy on his new Zeno, Nick took to shedding every ounce of gear that he could imagine, while in the air – in his own words – he kept falling off the back of the fast-flying gaggle after a few hours, at which point he would have no choice but to slow down and revert to cross-country, while the others kept dirting out in front of him. This pattern would ultimately reward Nick with the only 400+ kilometre flight (420km) during the period we were there.

Full circle

My own euphoria with my new national record was short-lived; after a day's rest I returned to the launch and duly followed Josh and Nick into the air. However, unbeknown to me, a link on the bar-end of my speed bar had apparently broken towards the end of my eight-and-a-half-hour flight. This became apparent as I levitated straight up and then began to get blown backwards towards the large antenna behind the Via Sertaõ container control centre.

As I pushed on the bar I felt nothing. Aware of the shouting going on at ground level below me, I gave the speed bar one more try, thinking I had somehow missed it, and then, sensing the large metal antenna mere metres behind my head, I finally peeled off to the left (as Paulo had advised me to do if in trouble) and ran off downwind over the back of launch. It turned out to be far less turbulent than I would have imagined, with a convenient sheltered LZ beside the road within glide.

I had been so close to getting wrapped around the antenna that the man who had been videoing the action dropped the camera because he didn't want to film me getting hurt. A close call like this one quickly brought my aspirations back down to earth, and while I tried to brush off the event, the increase in wind on launch each successive day (until we finally got blown out and went to the beach) and the difficulty of the flying continued to erode what little confidence I had left. I kept bombing in the first 50km to Magdalena each day.

Other pilots found it equally difficult: Jon Hunt ripped his beloved Icepeak 6 in half over a barbed-wire fence upon landing one day; while Josh Cohn's perplexity at his myriad of shortened flights was increasingly obvious, one of the most experienced competition pilots in the world forced to examine his usually calculated flying style.

Finally, on our very last day of flying, Josh flew 360km in 10hrs 45mins, breaking his personal best, and Jon Hunt had his first 100-mile day, salvaging something from a very difficult 10 days of flying. Of course, after we left conditions improved again: Kevin Phillip broke the Swiss record with a flight of 415km; and Juan Sebastian Ospina and the Venezuelan pilot Joanna Di Grigoli both flew 400km, all during the last week of November.

On the second-to-last day I bombed yet again before Magdalena, and when the Via Sertaõ driver found me, he had the same Brazilian pilot who I had met at the airport – the one who had flown 375km on his first flight in Quixadá the year before – with him in the car. With typical Brazilian enthusiasm he convinced me to return to the launch for a second try. On the ride up I asked him how he and his friends' trip was going this year, and his tanned face noticeably darkened as a rare frown appeared.

"It has been terrible!' he said. "Not one of us has flown more than fifty kilometres! Can you believe that? I don't think there has ever been a worse week in Quixadá!"

My second flight was as inconsequential as my first, but when I landed some 40km away, I realised that a botched launch had ripped off my helmet vario and somehow I had lost my tracking device as well. The heat was terrific, and as I slowly packed up in the shade wondering how I would contact Paulo, a couple of lads appeared on motorcycles and gave me a ride to their house which had wifi. The family had me set up in a hammock with a pitcher of cold juice and lunch on the way when Fifth-Gear turned up; unfortunately I had to leave.

It felt like I had come full circle. And despite my New Zealand open-distance record, I would leave Quixadá suitably humbled that I was not sure that I was really a good pilot, but merely a lucky one. I guess I will have to go back to find out.

A top-class paraglider pilot, James 'Kiwi' Johnston was a rebel spirit and a popular writer for Cross Country magazine, as well as being a leading figure within the psychedelics and Burning Man festival communities. He died in a paragliding accident in 2020. For more details of his life, see the story Finding Kiwi in this volume.

On paragliding and certainty

Allen Weynberg

Great wafts of sweet molasses fill my nostrils. A rich syrupy mixture of cloud and steam. Sensory overload as I start to accelerate upwards and bank hard. I can hear machinery grinding and crushing below as I glance down at the sugar mill. These industrial marks blot the northern Australian landscape. Each one with a prominent smoke stack that belches forth a frothy mix of smoke and steam. Tall plumes that provide wind information on the long drive south to the hill (we pass four at least). Now, on the flight back north, I'm joining the dots. Each one a thermal certainty.

In a sport that's all percentages, gambles and chances, the sugarcane factories beckon over the flatlands, shouting. Smoke signals for miles. Like an arrow in the sky: "UP HERE." My recent flights have lacked that certainty.

A solid bomb. I turned up new, keen and green. After brief conversations with the congregation gathered, I set up hurriedly and watched out of the corner of my eye as the first two pilots eked out enough height to leave on the first breaths of lift. The multitude hesitated wisely, but I took off. That sinking feeling immediately hit the pit of my stomach. Each little blip felt nowhere near enough. Down into the deserted valley below. First to land.

I spent the whole day watching other pilots wheel away into the bright blue sky. Comp wings, demo gliders, hangies, school gliders – I swear I saw someone on a bin bag around midday. I listened to it all for a bit on my radio, then I kicked that around the field, switched it off and stuffed it into the useless heavy bag that sat next to me like a millstone in the valley of doom. Eventually the bottom field claimed a few more and I got a lift in the back of a Byron Bay camper van.

Paragliding doesn't care. It is merciless. Imagine a parallel scene in the world of say, golf. A player moves to a new city and joins the swankiest club. He's got the required money, pieces of paper, handicap etc – whatever those golfies need besides a set of bats and some trousers. He arrives at the course on a shining Saturday morning, shakes hands with his new playmates and generously offers to hit off first. First ball dribbles off to the left and under a rusty park bench labelled "Failure's Viewing Platform." The rules of the sport dictate he must sit down and watch as all the others merrily drive, chip and putt away the day.

"Any chance someone could come and get me?"

"Nope, we all love driving, chipping and putting so there's no chance anyone will give it up at prime time. You wouldn't."

"Any drinks on the bench?"

"Nope. See you in the clubhouse later."

Golf would change the rules. Paragliding doesn't care, and that's not a dig at the participants. If you survive in this sport for even a brief time, then you will look at the failure bench and know you won't swoop down to give lifts or any non-medical assistance. We are all self-reliant and a little selfish. We have to be.

My hands are high up and quivering on the rear risers. In front of me a distorted mass of neoprene hints at a hastily stamped-on speed bar. A brief wave of reassurance, as the Flytec gives a speed of 5km/h, suddenly turns to nausea as I look down and realise that's backwards speed. I was first off the hill again.

A little height gain, and I begin to inch forward. Experience tells me it will probably be an all right but not very pleasant trip to the landing field. I sort out the pod, make myself more aerodynamic and settle in for the ab-crunching ride. Getting schooled about whether it's worth the risk to take off – if you don't go you won't know. One good whack and a heavy landing, and it's all over.

I hurry towards the hang glider pilot who's packing so I don't get left behind here and he has a passenger on her first flight. She eyes my harness and innocently asks, "Do you need all that stuff?" I look down at the assortment of phone, radio, vario, Spot, camera etc that I have just flown straight down to this field as fast as I could. "Need" is a relative term.

After the sugar factory plume spewed me out at base, I continued on down the track. Back home in Townsville I had the certainty of John following me and a certain lift home. Closest to the car goes to fetch is a rule, and I've never lost.

Next thing I'm looking down at an enormous dusty. I'm not flying over that so I skirt to the left and the inevitable happens. The dusty sucked up that field so I'm hitting the dirt in the adjacent one.

I enjoy the calm of packing under the shade of a gum tree. I clock John's icon on FlySkyHy getting closer. Then I see him float right past and I grin. There are no certainties in paragliding.

Allen Weynberg learnt to fly with friends in North Wales in 1994. He works as a high school guidance counsellor in Queensland, Australia, and is a columnist for Cross Country magazine. Allen's ambition is to fly 200km – but without making a plan.

Breaking three hundred miles

Larry Tudor

I had a big breakfast at 7.30, because I knew it would be my only meal of the day. Afterwards I called Wills Wing to tell them about my 200 milers on the two previous days. I also told them I'd be calling that night from Elkhart, Kansas, with news of a 300-mile flight. I usually take two aspirin before a flight, but I was still pretty sore from the last two flights so this time I took four.

Conditions in the morning looked good. A low pressure over Arizona was pushing into New Mexico, and a high pressure system to the east meant a good southerly wind all the way to North Dakota. The high would also cap off the instability that the low was pumping up.

I decided to launch at 11.00. In retrospect, 10.00 would have been better. The low was causing overdevelopment in the mountains 150 miles to the west, and some cirrus clouds were starting to appear over Hobbs airport. Surely they would shut down the lift.

Unfortunately, I'd agreed to let Ted Boyse launch first. When he didn't get away on his 10.45 tow and needed another, I figured I'd be lucky to even get out of the airport. At 11.13 I launched with cirrus cloud over me and got off tow at 4,800ft (airport elevation is 3,707ft).

The first thermal only took me to 6,100ft, but there was nothing to be gained by hanging around the airport, so I turned north towards the sunshine. Two or three miles later some birds showed me a thermal, before it dissipated and I headed north again, this time into real sink. A mile or two later I was 75ft(!) off the deck over mesquite bushes, oil rigs and power lines. I was scratching to stay even, and drift to a safe landing area.

After five exhausting minutes at 75ft, I caught a thermal. It eventually took me back up to 5,700ft before flattening out like the others. I thought the whole day was going to be like that, and decided to make the best of it.

I circled in zero sink and drifted a few more miles before the sky finally cut loose a bit. After scratching all that time so low, I figured that whatever happened from there on out was a treat.

For the next two hours I cruised at 9,000-11,000ft, trying to conserve precious altitude, and kept focused on the first rule of flatland flying: wind, not speed, gives you distance, and the wind is stronger at altitude.

75 miles into the flight I hit the strongest lift I'd encountered in the last three days. At 13,500ft, I realised how much the low save had taken out of me, so I started to fly fast between thermals. I was making my way north between the east side of Highway 18 and the Texas/New Mexico border. Heading into Clovis, New Mexico, the wind had picked up and turned south-west. This worked out well, because I needed to fly east of Clovis to avoid the controlled airspace of Cannon Air Force Base. I crossed into Texas at Farwell on a track that would take me north-east to Adrian.

By the time I got to Adrian, I was 175 miles and five-and-a-half hours into the flight. I was also down to about 7,000ft. This was bad news, because 50 miles of remote scrublands around the Canadian River lay ahead. It's all landable, but there are only a few unmarked roads and I didn't want to put any of us through another two-day retrieve like we had earlier with Ted Boyse. I told Ted (who'd landed after 50 miles), Pat and Josh in the retrieve vehicle that I might have to land in Adrian.

Fortunately I caught a 700fpm thermal to cloudbase at 13,000ft. It felt great, but I knew it was no guarantee. Soon afterwards, I got in the worst plunge of the day. After ten minutes of big sink, I was down to 7,500ft, in a worse position than Ted had been in when we lost him. I was right where the Canadian River meets Rita Blanca Creek, but there were no roads in sight and – worse yet – I had lost contact with the retrieve vehicle.

I finally found some zero sink, and after a few minutes it turned into my favourite thermal of the day. Ten minutes and 5,400ft later at cloudbase, I couldn't help exclaiming into the radio: "Do you know how I spell relief? 13,000 FEET!"

I stuffed the bar and raced for a good-looking cloud about six or seven miles in front. I lost 4,000ft getting there, but the lift under it took me right back to cloudbase over Charming, Texas. Near Hartley I got back to 13,000ft for the last time. 230 miles into the flight, things looked good.

Unfortunately, all the clouds in front of me were breaking up, so I started being real conservative with glide. At this point I was just drifting along in a series of zero sinkers towards Stratford, near the Oklahoma border. I worked a few bubbles, but basically I thought I was on final glide. But when I gained 1,700ft in a 300fpm thermal, I was back up to 9,000 and knew I wouldn't be landing in Texas. For the next 45 minutes I drifted and worked lift ranging from 200fpm up to 200fpm down, all the way to Oklahoma.

At 10,200ft I knew I had a shot at reaching Elkhart. But I also knew that if I hit the same kind of sink that I had on the way to Stratford, I was doomed to land somewhere in the Oklahoma panhandle, about 15 miles short of goal. I was 45 miles south of Elkhart in a light, sinking tailwind and having to crab against the south-westerly drift to maintain my north heading. I knew the lift was pretty much over for the day. I was on final – a torturous, frustrating final glide, because it lasted so long and because I knew how disappointed I'd be if I got this close to 300 miles and didn't make it.

The suspense was nerve-wracking. At one point I started cussing out loud because I didn't think I was going to make it. But the tailwind held out, and I caught my first sight of Elkhart just before flying over Crossroads, Oklahoma.

About halfway between Eva, Oklahoma, and Elkhart, Kansas, Elkhart started looking like a plausible glide. That's when I started seriously wondering whether I was awake. Nothing seemed real to me. The air was smooth as glass and I was so tired I thought I was in a dream. When I finally figured out I wasn't dreaming, an electric feeling came over my whole body from head to toe. Maybe it was the combination of exhaustion, elation and dehydration, or the effects of adrenaline and low blood sugar. Whatever it was, it got stronger and stronger the closer I got to Elkhart. By the time I had Elkhart directly underneath my wings the tingling sensation was like nothing I'd ever felt before in my life. The feeling lasted a full 24 hours after I had landed.

I figured I was in a position to go another 15-20 miles, but the area north of Elkhart is almost deserted and I was afraid I'd have trouble finding a witness. Rather than press my luck, I decided to settle for the 302-mile declared goal. So I spiralled down and started yelling "help" at the top of my lungs to attract landing witnesses. And plenty of witnesses there were in Elkhart, including one little girl who kept asking me why I was yelling for help when I obviously didn't need any.

Larry Tudor grew up in Denver, Colorado. He was an expert youth chess player before discovering hang gliding in 1973. Larry became the predominant US big distance flyer – being the first to break 200 miles, and setting records for height gain as well as distance. He later started paragliding in Stubai with André Bücher, whose instructions consisted of "links, recht, halt".

MINI STORY

Sharing the joy

Andrew Craig

After a desultory morning's flying, I was becalmed on launch in nil wind. I got talking to a passing father and his charming little girl, who asked me lots of sensible questions about steering, thermals and birds of prey. Then she wistfully remarked: "I've never seen a paraglider take off."

I told her I couldn't promise anything. I didn't want a sweaty walk up from the bottom, and the barbed wire fence right in front of me meant I'd need a bit of lift to get off safely.

Eventually I got my bag out to pack up, while the girl's father told her it was time to move on. But then a waft came through.

I stopped packing; they stopped walking.

I inflated my wing and made several abortive charges from the tiny slope of the dew pond down to the fence. And then a big, juicy thermal came through, and I stepped into the rising air.

"Bye-bye!" called the girl.

I gabbled a reply as I wrestled with the rough climb, and just about managed to give her and her dad a wave as I flew off.

That was twelve years ago.

I wonder if she's a pilot herself by now.

Andrew on trying to inspire the next generation

The King's Trail

Lenka Zďánská

The forecast for Tuesday and Wednesday promised sun, and, after a rainy week, the air had begun to smell of the promise of thermals. "Well, why not?" I said to myself. "Time to see if my big summer dream is feasible."

First, my 'small' bag, into which I would have to fit the following:

Paragliding equipment: Wing, harness and reserve. A GPS with vario, ball compass, map, helmet, jackets, warm gloves (it tends to get really chilly where I was headed), phone, video camera, and an unnecessarily heavy power bank for charging all the electronics.

Sleeping equipment: Sleeping bag, camping mat, tent.

Provisions: I opted for a minimalist, but relatively luxurious, strategy. My tiny titanium stove fits nicely into a cup, and the small bottle of liquid fuel is just enough to boil water for breakfast and dinner. I then took oats and polenta because you just pour hot water over that, and raisins, nuts and cinnamon to add to breakfast. I also went with salt, olive oil, a few cloves of garlic, and sun-dried tomatoes – enough to dine nearly as well as in a Michelin-starred restaurant.

And water: There's plenty of this here in the north, but carrying at least a litre is a good idea, right?

But how to squeeze everything in, when the bag's not inflatable? I removed the bulky foam protector from my harness and filled the space with the sleeping bag, the tent (without the poles), the sleeping mat and clothes instead. I wasn't convinced this would perform the same function as the original protector, but I couldn't think of another option. And it kind of worked. The bag's seams were tight as guitar strings, but everything was in. I decided not to weigh it though. Sometimes, ignorance is best.

But what was my plan? There's a long-distance hiking trail called The King's Trail (Kungsleden in Swedish), which runs down Sweden. It starts in the north in Abisko, which is 100km from Kiruna, where I live, and leads south across the mountains for more than 400km. One of the most rugged sections goes from Abisko, past Sweden's highest summit Kebnekaise (2,098m), to the village of Nikkaluokta. It's about 110km from Abisko to Nikkaluokta – and I wanted to fly as much of it as possible.

Nobody had tried it before – and I was about to find out how possible it was. But despite planning it for so long, studying maps, weighing up all the options and risks, and imagining what it would be like on my own, I felt incredibly nervous. What if I sprained my ankle in the middle of the mountains? Thankfully, my husband, David, is a rational thinker and he gave me understanding and support. He made it seem possible. "Let's do this!" I thought.

For safety, I decided to turn on position sharing on my phone. This smart feature is enabled by Google Maps – so that every time you get into an area with a signal, your position on the map is updated and viewable by anyone with a shared link. This meant that David would have at least a rough idea of my position – and could call in the cavalry if anything went wrong.

I gathered all my courage, put on my backpack, my only companion for the next few days, and set out into an unknown world, a world where, I hoped, even the most secret dreams could come true.

After sweating and scrambling my way up the hill above Nikkaluokta, I was really looking forward to relaxing under my glider – and I managed to launch before 11am. The first thermal took me a few hundred metres above the top, but my initial excitement quickly evaporated. I flew over the first valley but 'rotted out' like an overripe plum on the next ridge. Landing on some ugly, stony terrain cost me a stubbed foot and scratched elbows and knees. This wasn't going to be easy.

I sat on the top with the expression and the mood of a drowned rat. Would the thermals start working? Or should I just slide back down to the car, and try another day? I was desperate to chase my dream further, so I sat and waited.

Around 1pm some little puffs of wind began, and as they got stronger, I was soon in the air again. For a good half-hour, I hugged the rocky edge, and patiently waited for what would happen next. Finally, it came – a strong thermal, and I let its wave carry me above 2,000m. Those nasty rocks that tore my elbow, my knee, and my favourite jacket were far below me. I finally felt safe and relaxed.

From there, I managed to glide to the valley which leads to the Tarfala cabin and a lake which is free from ice for only one month a year. It's a hard place to climb out from, as the slopes are gentle and the valleys wide. But then a bird of prey flew past me and started rising. "Thank you, my friend!" I shouted as I followed my new companion skywards.

I flew past the Kebnekaise fjällstation mountain cabin and headed daringly on. The summit of Sweden's highest mountain, Kebnekaise, was now almost within my reach. Here, the slopes are much steeper and the thermals stronger.

Above the glacier, which was being crossed by a group of climbers, I met a magnificent mountain eagle – and I was getting ever closer to the wall of Kebnekaise. Another climb took me to 2,500m and I had the whole ridge of Kebnekaise beneath me. In fact, I was so high that I could barely make out the human figures that had managed to scramble to the top.

"It's now or never!" I thought. So I steered my glider towards the north and flew into the unknown. What lay ahead of me now, I knew only from the map.

A view of endless mountain ridges and mighty snow carpets opened up in front of me. In the valleys, lakes that had only just begun to thaw were sparkling blue like sapphires. Glaciers licked the rocky feet of the mountain giants. The whole landscape looked like it was just waking up from its winter's sleep.

To my left, I could see a single green valley. It is so wide that it allows rays of sunlight to caress it, bringing spring a month early. And it is this valley that Kungsleden passes through. I tried to keep it in my sights, but the steep mountains, pristine lakes and glaciers attracted me like a magnet. I changed my plan and turned towards the Stuor Reaiddávaggi valley instead.

I jumped from one ridge to another and flew over the Nallostugan mountain cabin as the air got colder. Thick snow and ice isn't the best breeding ground for thermals, and I started to wonder whether I had been a bit too adventurous. Especially when I had to land by the frozen lakes of Nállojávrrit.

I packed, consulted the map, and set off across a small glacier to a nameless peak lying at 1,807m. The journey to the top, over the glacier, was freezing and exhausting, and my hiking boots got soaking wet and heavy. Heading up the steeper parts, I had to jab my boots into the snow and ice as if I had crampons.

But looking out from the summit, I forgot all about the weariness and cold in the blink of an eye. The sun warmed my cheeks, but it was getting late and this would have to be my home for the night.

To know that someone will be worrying about you is a horrible feeling – especially when you can't let them know that you're alright. But, to my surprise, my phone suddenly connected to the network and I was able to contact David. It was a feeling of immense relief, swiftly followed by a wave of desperate hunger. I put on the stove, made dinner and set up camp. And then I slept like a princess. Spending a night in the open air, above the Arctic Circle and at 1,807 metres, is a real novelty. What a shame I slept through it all.

In the morning, however, it was clear this wasn't the easiest launch. Glider lines tend to get stuck behind – and even cut by – protruding rocks, and I had to fine-tune the take-off. After half an hour of tidying up and rearranging the stones on the summit, I felt like a tile setter. And I still struggled to launch. In the end, it took me an hour to get airborne.

After the first morning flight, I discovered that there was strong wind higher up, which blew apart the thermals, making it almost impossible to centre them. I landed in a neighbouring valley and climbed up to take off again. Perhaps I would get a bit further this time. I soared the edges of the ridges in the wind in the hope that I could make it to the next valley, but eventually I chose the cowardly strategy of retreat – and instead went on through the Aliseatnu valley to the east. I landed after about 20km – and started hiking. "You can't always fly, Lenka," I told myself. "Sometimes you have to work for it a bit, too!"

I jumped over streams that gurgled over pebbles, as well as bushes of dwarf willows, before wading through the last big river. How pleasant and refreshing! The mighty, roaring Aliseatnu river was hurtling through the valley like an unstoppable element. It was an overwhelming sight. But this magnificent green valley had its downside, too. Bloodthirsty mosquitoes appeared, buzzing with delight at the arrival of a walking blood bank.

At last, I reached the foot of Báhkkabahkčohkka mountain. I quickly put up the tent, and dressed for dinner in my mosquito-proof Gore-Tex jacket and head net. Even then, I had to stage my second retreat of the day and hide in the tent.

The following morning was quieter; the mosquito gang probably still asleep. So I packed and marched slowly on. The vegetation was quickly disappearing, and my insect tormentors with it. I could finally allow myself the luxury of breaks to catch breath.

The weather was scowling, so there was no point in waiting. When I reached a suitable launch, I took off, meaning to glide down towards my destination: Abisko.

At the bottom I ran into some tourists, and it was nice to meet somebody of the same species again. We chatted merrily as the sun lit up above the valley. I gathered my last strength and set off to climb up to what I hoped would be my last take-off.

That last glide got me to within approximately 2km of Abisko. The air had started bubbling with late afternoon thermals and had taken me further than expected. After a smooth landing, I realised that I had made my dream come true – and survived.

I learnt that everything is possible if you gather enough courage and make the first step. It's not easy to set off on a journey into the unknown, but, trust me, it is truly worth it. Besides, if you do it with your heart, nature seems to find a way of helping you along the way. Thank you, universe.

Lenka Zdánská learned to fly in her native Czech Republic in 2012, and now lives in northern Sweden. She works as a geographic information systems engineer.

The ballad of Robb and Joe

Matt George

Fort Funston, then. It was surprising to me that I was not frightened. But someone stepped in for me anyway.

It was Fort Funston on the beach in San Francisco. It was spring, 1971, and we were surfers, my brother and I. Older brother Sam was just fifteen. I was twelve at the time. Sam had cadged us a ride to the beach with a couple of seniors from his high school. I stood on the dunes, facing the sea, taking the weather in the teeth.

The surf was inhuman. Huge, deadly looking, arctic cold and laced with malice, hissing like a monster in pain. A northwest wind was screaming in, blowing the whole world to smithereens. From shore to horizon the sea looked like a flock of giant, stampeding sheep. We held our jackets up and leaned into the wind. I got to about 45 degrees.

I saw them first. A group of hippies wrestling what looked like a plastic-wrapped wooden Christmas tree up from the spot where they parked on the Pacific Coast Highway. Sam and I watched as they fought their way to the top of the dune and unfolded the thing like an origami butterfly. The contraption was made of clean, split bamboo and clear plastic sheeting, and it became evident that they were going to try to fly it into the wind. Manned.

Sam and I approached quietly, being younger than the hippies, and sat in the sand to watch. Being daredevils ourselves, to our eye and to our hearts the machine and the mission made perfect sense.

And God knows there was enough wind. The hippies, a mixed bunch with one very pretty girl in a Janis Joplin jacket, finally got their machine together. They surrounded it, braced it and levered it into the wind. I was holding my breath at this point. The biggest hippie crawled under it, grabbed the bamboo bars and at his order, he stood up, lifting the craft free of the sand. Someone, somewhere, honest to God blew a whistle and the big hippie was off, running directly into the wind towards a 12-foot drop over an old bunker left over from World War Two.

So this big hippie, he tears off for all he's got and the pretty girl shrieks encouragement and the guy bounds along and then leaps off the lip of the bunker and for one second it looked like it might just work. He was suspended, airborne, hanging vertically with the bamboo bars under each arm, his shoulders up around his ears, his eyes like a horse in a barn fire.

Then the shuddering stall. Then the nose dive into the sand. Pow. Pathetic really. All that work.

I could tell he really wanted to impress the girl. She was the first one he looked at when he got out from under it. They all hauled it back up the dune like bell-bottomed ants, and took another whang at it. After about five of these attempts the guy was pretty beat up. Had a nosebleed. Torn his pants in the crotch. Broke his glasses. At that rate… well, that's when he announced he was just too damn heavy and the girl was going to have to do it.

You might as well have asked her to go catch a snake.

So like I said, I was surprised that I wasn't frightened. And I was the smallest human on the beach at that moment. So I stood up and said I'd take a shot at it. Everyone loved this idea. Everyone but my older brother. He stood up next to me, waved me off in our secret language.

The hippie with the nosebleed came over. Asked us what we weighed. I didn't know. But my brother was a springboard diver, so he knew what he weighed, and even though he had five inches on me, he hadn't filled out yet. So Sam said he would take my place. He always was protective of me. Still is. The hippies sized him up. And I'm not sure, but I think the pretty girl kissed Sam on the cheek right before he tested fate.

Readied, they all ran like hell for the ledge and Sam shoved off.

It was a miracle to me, watching my brother fly. The whole craft, with him hanging below it, described a perfect flowing arc off the edge of the bunker. Suspended, he joined flight history and crash-landed unharmed down in the flats after about seven seconds aloft.

The second flight was nine seconds. That really turned the trumpets on. But the third flight was just too much for the bamboo and the plastic sheeting, and the main braces gave out and Sam fell out of the sky.

The aircraft was crumpled. My brother was banged up too, but happily accepting handshakes all around. Sam got his second hug and a kiss from the pretty girl. She had tears in her eyes, but that might have been the weed she'd been smoking. I was close enough to smell that. That's when we found out the hippies were a group of postgraduate engineers over from Berkeley, spending grant money, developing a manned Rogallo wing for some big engineering design competition.

By Christmas of 1972, people would be jumping off Half Dome in Yosemite Valley with these hippies' design and my sister's boyfriend, flying in an early competition, would hang dead in his rigging in the upper branches of a redwood tree.

Kagel Mountain now

Flight had always remained a constant in my life. My Father had been a Navy man. Pilot. Spent World War Two in the cockpit of a Grumman F6F Hellcat. He'd bought a couple of aeroplanes after the big show was all over. A North American AT-6 SNJ Texan, and then a Starduster biplane beefed up for aerobatics. We had some adventures in those goddamned things. Some I'd like to forget. Running out of fuel over the San Francisco Bay in the Texan, and a pitch pole landing in the Starduster after my dad bent the wings doing Immelmanns.

Mind you, I had never learned to fly. It just wasn't me. But I'd go up with the old man, sure. Support his passion. His fourth wife hated me for it.

It went on, this flight thing and me. My abortive attempt at flight school, where I quit after I ran out of money having learned how to take off in a Cessna 152, but never learned how to land it. Then the rides in the bush planes all over hell looking for surf. Mexico, Africa, Java. I got shot off the catapult of the USS Ranger in a turbo-prop SEAL delivery aircraft. Zero to eight in an instant. Gs, that is. I thought my teeth were going to fly out of my mouth. That'll age you. Then there were the helicopter ops for the UN during the Pakistan earthquake of 2006. No pilot, me, just running the show and delivering high-altitude supplies in Kashmir out of Abottabad. They'd find Osama Bin Laden hiding out there later on, and we all know how that went. And I guess the skydiving would count.

But nothing prepared me for Kagel. Or the men who took me there. Kagel Mountain stands rampart over the inland empire of the Los Angeles area. From the ocean side of the valley, it looks like a footprint crushed into the edge of a caramel cake. Private pilots trying to find a place to land navigate by it. My friend Robb Derringer lives near there. He is, among other things including a successful Hollywood actor, a pilot. I met him in Hawaii when he was acting on a television show that I wrote for NBC.

First sight, I could tell by the way he walked he was a pilot. That swagger. It was one of the reasons we hired him to star in the show in the first place. As a producer, I wasn't really supposed to fraternise with the help, but I was drawn to him by the fact that his acting came second to his flying adventures. After a difficult childhood, Robb found freedom in the sky. He tried the air force, and that was like jail. So he cashed out and returned to recreational flying, always keeping his licence current in rented 172s. Robb took me and my Aussie girlfriend up a few times. I would hang on for dear life and try not to vomit. We became fast friends.

Back from some Indonesian travels recently, I caught up with Robb. I was writing for Hollywood again, and Robb had just landed a big role on General Hospital. He had started hang gliding the year previous, and had never been happier with his flying life. He told me he particularly liked flying with red-tailed hawks at his wingtips. It was that freedom that he was looking for. I always stay at his house while I am visiting Los Angeles, and I read all his hang gliding magazines and feed his pet. A big, black rescue raven with a shattered wing.

One morning, Robb sprung it on me that I was to take a tandem hang gliding flight. Take it with the legendary pilot Joe Greblo. A privilege,

I was told. Up at a place called Kagel Mountain. Still being a bit of a daredevil, I said yes. And an hour later, I found myself sitting on Joe Greblo's lawn right next to the Sylmar LZ. A briefing on what was about to happen to me.

I listened to Joe like a child at the feet of Buddha. Joe was comfortable in his element. Competent. A master. With a bubbling enthusiasm barely held back by pilot protocol. Safety first. Play things down. Stay frosty. I've always had the feeling that underneath it all, pilots would rather just jump up and dance around and sing about how much they love flying. But they can't. It's against protocol.

Up at the launch site, I looked out over a big piece of California. It was both beautiful and hard to believe. After all, I was about to jump off a mountain belly first. Robb was there, quietly helping Joe Greblo get me all strapped in, triple checking everything, keeping me calm. Robb was going to launch right after us and join us up there.

In the last seconds, I listened to Joe, he was my whole world at this point, and I did exactly what he said. And my brother didn't step in for me this time. This time, I stepped off into eternity all on my own. And I found myself soaring with Joe, above all the troubles in the whole damned world.

Funny, with pilots like Robb and Joe and the ghost of my father at my side, for the second time in my life... it was surprising to me that I wasn't frightened at all.

Matt George is an acclaimed surf journalist and screenwriter. His book In Deep covers four decades of his storytelling.

Stewart's story

Hugh Miller

Stewart Midwinter's is perhaps not the obvious kind of inspiring paragliding story. But Stewart lives very much as a pilot, as a member of our community. Just last summer he contributed to Dave Turner and Gavin McClurg's Alaska expedition efforts, tasked with sending them daily weather updates.

Through my own 25 years in flying, I'm mindful of how many pilots I've heard about who've suffered life-changing injuries, and whose stories get cut short. It's as if they fade to the edges of our consciousness as we keep on keeping on. A lot of what follows doesn't make for easy reading. But Stewart's experience is a pilot's life, and if we are to honour his experience as a fellow pilot, his story should be told just like anyone else's.

I first met Stewart in Castejón de Sos in 1997. It was my first World Championships, held in the harsh, mid-summer heat of the Spanish Pyrenees, with plenty of reserves being tossed over jagged peaks. No official record was kept, but at least 15% of the field either threw their chutes or were injured during the contest. Stewart was a judge at the time.

"That's right," Stewart recalls. "It was a tumultuous week in many ways. I met this woman and I had an affair with her. It ended my marriage and completely changed my life, and I don't regret a moment of it. That distraction helped me get through the ugliness of the record number of protests that the jury had to deal with.

"In terms of competition paragliding safety, I think we've since come a long way. We just haven't had that level of carnage since. Pilots are now way better trained, and wings are more solid."

Now aged 61, Stewart lives in Calgary, Canada, in a small community for people with life-altering conditions. He fell for the Rockies as a university student. "As soon as you see the Rockies, you just think: 'I've got to be there' – especially as a hang glider pilot," he says. "I remember the exact date I first flew: 23 October 1974."

"It feels like a lifetime ago. And when you look back at photos of those gliders, I'm like: 'Man, really?' They were just so horrible to fly. When the double-surface UP Comet came out in 1981 that was it, that was the watershed moment."

"I started paragliding in 1987. My first wing was a modified freefall parachute. All the lines were three-millimetre-thick nylon like you see on reserves. It had a glide of about 2.5 to 1. We ran off the hill, and kept running – we could barely get to the bottom, but after two flights I thought: 'This is the future of aviation'."

Stewart continued to fly hang gliders too, and was one of the first to fly the Class 5 Swift. He went on to set five FAI world records. However, soon after returning from Castejón de Sos, and with his marriage in tatters, he found himself in a flat spin crashing into Mount Swansea, and was lucky to walk away without a scratch.

"If your personal life is in turmoil, you really shouldn't be flying," Stewart says. "That's what I believe now. When you get into a crisis in the air and it's a do-or-die situation, you have to react instinctively. If you've just got fired, you're stressed, you just got divorced, or your mother died… your brain won't be alert or functioning well enough.

"If you spin a sailplane at low altitude, you're dead, so really, I was lucky to survive. I wrote an article for Cross Country titled An Interview with a Dead Man. I talked about that idea with Michael Robertson, a long-time instructor in Canada, since Michael had come up with his 'Robertson chart of reliability.' Basically you should do a proper self-assessment before you fly, including all personal factors."

Stewart would go on to enjoy another 14 years of incident-free flying before he suffered his life-changing accident on 13 August 2011. But like his accident of 1997, things were on his mind in the hours leading up to his crash, and he believes this contributed to what happened.

"I'd started dating this woman – now my fiancée – about three months earlier, and on 11 August she rang me to invite me to a family barbecue at her ex's house. It just felt a little strange, you know, I mean nothing that weird – they'd been split up 20 years – but it just knocked me a bit.

"Also, the day before I got hit by an unexpected garage bill, and as I was pulling out from the garage I saw flashing lights from a police car. I got pulled over and got told I don't have a current licence plate sticker and handed a stiff fine. Things were bothering me a little, I guess."

Will Gadd had posted an invite for a hike-and-fly at Canmore the following day, and Stewart decided to take him up on it, packing his 18-metre mini-wing for the trip. He'd flown his mini-wing for over a year, with several flights to cloudbase, and loved it, but remembers that even a mild day could feel like really big air.

"You know Will, right? This guy is an uber athlete. I figured the only way I'd keep up with him is by taking my light gear, my mini-wing, despite the fact I knew I'd be taking off into pretty big air in the middle of the day later on."

Stewart set off with Will, but Will was on a mission: "I don't think he can walk slowly enough to stay at my pace!" joked Stewart. Stewart soon felt burnt out trying to keep up, ran out of water and food, and told Will to go on ahead. By the time he got to take-off, Will was inflating and off, so Stewart was alone on the mountain.

"I was late, and I thought: 'I gotta get in the air, gotta get in the air, he's getting away,' and I didn't really think about the conditions. I mean, it was light wind, but I didn't have much of a plan," he remembers.

Thirty seconds after take-off, Stewart took a big asymmetric collapse. "For whatever reason I didn't look up," he remembers. "I corrected, then over-corrected – the wing was so loaded and so responsive. My muscles were hard-wired to dealing with the docile Nova Mentor 2 that I normally flew. It got worse. I looked down, saw the rocky mountainside and thought, oh crap. That's the last I remember, but I probably pulled brakes to slow my descent and might have stalled the wing."

Stewart landed on his head, dislocating his C4 in the spine in his neck by ten millimetres. A thousand feet overhead, Will remembered hearing him bounce and concluded that no-one could possibly have survived such an impact, but spiralled down to assist.

"I was face down on the slope, my wing caught in some trees," recalls Stewart.

"I couldn't get up, right? …This is pretty hard to talk about…

"I could barely lift my head. I thought: 'I can't feel my left arm, why's that, maybe it's broken?' I took a look, to my left, and my arm looked OK. Then I thought: 'Why can't I move my legs? They must be jammed in the dirt, that's why.'

"A part of your mind cannot accept the reality, which is paralysis. Although another part knows exactly what's going on. I lay there, and people ran down the mountain to help me. One of them was a nurse. She knew what to do, stayed with me, gave me sips of water. "About three hours later the Banff Parks rescue helicopter showed up. The hospital was right below in the valley. As they long-lined me off the mountain, I still had the presence of mind to think: 'Hey I'm having a longer flight now than I did with my paraglider'."

Hugh Miller: What has happened to you, there's no denying it's something that could happen to any single one of us who flies. And there's an aspect of this I'm interested in. We at Cross Country magazine naturally mainly focus on pilots doing great things, flying far, enjoying competitions. We don't hear about pilots who get hurt and can't fly anymore… they kind of get swept to the sidelines. It's like an unconscious: 'Yep, we don't want to know about that.' But those pilots' experiences are a very real part of the fabric of the sport. And many, including you, feel, and are, in your very core identities, pilots until you die. It's in your blood. So I'm interested in bringing it more to life, that diversity of experiences we share.

Stewart Midwinter: I thought, "Wait a minute, this is not my life story. I'm a pilot. I'm an experienced pilot and I'm going to be flying when I'm 70. Flying is my life. No, no no. This is a mix-up. This is not my story. Wait a minute, I want my money back.

"Too bad, you made a mistake," comes the reply from the other side of my mind. Buddhists would say 'OK, let go of the story'. We're not following a script through life. You just need to be present and aware of everything. Well, that's easier said than done. And yes, that point you make about not hearing about the stories of those who have accidents is really valid.

I went to the Banff Mountain Film Festival last year to watch Will [Gadd] and Gavin McClurg speak about their Rockies trip. You go through the foyer where there's all these people wearing their Patagonia jackets, looking healthy, talking about their latest exploits, and here you are in a wheelchair. Firstly you're shorter than everyone, so they're tripping over you in a crowded hallway. They either don't see you, or they see you too much. You're either invisible or you're a spectacle. I went with a friend who's also in a wheelchair. After it was over, she told me she'd wanted to scream out: "Hey you know, I'm not just some CRIPPLE. I'm one of YOU guys. I'm a part of this tribe!" And nobody sees it.

When I was 20, a friend had a flying accident and was paralysed and I didn't know what to say. I'd like to think now I'm older it's OK, I don't have that awkwardness, but I think I probably still do.

We don't know how to deal with suffering and other people's suffering. A lot of my friends never came to see me in the hospital. Or they came once, had tears in their eyes, and never came back. There were precious few that came twice, and I can count on the fingers of one hand the number that still visit me. People don't know what to talk to you about. Maybe they feel: "Jeez, I can't talk to him about flying cos I'm going to make him feel bad."

I guess people are second-guessing, trying not to upset you… but that doesn't do anyone any good, I guess. Yes, they feel they can't talk about the great flight they did two weeks ago so they don't come by, and I think that's sad. As you say, I'm still the same guy, I'm still fascinated by flight. I've been up in a glider a number of times since the accident, I've had some stunning flights, but obviously I'm just a passenger. It's a little unreal from that perspective.

My suggestion would be: get past whatever barriers you're putting up and talk to people about your passions, share them so they can live them vicariously.

This guy, a quadriplegic, wrote some advice recently. He said, instead of saying: "I'm so sorry for what happened", or: "I'm so sorry for your loss", instead of sweeping away the pain and the horror, acknowledge it in some way. Say instead: "You know, this must be terrible for you at times, but I'm here for you, if there's anything I can do to help, let me know." Don't sweep it away. It's part of the human condition. Recognise we are doing something that's risky, but at the same time most spinal cord injuries happen from road traffic accidents, or getting smacked by an ocean wave into the sand. You're not doing anything wrong by flying! We just don't want to realise how ephemeral our continued good health is.

The mountaineering community really understands the nature of risk much better than the flying community. It's more obvious. With high level climbing, that risk is with you every moment – you can be killed by objective hazards like rock falls or avalanches. Shit happens.

Will Gadd made the point that when one of his climbing friends gets killed, you get together, have a memorial, share pictures and memories, and sooner or later you move on, and you get on with your sport.

But with me, well, I didn't die. And I'm still here in people's faces so they can't really avoid having to deal with the reality of what our sport can imply. A lot of people can't deal with that.

I backed off and started just flying EN-Bs a long time ago. I didn't really comprehend that a mini-wing could turn into a D, or worse, if it collapses. I think we have a duty to each other to point out if we think our friends are taking undue risks. And it's hard to tell people in a polite way, without often getting a rude response – "Who are you to tell me I don't have the skill to fly this wing?" – that kind of thing.

I remember Robbie Whittall standing up at a European Paragliding Championships and saying, "Most of you pilots are not up to flying the comp wings you're on." That went down like a lead balloon, but he was right.

Not that I was over my head when I had my accident. My problem was I wasn't present: I was too distracted. That's the thing about mindfulness – when you're not mindful, you're not mindful enough to tell that you're not mindful.

You're very right.

I wasn't on my game and I didn't know I wasn't on my game. Maybe Will might have picked up on that and told me, and for a while it felt like he was avoiding me, but at the end of the day I'm responsible for my actions. Of course it's not Will's fault.

But I guess what you're saying is: take this seriously, look out for each other.

Yeah, it seems too simple, but because flying is such an individual sport, a lot of people object to that. We currently have a hang glider pilot in Golden flying a 30-year-old hang glider. The cloth is like silk. He's got duct tape up and down the leading edge. His harness is stitched together. And a lot of people have told him it's only a matter of time before it falls to pieces. Then others say: "No, who are you to tell him what to do? We're all pilots taking our own responsibility." But the day he dies, others will say: "Yeah why didn't anybody stop him?"

But in our sport and the sport of climbing we encourage risk-taking. We reward Alex Honnold for climbing solo up these insane walls and Nevil Hulett for breaking 500km flying in incredibly strong winds. And what happens when you get injured trying one of these bold moves? Well, the accolades fade away.

But you know, I remember a local pilot who crashed in 1984, became a paraplegic. I didn't know what to say, I didn't visit him, I couldn't deal with it, couldn't bear it.

It's a really difficult topic. These are very uncomfortable truths.

The first six months of my injury, I remember thinking: "I can't even commit suicide, I can't even hold a gun because I don't have any hand function. How can anyone live like this?" I was on anti-depressants and sleeping pills, and it was very, very hard.

I was a really active guy, riding my bike to work, running at lunch time, skiing, rock climbing, sea kayaking. And suddenly it was like being in a psychiatric hospital strapped to your bed. Every night it was the same nightmare. I'm at a picnic on a warm, sunny day and I lay down on the grass under this tree for a nap, and when I wake up I go to stand up and my legs won't move. I try again, my legs won't move… and I start screaming, and that's when I wake up and the nightmare is reality, but reality is worse because in the dream I can sit up.

I had so many times of just breaking down uncontrollably, and after six months or so I just thought: "Stewart, you're losing it here, you have to try and get a grip". Grief isn't linear, it just keeps coming back and hitting you when you least expect it.

Everybody says, "you're so strong", or "you're such an inspiration". I really loathe that word now. I'm an inspiration for simply waking up today? Or they say: "It's so good to see you out." Like I conquered some record by getting out of the door. I don't want to be special, I just want to get on with my day the same as everybody else, and be treated the same as everybody else.

Being called an inspiration – I guess that's a hard package to receive, to sign for.

Psychologically, the way I try to deal with things is to think I did die, and now I'm this reborn Stewart. That's what my yoga teacher told me. "Pretend every day you've got a new body and don't have any expectations. See what you can do." It's not easy. And the adventures are so much smaller nowadays, but they're still adventures. My fiancée and I will go out down the river, see the ducks, go out to see the hills. Guess what, I'm still a risk-taker, and just getting on the bus on my own and going into town is a proper adventure.

When you get this injured, it's easy to feel totally useless. The thing that helps me immensely is when pilots recognise I have something to contribute from all my years. Each year I give a briefing on flying Golden at the Willi Muller competition, and I watch the Spot trackers, keeping an eye on things.

I also did the met updates for Gavin and Dave's traverse of the Alaska Range. Holy crap, now that was a responsibility! A great honour but also a great responsibility. But I really am touched that they valued my input. In the US they have Jeff Huey, who's a former team pilot and now a paraplegic. He's a meet director at many of the US comps, including the Rat Race and the US Nationals. He's fully involved, as he should be with all his experience.

Earlier on, you identified some of the factors you believe contributed to your accident. Do you think there's a general malaise of not taking risk seriously enough in free flying?

Maybe. Speaking personally, I've never taken an SIV course and in retrospect that seems like a huge mistake. Twice in my life I've been in a panic situation and not done the right thing. And if I'm really honest, and face up to the truth of it, that means that my flying career has always had this Achilles heel… I've never been properly prepared to react in the right way. Even if you're a calm-air pilot, do an SIV course. You need to know how to recover from situations. And if you can't cope with that you shouldn't be in the sport.

Astronauts look at every single possible thing that could go wrong, and they ask, "How is this spaceship going to try and kill me today?" And they practise dealing with that, repeatedly, in simulations, and find their weaknesses, and work on them. We need some of that discipline in free flying. You know, it's really hard for me to be a cautionary tale for other people. Maybe all the bad luck got channelled through me, and now very few pilots fly mini-wings in strong conditions in Canada, at least. But maybe that's a way of rationalising it.

I've been struck by your honesty in talking so openly about what you've been through. I'm also taken by the straightforwardness of your appeal to fellow pilots to continue to be included in the conversations about what we all love to do.

One of the things I've learnt since my accident is this: everyone has a burden to bear. I've learnt to treat everyone with kindness, and take the time to talk to people. And I do now because I haven't got a job to rush to. The other day I got chatting to an 80-year-old lady at the bus shelter, a Native American. Normally I wouldn't, I'd think: "Nah, she might be asking for money, move on," but I did and next thing I'm spending half an hour learning about her upbringing on the prairie as a child. Just wonderful. That's joy – making connections to other people. More than anything.

Also just going out in the mountains in the car, looking at the snow-covered peaks, I think: "I'm so lucky to be alive now, living here, seeing these views." There are so many people in the world in the midst of war, with no drinking water… what have I got to complain about? It's the very simple moments, mostly being outdoors, that bring real joy. Getting out of the house on my own, without a chaperone – that brings a lot of happiness. Connecting to nature and to the earth is one of the deepest joys you can have.

There's a facile saying that you never know how strong you are until you have to be that strong. I've had a pretty easy life, I've never had any physical or mental health issues myself or in my family, I've got to do loads of sports, and I've had the money and time to do them. But I mean, how can you ever think you have the strength to get through a life-limiting injury? I guess it's the ultimate competition task.

Stewart Midwinter is a highly accomplished paraglider, hang glider, sailplane and light aircraft pilot. One of the pioneers of the Canadian scene, Stewart has also been a respected competition judge for many of his 40 years in free flying. In 2011, Stewart had a flying accident that concluded with neck-down paralysis.

Hugh started flying in 1992, and continues to have his head very much in the clouds

Dosti

Jim Mallinson

The 2008 autumn season in Bir was the best yet. Cloudbase was high most days, allowing plenty of new routes to be forged, and more people took the high road to Manali than ever before. However, for me it won't be the great height gains, beautiful bivouacs or previously unflown lines through the snowy wastes that stand out in my memory, but one particular incident that reminded me how flying paragliders can still inflict on me bizarre and intense emotions, and how, in return for taking over my life, it's given me a very special bunch of friends.

November 4th, 2008. Feeling virtuous, Eddie and I decide to walk up to Billing for a change. To our surprise, the thousand-metre climb is not too tough. The path runs past ploughed fields dotted with mounds of as yet unspread compost before heading straight up through a shady rhododendron forest. The tiny wooden shack that is the temple of the goddess Satyavadini, "She who tells the truth", provides a welcome excuse for a rest before the final push along the spine, now exposed to the morning sun.

By half past ten we're at take-off, the first pilots of the day to sip Chachuji's chai. Soon vanloads of Russians turn up, followed by a handful of Bir regulars. The conditions are looking good, nearly as good as yesterday when Mani and Paolo made it to Manali. I'm going back to England soon and have only one or two flying days left. A last visit to the big mountains beckons. I want to get over the snows and up close with the rocky wastes atop the Thamsar massif. Not all the way to Manali, though. I flew there last week, and anyway I have to be in Bir tomorrow and don't fancy the six-hour bus ride back. I'll go some of the way there, to Danesar lake, an icy pool hemmed in by fearsome swords of rock just beneath the 4,200m col which is the gateway to the Kullu valley. I'll top-land on the huge grassy meadow sloping away beneath it so I can enjoy a few moments of physical contact with the high Himalaya, then relaunch and fly south towards our regular campsite at Phuladhar (known to pilots as "360" for its stunning panoramic view), where I can reconnect with the front ridge and have an easy ride home to Bir.

There's plenty more ambition buzzing around take-off. Lots of pilots want to join Mani and Paolo for a soak at the Vasisht hot springs near Manali. The first gliders launch and climb well. Before long a gaggle made up of Debu and Flo on their tandem, Bruce, "Hairy" Dave, Mike, Peter and Robinson is disappearing over the back. But there's still no sign of our gliders. We'd left them to be put on a taxi so we could enjoy the walk unencumbered. An anxious telephone call elicits bad news. The gliders are in Bir, but will be coming "soon". There's been a mix-up and I'm fuming, but there's no one to blame but myself. It's nearly midday.

The gliders don't arrive until quarter to two, too late for us to do the big flight. I try to put my frustration behind me and concentrate on making the most of the couple of hours left in the day. Eddie and I rush to launch and are soon climbing above the peak at the top of the spur that runs up from Billing. Eddie glides over the back and I follow, a little hesitant after landing out a few days earlier and only just making it off the mountain before nightfall. Eddie gets up quickly. I have to work a little harder, but before long we make it up to a 4,000m cloudbase next to the snow line. The bitter cold and lowering sun cut short a full traverse of the Thamsar massif and we glide back to the front ridge, about 10km north west of Billing.

Once we've thawed out, we climb to just below the 3,700m Waldo peak, relaxed now that we are within an easy glide of Bir. I head towards the valley, anticipating an easy cruise home as I follow the line of the spur that runs down from Waldo and surf the air coming up from both sides. I feel a strange turbulence, look up at the glider and then, as I look down, a falling yellow shape catches my eye. It's my first aid kit. For a few seconds I watch with amused surprise as it plunges like some fluorescent falcon into the forest below. Then a growing panic grips me. How could it have fallen out of my harness? I let go of the brakes and reach behind me with both hands. The main pocket of my harness is empty. Shit. In the rush to take off, I can't have zipped it up properly. Shit! What was in it? The first aid kit and... the glider bag. In that? Oh shit! My bum bag, in which are my passport, satellite phone, credit card and cash, too much cash, all my cash. Shit, shit, shit!

I grab the radio, which has been crackling intermittently and indistinctly, and yell to Eddie, but I can't make out his reply beyond the fact that he knows something is up. He starts soaring an area of forest a little further up from where the first aid kit has fallen, at one end of which is a small clearing. Once I've pulled myself together and stopped clenching my fists and shouting curses, I make a couple of passes of the clearing. Perched at 3,000m, it's steep and rocky, tricky to top-land and even trickier to launch from. There's not much left in the day, and we've got no food or sleeping kit. We glide back to Bir. I sit slumped like a sulky teenager in my harness, head spinning with possible scenarios but always returning to one: I've lost the bag for good, I'll have to pay a visit to the local constabulary and coax them into giving me a police report, after which I'll have to borrow some money to get to Delhi and then do my best to get a new passport before my flight home, where I shall then jump through all the hoops in the vain hope of getting something out of my insurance company... But there's still a minuscule hope of finding the bag. I have to try.

First the gliders didn't turn up, then I dropped the bag. These things come in threes, they say, so I land with extra care before slipping out of my harness and running over to Eddie. He saw the glider bag fall. When he heard from me on the radio what was in it, he went to mark the area where he thought it had landed. I'd been flying slightly to the north of the spur and three hundred or so metres above it, over an area of forest about one kilometre long, between two gullies. We'll sort out our bivi kit, fly over there tomorrow, search from the air for a while, then top land as near as we can and go and find the bag.

Eddie's optimism and pragmatic approach to the task in hand are infectious, and my anxiety eases. It's bad, but not so bad – no one has been hurt, and everything that's been lost is replaceable. "Worse things happen at sea" as my father, a sailor, would have said. It occurs to us that we're going to need all the help we can get. As if on cue, Antoine appears overhead, throws down some acro shapes and then wingovers into the landing field. He's a paragliding genius, one of the best pilots I know, and we need him on board. I tell him what's happened and what we're going to do. Before I can hint at wanting him to join us, he growls with his usual Gallic sangfroid: "OK, so I come too. I take ze tandem and bring Lynn." Perfect. Lynn, Antoine's Scottish girlfriend (vive the auld alliance!), is the epitome of positivity. The two of them are fresh from making the first tandem flight to Manali ('on-sight' as they say in the climbing world – Antoine hadn't even flown there solo), and ten days earlier Antoine had pulled off the daring evacuation by tandem of a pilot who had broken both his legs top-landing at 2,600m in the middle of nowhere.

We pack our gliders and walk up to Vimla's chai shop in the Tibetan colony. After the morning's exertion and the trials of the day we're famished and wolf down heaps of rice and dal. Word of my predicament has already got out and Chicco and Jess appear at the chai shop, concern written across their faces. As soon as Chicco has verified the rumour he joins the team and says he'll bring Jessica on the tandem. Fantastic, two more pairs of eyes and a whole load more optimism. Jess, in true Californian style, is driving home to me the importance of staying positive: "You will find the bag!"

Most of the Bir regulars, many of whom would no doubt have been up for the mission, made it to Manali and aren't coming back till tomorrow, so the talent pool is small, but we're doing well. Jitka, a petite Czech long resident in Scotland and renowned there for having "balls the size of haggises" (a judgement confirmed by the new routes she 'on-sighted' every day of this, her first trip to the area) and Dominic, a solid, honey-voiced Scot whose low airtime belies his prodigious flying talent, overhear our conversation and sign up without hesitation. They've been planning a vol bivouac and the prospect of combining it with a mission is just what they're looking for. I'm delighted but worried. The top-landings near where I dropped the bag looked difficult, to say the least. All these friends flying there for my sake, four of them on tandems – I hope no one crashes. I voice my concern, but they're all level-headed pilots and no one is going to compromise safety. I need this day to end, so Eddie and I return home where, after I top up my pocket money yet again with a few games of backgammon, we get an early night, anticipating a big day tomorrow.

November 5th, 2008. Before heading up to Billing (by taxi this time), Eddie and I go to the Tibetan colony to get provisions for a night or two on the mountain. We're going to give it our best shot, even if it takes a few days. Jitka and Dominic are also prepared to stay out, but the others need to be back in Bir by the evening. While stocking up on Maggi noodles, porridge and chocolate we hear on the television news that Barrack Obama has won the American election. A good omen if ever there was one. Thirty metres of rope completes our kit – the bag could well be dangling from the branches of a tree.

We break up the taxi ride with another visit to the goddess Satyavadini, this time taking some sweet-smelling incense sticks as a propitiatory offering. We need all the help we can get. At Chachuji's chai shop we tell him what's happened and what we're planning. He knows every inch of the mountains for miles around Billing. After a pensive scratch of his head, he tells us that there won't be any shepherds where we are going as winter is approaching and they will have already moved down. The only people likely to be around (and who might already be enjoying the bag's contents) are hunters. Hunters? What are they hunting? Bear and musk deer. With guns? No, with traps. Shit, that spices things up a bit. Not only are we going to try to fly up to 3,000m, top-land and then search a large and precipitous area of Himalayan forest for a black glider bag (needles and haystacks don't even come close), but the area is likely to be dotted with rusty iron beartraps.

The second chai tastes particularly good and the mission seems correspondingly more daunting. Eddie and I wait for the tandem crews to arrive while the ever-keen Jitka and Dominic launch as soon as the first decent thermals bring the resident Himalayan griffon vultures above take-off. The conditions aren't as good as the last two days – the weather is still clear, but it's more stable and the climbs are weaker and broken. No hope of anyone going over the back today, but we should be able to make it to our goal. Jitka and Dominic are well on their way by the time the tandem crews arrive. Eddie and I leave them in the chai shop, nervous excitement preventing us from putting off our mission any longer. Eddie takes off and muscles his way through the chaotic crowds before climbing along the spur above Billing. I, brave Sir Jimmy, run away immediately after launching and scuttle off low to the next spur, unable to focus simultaneously on collision avoidance and the task in hand.

Having extricated myself from the swarm of Slavs, I relax and let myself enjoy the flight. I slowly climb to nearly 3,000m, fighting close in to the terrain to break through multiple inversions, and then continue on my way. After a couple of glides and climbs I find myself just above a grassy spur leading up from Tatopani, a hot spring deep in the valley below where the bag fell. I'm relatively high, 2,600m or so, but in these huge Himalayan valleys perspective is misleading and it feels as though if I don't climb soon I'm going to have to land in there. Then a massive thermal releases and I corkscrew up vertically, leaving the land behind and stopping only once I'm level with the ridge where the bag fell. Eddie has sensibly taken the high route and glides across the valley above me.

When we reach the clearing nearest the area to be searched, we see that Jitka has already landed there. Haggises indeed. It's harder to stay above the ridge than it was yesterday and, after struggling to get over the search area, which at this time of day is in shade and giving no lift, we give up on the aerial recce. I make a pass of where Jitka has landed. Close in I can see that the flat areas are strewn with boulders and there's just a small steep grassy area where I might be able to slope-land. Each time I go in I'm either hoisted back above the ridge or flung down into the wooded bowl below. After a few attempts Eddie and I look for somewhere easier further along the spur.

The prudent choice is right at the end, a beautiful bald promontory commanding a panoramic view of the Kangra valley and the plains beyond. The only problem is that it's a good two kilometres from the area to be searched. Laziness and lack of time demand somewhere closer. Dom has landed there and is already walking along the ridge, but Eddie and I keep milling about indecisively. Then the tandems arrive. Antoine is a master of top-landing – I've seen him get into slots smaller than his glider – but this time he's hampered by flying a tandem, and I reckon that I should at least be able to land my solo wherever he can get himself and Lynn down. There's a lovely grassy glade about halfway between Jitka and Dominic's landings, but it's hemmed in on all sides by evergreen oaks and pines, and there are thermals constantly pumping up all around. I've already overflown it once and given up on it as it's a one-chance-only sort of place: miss it and you're in the trees. But Antoine blithely sneaks in there when I'm not looking and then talks in the rest of us. To avoid being lifted up too high we have to glide in below it, through the V made by two chilgoza pines, after which the gentle upslope of the clearing is easily, if unceremoniously, embraced.

So that's the most dangerous part of the mission over: we have all landed safely. Thinking that it will be an easy stroll between here and the search area, we bunch up our gliders and take only the kit we think we might need: rope, radios and torches. Dominic is waiting for us and we set off along the spur. It's already half past two. We soon learn a lesson: in the Himalaya, what looks from a paraglider like a level kilometre on the ground is nothing of the sort. The path through the forest is good – frequent fireplaces encircled by carpets of sheep and goat shit show that it's not long since the shepherds passed this way – but there are plenty of ups and downs and it takes us the best part of an hour to get to where Jitka landed. We call for her but our shouts are unanswered. She responds to the radio and is already some way away, searching for the bag. Dominic heads off along the shepherds' path to help her.

The remaining six of us walk to the north side of the ridge and peer down into our objective. It is very steep… and very wide. It must be a kilometre, a Himalayan kilometre, along the ridge to the far gully, the limit of the area to be searched as reckoned by Eddie. Eddie also estimated that I might have been as much as fifty metres to the north of the ridge when the bag fell. It doesn't take trigonometry to work out that fifty metres wide of the top of such a precipitous slope means a long way down. Eddie, practical as ever despite the mounting odds, gets us to fan out. He and Antoine sideslip their way down the grassy mountainside until they disappear from view. Lynn, Jess, Chicco and I take the higher contours and so start two of the most beautifully surreal hours of my life. The sun is already low, casting a delicious warm orange light onto the forested slope but blinding us when we look to the left. I start traversing a grassy gully, following inch-wide animal trails (deer, I hope) towards the trees, and realise that the animals have got it right: four limbs are needed here. Progress is made by clinging on to whatever I can and stopping thankfully every few metres to scan the forest. Chilgoza pines reach up above me, those to my right glowing majestically in the dappled sunlight, those to my left brooding sillhouettes. My black and red Ozone glider bag will be perfectly camouflaged here, whichever way I look.

Before long I am in the trees and alone. Our attempt at an orderly search is made futile by the topography. Where we're searching is a uniform mountain face when viewed from a distance, but close up it has its own micro-geography. Cliffs, gullies, bowls and ledges separate us. We shout intermittently to keep the others aware of where we are. The radios, as ever, are unreliable and messages are relayed in a confusing game of Chinese whispers. Soon they and we fall quiet. I take stock of what I am doing: standing alone perched on a vertiginous slope in a Himalayan forest at 3,000m with nothing to do but look. Somewhere I would never normally have reason to go, somewhere astonishing in its pristine perfection. The mad futility of our mission only adds to the surreality, and I enter a heightened state of awareness. My hands grasp at clumps of grass or cling on to tumbling dreadlock trellises of gnarled roots, my feet pick their way from foothold to foothold, uncannily finding hard stones embedded in banks of crumbling earth. I am covered head to toe in grass and pine needles, my hands are caked in a rich humus. Now the only sound piercing the silence is the occasional accusatory, derisory caw of a crow. "Haaaa! Haaaa! You think you can come here and find your bag! Haaaa! Haaaa!" Crows in India are said to divine the future; holy men can interpret their calls. I, in my unholiness, am not encouraged.

A rhythm develops: I scramble a few yards, taking whatever route is offered to me by the terrain, then stop to scan the trees and mountainside. Sometimes I feel like an intrepid adventurer exploring hitherto untrod realms, sometimes a gormless, gawping fool. The latter sentiment starts to win out when the light begins to fade, and it's compounded by the responsibility that I feel towards the others. They're all here on my account.

It will be dark by the time we've climbed up and reached the path, let alone by the time we find somewhere to camp. Half of us are completely unprepared for a night out. We have little food and less water. OK, time to stop searching and start looking after our basic needs.

I reach a buttress criss-crossed with tree roots, a ladder on which to climb back up to the path. I hear Eddie and Antoine talking below me and call out to them, but an acoustic quirk means they cannot hear me. Their edgy chatter tells me that they're having difficulties negotiating the terrain. I wonder whether to wait for them, but opt against it. It's getting dark and they may take a different route. Before too long I'm on top of the ridge, in the twilight. I head along the shepherds' path towards where Jitka landed and meet up with Lynn, Jess and Chicco. Spirits are still good. We are paraglider pilots after all, accustomed to absurdly high hopes coming to nothing. We'll return the next morning for a more thorough search. The chances of finding the bag are slimmer than a microline, but, hey, we're having fun.

We await the others in the gloom. The radios, fickle as ever, get no response. Then Dominic's mellifluous brogue, all bass tones and rolling Rs, interrupts our idle chit-chat: "Can you confirm that you have found the bag?"

We look at each other and frown. I reply into my radio, "Er, no, Dom, we haven't found the bag."

A moment later Antoine's voice, mild hysteria modulating its usually gruff tones, puts paid to our befuddlement: "WE 'ave ze bag!"

Eyes and mouths owl-wide with incredulity, we scream and jump and hug one another. "Nooo!" hoots Lynn, "I don't believe it!"

Ten minutes later Antoine and Eddie come striding along the path, the beam of Eddie's headtorch heralding their approach. Once the high-fives and hugs are over, I ask them how they had found it, still not quite believing that they have, even though there it is on Antoine's back. They had to climb up a cliff face to get up from where they were searching, which must have been when I heard them. Hauling and pushing each other up the more difficult sections, they reached a small plateau at the cliff's top. Antoine, in front, looked back to make sure Eddie was OK and there behind Eddie on a ledge was the glider bag. The bum bag was still inside it; luckily I'd done a better job of zipping up the glider bag than I had my harness.

Dominic and Jitka appear and join in the celebrations. Elated, we turn to our next task, sorting ourselves out for the night. Normally that would have been somewhat daunting, but now we feel as if we can do anything, Antoine perhaps more so than the rest of us; he is keen to fly himself and Lynn off the mountain. In the dark. With no known landings in gliding range. And no take off nearby, for that matter.

Buoyed up by our success we float back along the path to where we have left our gliders. My subconscious had already given up on finding my stuff and I'm still coming to terms with the realisation that I don't have to go to the police station, I don't have to borrow lots of money, I don't have to leave early for Delhi and I can just enjoy my last few days in the Himalaya. Despite our elation, in the dark the walk back is difficult and tiring. Only half of us have torches and the path is not always clear. I'm very glad that we don't have to come back this way in the morning – our mood would be very different.

There was a clearing with some deserted shepherds' huts not far from where we landed. The bunched-up gliders are drenched with dew so Antoine and I decide not to pack them but carry them open to the clearing. Now that it's almost pitch dark – the new moon has already set – Antoine has said that he won't fly down, but with his glider still open I'm not convinced that he's given up. He, Lynn and I go ahead, leaving the others to sort out their kit. After half an hour the fabled huts have failed to materialise and we are a little concerned. We press on, hoping to find somewhere else, but the occasional shepherd campsite by the path isn't very appealing: the tandem-wallahs, having no bedding, are keen to find shelter.

Suddenly Lynn, a little ahead of Antoine and me, who are struggling with our bunched-up gliders, screams and runs back towards us. "A bear! There was a bear right there in front of me!" She's shaking with fear. Antoine and I try to reassure her – and ourselves – that the bear will be scared off by us and our gliders. She walks between us, and I light the way from the rear, the beam from my headtorch now feeling rather puny. At the next clearing we pack our gliders – the walking has shaken off the water – and wait for the others. Eddie appears first and joins us for a welcome rest. Silent and still again, I notice a shape move high up in a pine tree just in front of us. "Hey," I whisper to the others, "it might be a flying squirrel." Eddie trains his torch on it and like two laser pinpoints glowing red its eyes shine back. We stare into the darkness for a minute or two then suddenly the shape launches out of the tree and plunges into the valley. Its glide angle is barely 1:1, no better than a wing suit, and it disappears below our field of vision before we can see it level out.

The other four join us. With just one torch between them, they have been making slow progress and it's time for a decision. The only decent campsite we can be sure of reaching is at the end of the spur, where Dom landed. The shepherds' path leads there, and it's the perfect place to take off from in the morning. We're tired and it's another half kilometre of ups and downs, but the path is now narrow and we don't have much of an alternative. We set off and learn a second lesson about the Himalaya: what looks like an easy path by day is nothing of the sort by night. We lose our way twice, but by a stroke of luck Dom kept his GPS on after he landed and we're able to play join the dots to follow his track back to the campsite. Once there we spring into action. Antoine creates a tent by stringing the rope between the branches of a tree and hanging one of the tandems off it. The other tandem does the job of bedding. It doesn't look very warm and I offer my sleeping bag but it's turned down. I promise to keep the fire going all night. And what a fire. It's the fifth of November, remember, bonfire night, Britain's anarchist anniversary, so we have a good excuse to burn up all the wood we can find. We scatter in all directions and build a huge pile of logs. Once the fire is blazing, we pool food resources. Between us we have eight packets of Maggi noodles, three potatoes, two carrots, nearly a kilo of porridge oats and Eddie's impressive stash of chocolate. Sorted.

While dinner is being cooked, I check my bum bag. All present and correct. I nervously try switching on the expensive, rented, uninsured satphone. It gets a signal straight away. I call Debu back down in Bir to tell him the good news.

There is now a circle of very happy faces around a roaring fire. We did it. It's late already, after ten by the time we've each taken our turn to eat out of the cooking pot, but the laughter and stories go on into the night. I just about keep my promise to keep the fire blazing, although I do remember seeing Dominic, who was so cold he was sleeping in his boots, stoke it once or twice. The tandem wallahs sleep soundly.

November 6th, 2008. Breakfast follows a high-altitude yoga class from Lynn. Once the porridge is cooked, we're almost out of water and there's not much left to do but fly. We take off early, before the thermals have got going, and for a while we struggle to stay up. Then everyone heads off on their way. Jitka and Dominic turn west towards Dharamsala (and that was the last time I saw them), Jess and Chicco head out to Baijnath, and Antoine, Lynn, Eddie and I fly east, back to Billing. At Chachuji's we gulp down chai after chai. The only lunch on offer is Maggi noodles. They tasted pretty special last night, but real food is calling. We fly down to Bir and hurry to Vimla's. There, after another mound of rice and dal, I call Claudia, my wife, back in England. I hadn't dared tell her the bad news the day I lost the bag for fear of the ticking-off I deserved. Now it doesn't seem so bad. I get my ticking off and then she tells me how lucky I am to have such good friends. Too true. Thank you, my magnificent seven: Eddie Colfox, Antoine Laurens, Lynn Jones, Chicco Patuzzi, Jessica Love, Jitka Polechova and Dominic Job.

Jim Mallinson is an academic and an expert on the history of yoga. Fluent in Hindi, he has also worked as a paragliding guide in India. He lives in Wiltshire, and captains the South in the annual North-South Cup, a light-hearted flying contest between the northern and southern halves of Britain.

MINI STORY

One hundred and eighty three kilometres
Frazer Wilson

I followed ley lines.

I used a hazel dowsing rod to avoid damp patches in the ground.

I ate a LOT of flapjacks.

I bloody love this game.

Frazer describing his personal best

Je suis un test pilote

Andrew Court

I was on my way to spend a few quiet days with my old friends Amy Anderson and Bruce Goldsmith in the Alps to do my first gentle Alpine flying – or so I thought. It turned out they had assigned me as passenger for the new Airwave dual glider that was to be put through the ACPUL tests. I'll never trust a Frenchman's smile again...

As a relatively new pilot, I was always looking forward to my first flight in the Alps. As we approached Annecy the mountains looked beautifully clean and still, and the air was calm. I went to bed dreaming of clouds. The next morning I awoke with the same anticipation as on the first day of a skiing holiday. The sun was out and the sky was blue.

We met Bruce in a small car park next to a bit of grass. "This is the landing site," he said.

This was when I first began to worry. We're in this lovely big valley and the landing site had high trees on one side, a road on the other, a house on the approach and power cables to stop you if you overshot. If I'd been on my own, I would have gone fishing or for a walk on the beach or even shopping, but my apprehension was lost amid the bustle and hurry to exchange kit from one car to another. I secretly began to feel a bit wet behind the ears, and wished I'd brought my reflective wraparound shades to hide in. Much French was spoken between Bruce and the other pilots, who turned and smiled at me.

We were off up the mountain in convoy. My automatic Montego estate with my son Tom and wife Sally, and me with no shades, a cheap pair of walking boots and a cagoule from Millets, followed the cool French pilots. What a cheeser! Little did I know what they had in store for me.

"This is the take-off," said Bruce. This was not funny at all. It was a piece of carpet nailed to the side of a mountain. Trees were all around except for a chink in the forest just below, looking as if it had been created by previous pilots who didn't quite make it. I hastily went for a wee in the bushes and took a sneaky look over the edge. This was a big mistake, like testing cold water before you jump. I retreated to the family for support, but neither Sally or Tom were having any of it. They had come all this way to be entertained, and this was better than they had expected.

"Meet Patrique," Bruce said. "Can you fly the dual Duet with him for a while? He wants to do a few tests, and you're about the right weight."

"OK. Bonjour. Ça va?" I said in my best French. Patrique was not impressed. I could see my cheesy smile reflected in his shades, and I understood why.

I had never flown tandem before, and I thought this would be a good way of getting down to that very small landing patch that Bruce had shown me earlier. All clipped in and ready to go. Sally had briefed me on the French word for 'help', so I was as ready as I was ever going to be. With 100% commitment on take-off, we just cleared the trees.

It was breathtaking, just as I had imagined. The views, the sounds, the smells, the feeling of freedom as high as the clouds. A hawk soared beneath me, and I felt like a bird myself. Soon we were over the blue lake, and the fun began. Patrique whistled into his mic: more French to ground control. I looked up and could see him applying the brakes. More and more brake and then releasing the left-hand brake quickly and wheeeeeee... a spin!

Down and down, round and round at great speed faster and faster. The lake appeared to get bigger quite quickly. How much longer, I thought? I hope he knows what he's doing. Then we pulled out of the spin as dramatically as we had entered it. We stopped our downward motion and pressed hard into the harness, rapidly followed by a violent swing up to the point of weightlessness and further. I thought that I had left my partner as I fell free though the air. The reserve was on his harness. Oh no!

He whistled in to the mic as we resumed normal flight, and began to apply the brakes again. He didn't even ask if I was OK. Down and round we went again, flailing and twisting out of control. This time, obviously confident in the glider, Patrique was really giving it some stick. I was nearly sick. I could see the rescue boat below which, strangely, didn't fill me with confidence. Small cars moved along the road and the houses, which looked like models, spun round like a computer animation.

Then we were back to normal flight again, but not for long. My analytical mind had gone. I'm not sure which procedures we did next. I was lost in a new world of speed, wind, total exhilaration and the blue of the lake way down below. All the worries of the world had gone except one and that was out of my hands. Just when the small ripples on the water were plainly visible and I was ready for a dip, there was another whistle.

"C'est fini," Patrique said, unperplexed. The landing field looked like an old friend, and now somewhat larger than I had imagined. The undercarriage felt rather shaky as Patrique pushed me forward in my harness. On landing (perfectly, almost into the boot of the car) I was even higher than on take-off, but no one seemed to care. I tried to be cool but it didn't work. Not being able to undo the harness because of a severe case of the shakes gave me away. Patrique didn't say a word. My first time and he didn't say a word. I had been used.

"Encore?" he asked.

Well, I just had to go. The trip up the mountain was probably as dangerous as the one down, screeching round the corners and being thrown from side to side. A large sandwich was thrust into my hands, the size of a loaf with a whole Stilton inside and some ham. I had no choice. The day was well out of control already. Eating a sandwich is not usually regarded as a radical thing to do, but on this day it was pretty silly. When we reached the top Sally appeared from under the Montego with oil on her hands. Things didn't look too good. Again, jumping looked the better option.

This time the trim tabs were off. Believe me, it makes a difference! I don't know if it was the weight of our lunch, but we went very fast indeed. On the second spiral dive my cheeks began to flap and I found it hard to breathe. I assumed that Patrique was wrestling with the controls while I wrestled with lunch, which was trying to escape as we went weightless again. We dropped 3,000ft in a minute, which felt pretty much like free falling. On landing Patrique still said nothing. This time I was much cooler, I undid my harness, sat down and picked the remainder of the ham from my teeth.

By the end of the day I had done eight test flights on the Duet. Fortunately the glider was a good one, and so was the pilot. We did the complete AFNOR tests: spins, asymmetric collapses, spiral dives, the lot. It was an unbelievable experience and an important lesson in flying. Go for it if you get the chance... but don't have a large breakfast.

Andrew Court learnt to fly in the late 1980s. He continues to paraglide on the Isle of Wight, as well as enjoying life on the water with his son Tom, a professional kitesurfer.

Chasing the dragon

Craig Morgan

OK, so we know many top pilots head to northeast Brazil to chase world records from the tow winches prepared for hardcore distance flying. But how about you? Would you? Could you? Should you? Here's a taster.

Northeast Brazil is hot, dry and extensive. Its reputation is one of minimal infrastructure, poor communities but warm welcomes. The sertão ("back country" in Portuguese, and pronounced sehr-towng, like a cat's miaow) terrain is half bush, half desert, and huge areas of inaccessible wilderness scrub look 'worrying' to fly over. The air is big and the flying demands full commitment. Infrequent tarmac brings relief and occasional dirt roads rekindle confidence.

It's super challenging, yet the cross-country potential feels endless and offers a major hit of the adrenaline shot that we paraglider pilots seek. To the untrained eye this place is arid and unwelcoming, yet to those of us that "know", it's a thermic nirvana and the epic skies confirm it.

As a 'regular' pilot I took to these Brazilian skies in late October with my mates Guy Anderson (top ranked PWC pilot and Brit team member), Seb Ospina (Colombian Champ and pro tandem ace), Harry Bloxham (British Champ and techie guru), and Charles Norwood (father figure). My previous personal best XC distance was 187km in the UK, so I supposed flying 300 would be splendid, 400 would be mental and 500 would be off the chart!

We booked with Simon Penz, an Austrian who runs Flight Connections Arleberg (fca.at) and his Swiss partner Martin Portman. Together they provide the excellent infrastructure of Slovenian winches, local retrieves and coordination through their FlyTrack organisation, based in Assu in the state of Ceará. They got us airborne into this epic playground, but it was stamina-based flying the likes of which I'd not experienced before.

Our basic remit was up at 5am for a spot of breakfast, then head down to the dried-out lake bed at 6am to sort gear and gliders. Fifty minutes later, clip onto the end of a 2,000m spool of Dyneema attached to a winch strapped to the back of a Toyota Hilux. In the thermic gusts, trust your three grinning fluffers to pin down your fully inflated, coiled spring of a glider.

On your count of "três, dois, um", they release and you get yanked brutally skyward on the winch line. Ascend rapidly to 1,000m, release, fly all day, and I mean ALL DAY, eat, navigate and urinate on the wing so to speak, then put it down just before dusk so your long-distance effort can be validated. And if all that isn't enough – do it all in a howling gale. What could be simpler!

My first practise launch felt like a rodeo – the glider exploded into the air and I was immediately off my feet, wide-eyed and working hard to keep symmetry. Simon was launch marshal and held onto the lead line to assist where needed and to dampen any shock loading. Then I was off – the Hilux accelerated, the winch paid out and I zoomed up – pronto pronto!

It was a case of sensory overload really. My Enzo was straining behind me – surging, pitching and fully loaded. Unnerving noises rumbled up the Dyneema and made the tow bridle shudder and groan, occasionally creaking with the angle change.

As a precaution I closed my eyes until it was safe to open them one at a time. I'd also tied my right bootlace to the XCPee tube just in case my false leg fell off – didn't want to lose that! Slight correctional dabs on the B's kept me straight – stay off the brakes when there's this much strain.

A couple of emotional minutes later I pinged off into the calm at 950m, flew around a bit and soothed my ragged nerves. A short battle into wind followed, ending with my first backward landing at the launch tarpaulin. Nothing like the winching I'd done in the UK, and it clearly felt like we'd stepped up an order of magnitude in the power launch stakes!

Through my first couple of warm-up flights I became familiar with the different stages of the day. After a couple of short 'bomb-outs' for me at 225km and 285km respectively, I nailed a 350k and 390k, and was getting stoked. However, the retrieve that FlyTrack provided was equally impressive. Every time I landed farther than 250km, within minutes a friendly retrieve driver rocked up and gave me a hand to pack away.

I was massively impressed not to have long waits or walks in the baking heat. But, oh boy, were the drives home fast. At times I felt like I was in a video game – Grand Theft Auto maybe. Our man was on it, rapidly downshifting through the auto gearbox before hitting our heads on the roof going over speed bumps, hammering down the long straight desert roads on a state of high alert ready for the foolhardy cars and mopeds choosing to night ride with no tail lights. After a 2am return on one particular retrieve I asked the driver if he was professionally trained or a racing car driver, he just chuckled and replied, "No. Motocross!"

The next 'big' day had shaped up on all the meteo models that we researched the night before. Mitch Riley (USA pro guide) and Alex Robé (Austrian XC league champ) both offered good resources and insight during our route planning. Down at the tarps, nervous excitement oozed through me as I initiated my Garmin inReach, tested my tow bridle and squirrelled away my in-flight nutrition. My teammates sorted their gear and instruments, then we watched and waited.

06.45: small cumulus popped to the south as the convection gently moved towards us in the dawn glow. Birds began to circle instead of flap, and a faint breeze countered the already oppressive heat. My neck hairs bristled as I could feel a change in the air.

06.55: it had become locally thermic and was time to go. Ever-keen Mitch and Seb took the first two rides, then the rest of us piled in on the two winch lines. With seven-minute rotations, most of us were airborne by 07.30. Game on.

Each day I had a love-hate relationship with the first hour whilst in survival mode. Weak and broken climbs would drift erratically in the wind. Anxious low saves were the norm, but the urubu vultures were also keen to get up and gave us welcome visuals. My 'feel receptors' were on high alert for any and all indications of lift. These moments are gold dust. Get good at these and you're well on the way to XC stardom.

Generally, the first hour was in proximity to your winching partner, whoever that was. Good technique dictated a broad search pattern, which required bravery and self-belief. However, it wasn't always the case throughout the day, and those that repeatedly pimped got humorously then ruthlessly called out over the radio.

To my relief point-fives turned into twos and threes, and an hour later, as I rounded Mossoru airspace, a river crossing created a consistent trigger where other pilots waited, and some caught up, as planned, to form our super gaggle.

Base had now risen to 1,500m, but we rarely touched it as the strongest pilots continually pushed on to gobble up distance. It was relentless. Climb hard then push on. Always directly downwind, always on full bar – don't muck about – push push push.

Leapfrogging was cool, so was piling in on a low glider out front – that was their contribution. Sometimes I'd miss a cycle, curse my luck and push on looking for the ripper to put me back at altitude and in the mix. Separation inevitably occurred as the strongest pilots stretched out and worked different clouds, but the sky was huge, comms were good and our plan was to try to fly together. I could often make out Mitch or Seb five kilometres away and, ever the generous pros, they would occasionally take a breather and nurse our fractured flock back together.

At times we numbered 10, but not everyone was on our hymn sheet. Glide lines were often sweet as we paid much attention to the predicted areas of convergence when route-planning. So much to learn with a perceptive mind. Alex Robé, calculating and analytical; Cazaux, brave and efficient; Anderson, consistent; and Bloxham, from his sailplane experience, always choosing the best part of the cloud to fly to – this refined aspect I probably learned most from.

The early north star was a town called Quixadá (kee-shada), where stunning dome mountains punched out of the billiard-table plains to pre-empt the desolate high ground. Some 260km in and decision time, to go north or south of the lunar landscape. This town was an early pioneer destination for flying this area and carries a fearsome reputation with ridiculously windy, near-vertical take-offs – maybe you've seen the scary videos too!

However, rule number one for us here at this mountainous location was DO NOT, under any circumstances, fly lee side. Suicidal rotor in 30 to 40 knot winds. So we approached vigilantly. As if the preceding six hours of intense race-like XC hadn't been enough, my senses now had to absorb this outrageous topography. How does stuff like that happen? It felt like I was entering pre-history, and I chuckled as I thought about yet another experience that I just wouldn't be able to explain to my non-flying friends.

Boom! No time to get all philosophical though. The hot rocks were baking, we were flying over them and I was about to get smashed up outta the park! You know you're in a snorter of a thermal when the gliders close by choose not to join you as they disappear waay below. But you're in there, warp speed vertically, it's tough shit and you daren't come out until you've stopped all the screaming!

I don't know about you but I have an emotional, rhythmic relationship with my glider. Like my wife, when she's unfurled and in full refinement she's a thing of elegance and great beauty. I'm Welsh, she's my Dragon and together we dance.

In Brazil we samba'd to the beats. Powerful rhythms. I talked to her through the familiar tunes, screamed and hollered when the tempo hotted up, but every now and again, not often, a wack tune came on, we misjudged things, and slipped off the dance floor. She didn't like that when that happened and she got ugly! Screaming at me like Medusa and getting all outta shape. Action stations. So I'd change my tone and input. Coaxing and encouraging her back onto the dance floor, desperately trying not to spill our drinks before we got properly chucked out of the dance club. I digress but you get my meaning.

This Quixadá section was fast. Middle of the day stuff – strong climbs dripped off the wooded peaks, consistent winds seemed to smooth out the thermals as opposed to weak wind days when the climbs were noticeably rougher and 85km/h glides devoured distance – we were really motoring. But the terrain became more mountainous, so route choice became important. Safety and retrieve options were always associated with my decision-making. With the mountains came convergence where diverging wind flows slammed back together, spilled upward and created magic lift. No better place to be at 350km out, straight-lining for ten or fifteen kilometres doing my housework and having a chat with my buddies.

The preceding 10 days or so had put some serious hours (40-ish) into my kit in hot dusty conditions. My harness now looked like a camel's flip flop, and my once beautiful glider was so dirty it resembled a shit-house floor mop. My speed bar had been ragged out and replaced once, and added to that one of my A's resembled a hairy woollen weave line. As if that wasn't enough, a couple of misdirected XCPees had been blown back and introduced to my flying jacket, giving it that 'used' fragrance – I was definitely bedding in!

From the Quixadá mountains huge lakes came into view, glistening way beneath us, triggering yet more gloriously wide thermals which the ubiquitous urubu helped us centre. The day had changed again, and long cloud shadows now slashed diagonally across the sky. The sun was past the yardarm and was rapidly descending – something to do with the equator being more perpendicular to the sun at these latitudes, I believe. Dusk was coming and the landscape and horizon started to grey out. Gloomy but still warm – even at altitude.

Ceará hadn't finished with us yet, though. Some call it the glass-off, others say restitution, but either way the sun-baked sertão far below breathed out one long, last time. Like a reward for battling through the intensity of the day and making it this far, the last hundred kilometres were like a generous and calm offering from the sky gods to us intrepid mopeds in the sky. I whooped unashamedly as my instruments ticked past 400km for the first time – and I was still at 3,000m! A long final glide gave beeps on the vario which I daren't explore. We had to get down and land by 17.57, Ceará sundown, to validate our flights.

Our landing was classic. The option being to fly past a good tarmac road and milk another couple of kilometres into the boonies, or stick it down somewhere nice and easy for the retrieve. A no-brainer really. But as we came in low on finals on the previously empty road, a rickety old bus appeared and swerved through us swashbucklingly, intent on keeping to his schedule – not even a honk from the undeterred driver!

I had just flown 455km – an outrageous distance for any paraglider pilot to fly, and the craic on that hot asphalt was akin to postcoital ecstasy. I'd flown for 10 hours 16 minutes, a lifetime achievement that I never thought I could do, let alone have the chance of doing again in a couple of days.

As ever, our grinning retrieve driver Sandro cruised up five minutes after we landed, having driven 650km through the day chasing us down. We babbled our highs and lows to him – he just chuckled and said, "Iss Brazill mann – iss no for beginners!"

Craig Morgan has twice been British Paragliding Champion. He and his wife run a caravan park in Devon. Craig lost a leg in a non-flying accident as a young man.

Dust devil

Rick Brezina

"Ohhhhh! No!" [Scream]
"No! Careful!"
"Oh my God."
"Riiiiiicky!"
The dust devil rips through, throwing dirt and stones everywhere as she helps another pilot hang on to his wing as it tears into the air. It's like a tornado for a few seconds. Then silence.
"Is Ricky OK? Is he OK? [Sobbing]"
Another voice: "Are you OK?"
"No!"
"Did you just have a heart attack?"
"That's really scary. I don't ever want to fly again. Oh my God."

We were actually kind of surprised by it, how the video went viral. It's our first experience with such a thing. But most of the attention was just for the excitement. I want other pilots to learn from the whole thing.

We have our vacations pre-decided because we teach at a school. So it was the New Year school holidays. It's the fourth or fifth time that we've gone to Australia for this vacation, and we usually decide based on the weather where to go. We ended up in Manilla, and it was actually incredible – the weather for the entire two weeks was perfect. We were doing huge flights, I mean I flew over 2,000km in 13 days, the longest one was 270km.

This was a fairly normal day, as the weather wasn't at all extreme in any way. It was going to be another really good day. I'd spent the night before looking at the weather, so I knew in the morning the wind would be light northwest and it was going to change to south wind. The plan was to fly to the northwest, which is actually what I ended up doing that day.

But a day or two before, a very similar situation had occurred in the morning, when the wind aloft was light northwesterly. So the east slopes of the mountain were of course in full sun, and large superheated pockets had formed in the stagnant air in the lee of the hill.

It had been really rough on the east side of the mountain, and a bunch of dusties had gone through. So I was actually aware of that, and I was aware as we were going up that conditions were going to be similar. So I was just keeping that in mind a little bit.

But we were going up the mountain in the truck, about five or six of us, and somebody just decided let's go to the east launch: because even though the wind was still northerly, we were expecting it to change, and then fly when the wind changed. But I thought even then, remembering now, that it wasn't really the best choice because of the dusties. And actually people were already taking off from the north launch, without incident.

So we went up there and the wind wasn't good yet, so we were just waiting. And then a little dusty went through launch. And usually when that happens the dusty goes through and then wind comes in and you start flying, right?

So quite soon afterwards my friend Shane took off, and it was very, very light wind, and he went up. Meanwhile, all this while people on the north launch were launching, and we were thinking maybe we should even move over to the north launch. But then as expected the wind started to change.

So me and this one other guy set up. There were maybe 10 or 15 people on launch – fortunately most of them had their gear still in their packs. So we set up early, but I was really ready to launch. Shane had already gone off.

For a while the wind was really calm and not very good, and then it started coming from the southeast. So I immediately went to launch. I kited the wing but I got picked up by this funny gust and it was not so good. I stalled the wing and got dropped back to the ground, no problem.

When I landed I spun the wing, so it was on the ground with the leading edge towards the ground. And I was just holding it down a bit with the brakes. But it was funny because even as it was stalled it was trying to go up into the air, and I thought that was a little strange.

A friend of mine, Molly, was standing quite near and I realised what might happen. But at this time there was no clue that anything was going to happen except a bit of gusty wind, but that's pretty normal.

So, I was about to open my mouth and say: "Molly can you hold on to the wingtip?" And just then, it happened, out of the blue with no warning at all, the wind started getting violent and I got pulled off my feet.

Another friend of mine, Ollie, he actually tackled me and got on top of me, but we got pulled with such force there was no way that anybody could hold me, and he actually got hurt. He ploughed the ground with his head.

So he let go, and I could feel that I was in the grip of some really extreme forces. I felt I got lifted up, and it was a lot of Gs at first, getting lifted off the ground. When I got my bearings a second later, I looked down and saw that I was already more then 10 metres in the air and moving – I did a semicircle and was moving towards the west, that is to say toward the mountain over the launch. And right next to me as I looked, I could see the dusty, right next to me.

There was lots of dust and spinning – pretty spectacular! But after that I realised there was no way I could land and it was too dangerous anyway. And I also knew the wing was not really flying properly. I suspected it was in a parachutal stall, which it was.

So after that I just concentrated on looking at the glider and keeping it open and more or less over my head. The most I could do is I just held my brakes down a little bit.

In the video you could see that I was spun around a few times but actually I didn't even notice that. I was just trying to keep the wing open. But then suddenly I saw it dive forward and, as it happened, at that moment I did have good situational awareness. So I knew that at that time I had gone almost a full 360 around the actual dusty and I was facing outward and away from the mountain. And the wing just dove exactly in the right direction. So at that point I just let it fly and I flew away completely normally.

Actually, I'm much more nervous talking about it now than I was at the time. But I was completely calm, even afterwards you know how your hands shake or whatever? None of that happened.

For some reason I was completely calm and I realised I was going to fly away. I just thought, okay, well from now on it's a normal flight and I didn't think about it much.

Looking down it was pretty spectacular, because the other guy's glider got caught in the centre of the dusty. I went up like a rocket of course!

Leanne Brezina's side of the story

I guess I was much more affected by it than Rick was. I was also planning to fly that day, but I was going to be moving to the other take-off because I thought it was too rowdy for me to handle. I mean, people were set up and people were flying, but it was kind of like the big boys and everyone else was hanging back. I could see other people getting up on the other launch and yeah, I was not setting up, I was preparing to move.

I had been filming Rick take off every day. I don't know why, it's just something I do. And I could see it happening and in hindsight it's like, what the hell was I doing taking the video of it? I should have been there holding his glider and helping him. And that's something I learned from it too: that we should be more vigilant and, instead of taking videos, we should really be more present.

I thought I was filming his death. I thought, maybe this could be important, just so we know exactly what happened. I thought, oh my God, he's really going to die here because he was flung out of control and like a rag doll spinning around. It seemed surreal.

I spoke to Rick on the radio. Actually I wanted him to land because I was freaked out. I mean he just rode the thermal off the dust devil, he just kept on going up in that same thermal and I was just so creeped out. I wanted him to get away from the mountain, but he was all: "I'm going up, this is the right place to be," and I'm like oh my God.

I didn't fly, I went down and I retrieved. I flew the next day and my head was fine and Rick's head was fine. I mean we do a lot of flying and we do a lot of mountaineering and sea kayaking. We've been exposed to risk and dangerous situations before. We're both aware that these kinds of things happen, and we'll deal with it as best we can.

Rick went on to fly 193km over eight hours, the longest flight of the day on XContest. He was flying a lightweight Skywalk X-Alps (EN D). Rick is an experienced mountaineer and sea kayaker. He and Leanne live in Japan.

Out of practice

Matthew Whittall

Phew, what a scorcher! The hottest summer on record in the Alps: light winds, good thermals and lots of flying. It was a shock to the system, because spring in the Alps was cancelled this year. Until the beginning of June it was still snowing on the mountain tops; there was more chance of England scoring a penalty than me getting a decent weekend's flying. Then a week later someone flipped the heating on, the thermometer screamed up to 30 Celsius, and suddenly we were thrown in to the mayhem of full-on midsummer thermals. The transition was more than harsh in my eyes; it was like being hit by a cricket bat.

My preparation for the onslaught of thermic conditions this year was almost non-existent. By mid-June I had managed to amass a total of 13 minutes' airtime. Then along came one of those perfect forecasts and, trading in one of my precious wild cards, I headed off to the rolling green hills of the Vosges, in eastern France, with my ever-faithful friend, Alan. It was one of those days you dream about: no wind, nice cumuli bubbling all over the sky, and hot enough to fly in shorts. Looking up at the obviously pumping sky I was feeling more than a little rusty. I used to get worked up about losing my 'flying edge' over the winter, but I now consider the annual relearning process to be part of the pleasure in paragliding.

The first thing to overcome was that I was a bundle of nerves. I wasn't nervous about actually leaving the ground, or messing up my take-off, as despite my lack of airtime, I'd managed to get out groundhandling quite a lot, for a change. What really worried me was hooking into that first important thermal, or rather not hooking in to it and going down.

This left me in a strange predicament. There I was, risers in hands, ready to launch, watching pilots thermalling happily out front, yet suddenly I couldn't bring myself to launch. I argued with myself that I'd just gone through six months without flying, and a week of miserably low productivity at work, as I tortured myself studying classic skies and dreamt-of thermals, a 5am start, a rally-style drive up the hill, and a speed march to launch. I had sorted out my gear in record time, and there I was standing on a perfect launch, yet I seemed unable to see beyond copious reasons not to launch.

The wind was five degrees off for a start, and it could have done with being a little stronger, and although those guys out front were going up, it wasn't that quickly. And anyway, cloudbase was rising. Why scratch around when you can wait half an hour and have an easy ride to cloudbase? Suddenly I saw myself in my mind's eye, stood ready on launch, staring longingly at the sky like a child at a toy shop window, wanting but unable to reach out and touch the very thing he wants so much. I was laid out, ready, and in fact, blocking the entire take-off for others, while I continued to miss the very moments of ecstasy I craved so much.

The huffing and grumbling of an agitated Frenchman behind me brought me back down to earth – to exactly where I shouldn't be, terra firma. I ran. What a wonderful feeling, the glider pulling evenly against me as it rose symmetrically. A moment later I was flying out to join my brethren, and a few moments later still I was going up nicely. Locking in to the core of the thermal, my senses concentrating on the sensations of flight, all the tension, the worry and the nervousness started to melt away. By the second circle, I could concentrate on flying again.

Needless to say, I wasn't thermalling well. I was hurtling around like a skidding brick, overreacting to changes in climb rate and slight turbulence in the core. Just when I thought I was getting the hang of it, I was reminded that we were flying in the heat of mid-summer. The wing lurched forward, the wind noise doubled and the vario screamed 6m/s at me; my desperate attempt at 'active flying' began to make me look more like a bell-ringer on acid than an experienced pilot.

My reactions were slow, so my timing was always slightly out. One second the glider was banked at 90 degrees, the next I was kicked neatly out the core and flying straight again. I was happy to be going up, but why couldn't it be smooth? Nervousness began to creep back in and I immediately assumed the famous 'toilet seat' position – 15 years of paragliding and I still can't shake the habit of spreading my legs out and sitting up when I'm nervous in the air!

After about half a dozen of these thermals, I started to feel comfortable and, for the first time ever, I became aware of the sheer enjoyment of re-learning to fly. When I finally hit the sweet spot and had the wing cranked on a wingtip in the core, I laughed at how badly I would have coped in the same situation just half an hour earlier. I almost pity the expert high-airtime pilots that never go rusty; they forget about the raw act of piloting a glider. Flying by instinct and preoccupied with distance, speed, height and achievement, they completely miss out on the pure fun of turning a glider around in circles and trying to smooth out the bumps that Mother Nature is throwing at them.

I once read that Michael Schumacher sometimes made as many as six adjustments in a corner. Big deal. Even a middle-of-the-road paraglider pilot makes hundreds, maybe thousands of adjustments, in a thermal. And hey, most of us don't get to practise all winter either – that would make it too easy. So, Michael, take your millions, and when you feel like doing something difficult, give me a call!

I'd last seen Alan just after launch, scratching low down, just above the trees. I'd assumed he'd gone down, but suddenly the sight of him scudding across at cloudbase in front of me snapped me out of my thermalling reverie. I'm not usually one for going on about the spiritual joy of flying, but this was a wonderful moment. Those months of waiting and frustration were all over; we were firmly back in the saddle and loving it. I knew that Alan must have been fighting his own little battle, and would have gone through much the same kind of intense experience as me. I felt we were like two battle-weary soldiers regrouping after a particularly ferocious firefight, both proud to have survived, but equally elated to find out that our brother in arms had made it through too.

I was overcome with emotion but, strapped tightly into my harness and helmeted up, I had nowhere to channel it. So I did what we always do on the rare occasions we find ourselves enjoying a great flight together. I flew up close to him, hollered "Heeeeyyyyyyyyy!" at the top of my voice, and kicked my legs up and down like a five-year-old on a park swing. Childish, yes, but how else do you do it?

We Brits have never been big about expressing emotion, but after a while I started to go all American on myself, shouting "Bring it aahnnn!" when a strong thermal kicked in and tried to whip the brakes out of my hand. Worse still, when I landed and Alan walked over to me, I was so hyped-up that I broke one of my cardinal rules and thrust my hand up in the air for a high-five. The high-five gesture is, of course, designed for cool, young, athletically-built basketball players, not for two stiff-limbed, almost middle-aged Englishmen with sunburn. But somehow, a handshake and a pat on the back wouldn't have quite been enough.

We ended up having a perfect day's flying, and by the end of it we'd not only learned to fly again, but even had several hours of real airtime under our belts. Strong cores that had scared me in the morning were now just another way to out-climb somebody in the afternoon. In the space of a single day, we'd successfully made the transition from thermals flying us, to us flying thermals, and were proud of it.

Neither of us slept well that night. Not only because our minds were filled with the day's sensations, but because in our enthusiasm to get back in the air we'd forgotten a few basic precautions. I suppose we should have known better than to expose our bone-white arms and legs to eight hours of blazing high-altitude sunlight, but some things just don't seem so important when a good sky is beckoning.

Matthew Whittall has been flying since 1988, and writing about flying for almost as long. He's the less famous brother of former World Champion Rob Whittall. Matthew lives in Germany.

MINI STORY

Stuck at work
Andrew Craig

Telegram pings. I don't want to read it.
I don't want to know that my friends have succeeded
The forecast was good, but perhaps it was wrong
I'm evil – I hope that it's turned out too strong
Out of my window I see epic skies
While I write a memo on office supplies
My colleagues are wondering why I'm so surly
I long for the news that the gaggle's bombed early
My glider's been serviced, my parachute's packed
Half of me wishes I'd got myself sacked
My telephone sounds like a vario beeping
It's all I can do to prevent myself weeping
It rained all last week when I had lots of leisure
Today's fluffy sky gives me no kind of pleasure
I'm sorry to be such a miserable pill
But I hope you all land at the foot of the hill.

Andrew on the phenomenon of FOMO – fear of missing out

Girl gone wild

Kinga Masztalerz

"Hey sister! Can you hear me?"

I hadn't seen – or heard – a soul for four days of my vol-biv journey, and had gone all the way from despair to overwhelming joy and back to exhaustion in the meantime, so it felt like even longer. I had also started hearing things, so now I half assumed that this was just another imaginary voice.

But this one was real. It belonged to a bearded guy in pink Lycra, who was leaning next to his old-school road bike, as I clambered, with my 24kg backpack, over a fence marked with the sign: "Defence Area: No Admission." Oops! "Where the hell are you coming from?!" he went on. "From a place without fences," I answered. He didn't smile, but nodded slowly and looked towards the rolling fields and rocky mountains on the horizon. "That must be a good place," he said.

And he was right. I fell in love with New Zealand's Southern Alps when I saw them for the first time two years earlier. These remote, windy mountains, so different from the European Alps, have scared and fascinated me ever since.

The first time I flew here, I panicked. The second time, however, I carefully cruised around and accidentally broke the New Zealand women's open-distance record – 83.4km. But I knew there was much more to do. A day after that flight, I'd had dinner with the New Zealand X-Alps pilot

Nick Neynens, who'd just broken his own national record, flying a deep 200+km line, and France's Antoine Girard and Benoit Outters, who'd just returned from their own adventure across South Island.

Nick is a mountain goat crossed with a falcon, who was born and raised in these mountains. Antoine and Benoit, meanwhile, are amazing pilots and were also extremely lucky with the weather. The Southern Alps are famous for bad weather and for the prevailing northwesterly, which comes off the Tasman Sea and feels like the foehn in the European Alps. But these boys inspired me to fly deeper into the region's wild peaks.

So a vol-biv through the Southern Alps it was. When I said it out loud for the first time, it scared me. But it was also exciting. I knew I had to give it a go – and give it a go solo. Solitude scares most people, and it also scares me. It's way harder physically, logistically and mentally. You won't fall apart when you're with someone; you feed from each other. But when you're alone, it makes no difference whether you're a woman or a man – you have to do everything by yourself. You will hear all the voices you might not want to hear and you'll be alone with them. But you'll also find your own pace, trust only your instincts and take full responsibility for your own decisions.

To prepare for my Southern Alps adventure, I did some smaller vol-bivs alone and with my partner, Chris, in the European Alps and the Indian Himalayas. I hiked with my backpack, worked hard at the gym, and ate a lot to gain some extra mass, as I knew I'd lose a few kilograms – there isn't much food in these mountains.

Then, two years after that dinner with Nick, Antoine and Benoit, I spent a family Christmas on the North Island, packed my paraglider, camping gear and freeze-dried food, and the next day touched down in Queenstown.

Some good friends live in the area, but this time I didn't call anyone. Experienced pilots would have advised me, and more careful pilots would have expressed their doubts. I didn't want either; it was my trip from beginning to end. No stress, no fear, just go.

I hitchhiked to the start of a trail to Mount Crichton. I chose this starting point because it was close to Queenstown, but would also put me straight into the mountains. There is no bomb-out and because of airspace the only way to go is north, deeper and deeper into the peaks. I had never flown from here before, but I found a trail after some bushwhacking, was forced to do a little free solo loose rock climbing, then reached the top about midday.

It was a blue day, a bit gusty, but it definitely felt flyable. I took off after 1pm, immediately got a massive collapse and slid across the slope. Ugh... nice start. But despite this, I found a climb and slowly flew north. It wasn't pleasant, though. The thermals were broken and it was way windier than I'd expected. After 25km, I put myself over a leeside slope and landed vertically. I was disappointed, but also overwhelmed by being alone in these mountains. There were no trails, and the only way out led south, exactly where I'd come from. I was not going back.

It would be tempting to tell this story in usual paragliding style: how awesome it was, and how tough and heroic I was alone in the wilderness. The truth is that, at this moment, all the emotions were so overwhelming that I didn't know how to deal with them. Being truly alone for the first time, in the remote mountains, offline and at the beginning of an unknown challenge, made all the feelings pure and rough. There was no distraction, nothing to drown out the inner voices – I was forced to hear every one of them. I began to doubt myself and cried. In fact, I cried a few times during the trip – out of exhaustion, pain, despair – but this was the only time I cried because of my fear of the unknown. But then the beginning is usually the hardest part. Soon enough, I learned that the unknown is more exciting than terrifying. And that once you make the first step and really commit, your mindset changes.

I camped below the ridge, and next day life looked better. I took my time, made coffee, ate breakfast and launched at 11.30am. Probably I could have started earlier – but hey, it's my pace. Just after the first thermal, I felt the soothing confirmation that it was going to be a good day. It was easy to stay high, and I took a beautiful straight line over Mount Repulse to the Matukituki valley. Below, I saw some friends flying a regional competition in the valley – it was the only time I would see other pilots.

I crossed towards Mount Eostre, where it was rough and harder to climb. No stress, no fear, just keep going. But I also felt my blood sugar drop, and I was dehydrated. I planned to eat while crossing Lake Wanaka, where I was very high, but I chose the wrong line and the air was so sinky that I realised I wouldn't make it. If I'd landed, it would have been a beautiful flight, but it wouldn't have been good enough for today, so I turned back, stuffed a muesli bar into my mouth and scratched my way back up, deep in an unlandable gorge. Phew! I was back, refocused, and the next 60km all the way to Hopkins Valley went smoothly.

Entering Mount Cook airspace, I turned on my airband radio and reported to air traffic control. Just the fact that I had not carried this heavy-as-a-brick black box around in vain made me feel unstoppable. I crossed Dobson Valley rather low and deep, and the strong valley wind was killing all of the evening thermals. Still, I hooked on to a sparrow, and the vario beeped. The rocky mountains were impossible to top-land, and if I'd lost the lift, I'd have been touching down deep in a valley, probably backwards, and facing a very long walk out.

But not today. After 15 minutes trying every possible brake input, I finally got a decent climb and flew over the impressive Ohau Range. At the north end of it, majestic Mt Cook, the highest peak of New Zealand, was hiding in the clouds. I went for a long glide over the Pukaki valley and landed in the hills on the other side. I chose a place by a stream, because I desperately needed water, and quite low, hoping it wouldn't be so cold at night.

I was overwhelmed and tired. In fact, it was the most demanding flight I've ever done. But then I'd flown 173km, more than doubling my 2016 women's open-distance record. After all the doubts of the previous day, it was quite a plot twist. I cooked, ate, wrapped myself up cosy in my wing… and couldn't sleep until 1am. My mind kept processing the day. So, being on an adrenaline rush, I thought: let's go further north, perhaps all the way to Nelson?

Next morning, I hiked up to launch as a white veil of cloud gradually covered the sky. And after gliding into a headwind, I landed pretty much where I had the previous evening. I hiked another ridge, but I could see that the sky had completely shut down and the wind had picked up. Instead, I decided to hike towards Lake Tekapo and tried another little flight out of the valley. It was so windy that I could soar a little bush just a few metres above the ground.

Once on the ground again, I could see that the terrain that had looked so promising for hiking from above was actually uneven and covered in thorny plants and swampy streams. After a couple of hours, I could see the southern end of the lake, but I also noticed that the batteries in my Spot tracker were flat, so I decided to head towards a dirt road which was marked on the map. The 6km hike there took three hours, and the 'track' was a boggy trail. But I found a dry spot and set up camp. As I did, the hills turned dark blue while the snowy peaks glowed orange. It's hostile terrain, but this colourful light show made up for everything.

The night was cold, I barely slept, and it took me forever to start the following day. But after a couple of hours, I reached a dirt road and that man in the pink Lycra. I followed the road for another 20km and slowly entered a different world – cars, tourists and, best of all, a supermarket. I was so excited to see Coca-Cola and fresh fruit that I completely forgot about the batteries for my Spot and had to go back for them.

From Tekapo, I followed the Te Araroa trail (the main national trail across both islands) into a 65km/h wind. At times, my backpack felt like a sail. I needed a proper shelter.

I was exhausted and moving more and more slowly, but I eventually reached a hut. There were a few lovely trampers staying there and it was New Year's Eve, so we wished each other a Happy New Year and fell into our beds at 8pm.

I spent two nights in this tin hut waiting for the weather to improve. I repaired my gear, rested and had a beautiful time with trampers from all around the world. Once in a while, I'd climb a nearby ridge with mobile coverage to check the weather forecast and call Chris. But after a while it was clear that if I waited until the next epic flying day, I might be here all year. It was time to hit the road again.

I left in the afternoon, hiked along a picturesque ridge to Stag Saddle, the highest point on the Te Araroa Trail, and camped there, in my million-star hotel. In the morning, I flew down the valley before the wind picked up, and then kept hiking. But soon there was heavy rain and lightning and I jogged all the way to a hut which became my home for another day. In fact, it rained non-stop for 24 hours, and I started worrying that the nearby Rangitata River would swell and become impassable.

As the weather was completely unflyable, I hiked down and started crossing the labyrinth of streams and rivers. Some of them were quite scary, it was drizzling, and a cold southerly gale was smashing me mercilessly. I was wet and cold and all I wanted was to feel some sunshine. I didn't get any.

The next day was 30km of boring hiking with heavy grey clouds covering the sky. After the epic flying in Otago, I was a bit disappointed with Canterbury. The mountains were lower, the valleys were wider and way more populated, and the weather was awful. It wasn't the best start to the New Year.

But there were benefits. As I followed a dirt road, a few friendly Kiwis stopped to ask if I needed a ride. I even got a can of Coke and a sandwich from one older lady. I accepted any food with enthusiasm, as my daily intake was around 1,200 calories and I must have been burning five times more. But I had to turn down the rides. Once I'd decided the trip was hike and fly, anything else would have felt like cheating.

I set up camp and dreamt about Chris driving me back home. I was starting to get homesick and I began fantasising about leaving my heavy backpack at the side of the trail. I was weak, I'd visibly lost weight – but what's the point if it's all easy?

I got the odd short flight in the following day, but the weather was relentlessly bad and so I headed for another hut. The hike down the valley started well, but it became narrower and narrower and the trail turned into a stream, then a river. I kept crossing it at first, and then just hurried straight down the river, soaked to my waist, desperate to get to the hut.

But then the hurrying and tiredness caught up with me – and I sprained my ankle on the slippery rocks. It was getting dark, though, and I was almost there, so I carried on – and twisted the same ankle again. This time it felt much worse. I roared like a hurt animal – and then cried, cursed and hobbled the last 300m to the hut.

It was almost 10pm and there were two grumpy trampers sleeping inside so I cooked my dinner outside in a gale. The water didn't want to boil, so I ate the half crunchy, freeze-dried meal and limped to bed.

Next morning, my ankle was swollen and painful. Ugh. It was a vol-biv trip and I'd sprained my ankle hiking a river – not even flying backwards into a tree. I decided to wait in the hut, hoping it would get better. Which was just as well. It was raining heavily and relentlessly.

After three days of rest, my ankle felt good and I was ready to continue. But something had changed. After all that time in the hut, lashed by rain and wind, with nothing to read, no music and no-one to talk to, I'd had the time to look inside myself, and name the things that are most important to me.

There was no fear anymore, no insecurity nor doubt. Just calm confidence and the sense that I could take whatever these mountains threw at me. And because of that, I felt like my mission was accomplished and that the trip could come to an end. I had wanted to end the journey so many times because I thought I couldn't handle it anymore – but that was exactly why I'd had to keep going. But now I felt like I could handle anything... and that meant I could legitimately decide whether to carry on or go home.

I'd wanted to go on to Nelson, but thinking about the route through lower, wetter and more civilised terrain didn't turn on any emotion. So I hiked another 20km, hitchhiked to Christchurch airport and flew (in a plane this time) back to Auckland. Just like that.

On the way back home, I thought about that terrified girl in tears from the beginning of the trip. I knew her, I understood her fear, but I wasn't her anymore. Now I felt like hugging that girl and assuring her that there was nothing to be afraid of.

But that girl didn't need a hug. She needed to go out there, alone, and overcome her fear of the unknown and her doubts about what she is capable of. She needed to fly New Zealand's most beautiful line. She needed to suffer a bit to understand how much she can handle. To come out the other side a different person, the person I'd always wanted to become – the one who is not so easy to scare, who thrives on being alone in remote mountains, who smiles when the pain comes.

Now I can truly play, knowing that the end of this journey was just the beginning of another.

Kinga Masztalerz was born in Poland, but lives in New Zealand. She's a physicist by education, who nowadays grows tropical waterlilies and teaches the art of vol-bivouac to other pilots.

Kilimanjaro, 1978

Ashley Doubtfire

I was beginning to have a special relationship with Kilimanjaro. "Big brother" is a poor way to put it – but it gets close. The mountain was developing a personality. It seemed to say: "You are on me now; I have known you to be coming. You are frightened of me, and rightly so. You know that when you take me on you are putting up your very life for the pleasure and glory of flying from me.

"You hope that I respect you and that I'll take care of you. These rocks have stood here for thousands of years overlooking the planet's most primitive continent. Your blood would go unnoticed. All you can do is use all your knowledge and leave fortune to itself."

The others were resting, some asleep, when I walked over to the night watchman's shed 100 yards from the tourists' cabin. A lamp shone from the doorway and I stood on the threshold, adjusting my eyes to the light. Dark faces – lots of them – looked at me and there was a smell of stew. "Jambo," a greeting came. I returned it: "Jambo!" "Habari." "Habari!" "Msuri." "Msuri!"

The usual greetings led to discussing our health and trying to get Mr Lobonge on the radio at the bottom. No good. They offered me a seat and I reclined alongside the others. "Tek this," said one, "good for you." Smiles all round. We ate and talked for three hours about flying, God, religion, women, Amin, colour and politics. At least my mountain was being hospitable.

A cave marked the rest point between the long trials of five steps and rest, 12 steps and rest. I found that controlling my breathing was essential. The ski stick, which we all carried, acted as a support; when one had strained oneself to the utmost, one could then give out with one's chin on the stick and eyes closed.

The gliders, the rucksacks and four or five porters were all that I found on the top. The cloud was getting thicker, and the film crew needed to get some film of the take-offs. The success of the whole project depended on it.

After a while on the summit, I began to find it easier to operate, and began to think in terms of the flight. For a start, there was nowhere to take off from, which presented a bit of a problem! There was a choice between a scramble over nine-foot round boulders, or three-foot rocks with scree. I chose the rocks; I had to.

With enough build-up of energy by breathing hard, I reckoned I could get just enough momentum together to heave myself over the edge cleanly enough to dive into flying speed and get away. Only just, for there was hardly any wind.

I had a go at picking up the glider. It felt incredibly heavy and after five or six seconds I eased it back down again. In front of me was 15ft of rocks, below which was a sheer drop of 3,000ft to the saddle. I started breathing deeply and made my first couple of steps. The right wing lifted hard and the left wing lurched down. I stopped and set myself up afresh, with some help from the others.

At this stage I had to rest for nearly a minute. The tape recorder was already working, so I started to speak my thoughts, both for the recording and for the benefit of the others. I knew this time I had to commit myself, and made a supreme effort to control the glider, as I moved towards the edge. The drop off the last boulder put me cleanly away and I was gradually picking up airspeed and praying for some response from the bar. A happy sigh, and then a whistle, came from the glider as I watched out to my right for the fated outcrop. I was flying away from the mountain!

Relief is a poor word for what I felt, as I eased the glider round to the right, came out of prone and waved back to the others. Back into prone, I watched the crater rim slowly move by – now about half a mile to my right. Below me lay a beautiful fluffy white carpet of cloud, which gathered height and enshrouded Mawenzi. I looked ahead towards where Moshi must be lying somewhere below. A long dark gap is what I set my heart on. I tried to estimate my chances of making it. It was a worry, but I was so happy to be flying, so exhilarated with the general view that I just concentrated on getting my thoughts together. It was at this point that I remembered the tape recorder, so I apologised to it that I had not been saying anything for the last five minutes and started explaining what was happening.

This is a shortened version: "In front of me the cumulus is towering up nearly level with my present height. I am worried about making the gap in the clouds, but the view is amazing. In a minute I shall have to make a decision as to whether I fly right in order to avoid a large build-up of huge cloud to my left – or go the other way where there is more of a chance of reaching the gap before I sink into the top of the cloud."

Occasionally there were quite sudden increases in airspeed, without doing anything to the bar. I surmised that this was turbulence from Mawenzi, working on a large scale. My heart at this stage was continually in my mouth, because the changes in airspeed were tending to become more pronounced. I had read accounts of the sort of problems that have been encountered downwind of large mountains, and was praying that the wind was light enough not to cause too serious shears.

The path I decided on through the clouds worked out fine. There was no sign of the helicopter, when I got down (!) to cloudbase – it was another novel experience to approach cloudbase from above. I had some fun flying among the gentle wisps of cloud, then I saw Moshi in the distance and started looking for some good bases to thermal. Obviously it was highly overdeveloped, and although I maintained height during a few 360s, I felt it was wiser to try a straight glide towards the town. I looked back and up. Kilimanjaro had completely disappeared.

I had to rely now on Moshi, rather than the Mawenzi-Kibo set-up, for my orientation. As I lost height, I concentrated on clear areas for a landing. I had noticed a large green patch next to a housing estate. I positioned myself for an approach, turned back into wind and landed without incident.

The heat was overwhelming, as people started appearing from everywhere. As I unclipped and looked around, I found myself totally surrounded by inquisitive and unbelieving faces. Coming through the crowd was a police officer in khaki shorts, who eventually managed to get to me and asked me quietly for my papers. I explained that I had none and he asked me where I came from.

"From the top of Kilimanjaro," I replied. I watched him to see his reaction. He was looking down at the huge pile of my clothes, which had been heaping up as I had been stripping off. He gave me the faintest hint of a smile.

"In that case," he said, "Perhaps you may be excused."

Ashley Doubtfire flew from the summit of Kilimanjaro in 1978. A pioneering hang glider and microlight pilot, he sadly died young, although not from flying, in 1983. This is an extract from a much longer article he wrote that was originally published in the British magazine Wings! in 1979. It's republished with the kind permission of Skywings magazine.

Celebrate being alive

Haydon Gray

Adam died last week doing acro paragliding. He's the first friend I've known who's died. From the first phone call with Rob with the bad news, I knew I didn't understand death. I should have driven up the valley to check that he wasn't still there. I had an image in my head of Adam sitting on the road, lonely by himself, confused that everybody had got the news wrong.

I should have gone to the hospital. To connect with the idea of what death is. What it means. Not existing anymore. No sparkle in the eyes, no cheeky grin, no laughter. But it wasn't my place to go up the valley and it wasn't my place to go to the hospital. I couldn't distinguish the line between need and respect. I felt a lot of emotion about what had happened, and felt like I should be a part of it. But at the same time I felt there were more than enough people who would need to feel grief more than me, and that was how I would give respect.

Grief feels like an emotion that your body enjoys in a sadistic way, kind of like the pleasure of pulling a splinter out, but only after suffering the pain first. If you keep it in it will only fester. Sometimes I think our orderly lives are arranged to avoid too much emotion. We have outsourced emotion to the internet: to Netflix, Instagram, Facebook and porn sites. I guess I also missed emotion, and Adam's death made me feel it.

But for Adam, I told myself, I was in his second circle of friends. I met up with him when I needed help with my van renovations, but other than that our existence was one of chance. Being in the same place at the same time to enjoy some poor jokes, dry humour and a beer maybe. But I was second circle. For me, first circle was close friends, friends who contact each other regularly and put effort into relationships with each other. To me Adam was Steve's mate, and Steve was definitely first circle. The only thing before first circle was family and I guess sometimes even that line is very blurred.

I don't understand death. And I didn't understand Adam. He was a character. Loud, boisterous, exuberant, selfless, generous and switched on. He knew how to have a good time; how to impress girls; how to make people smile; build a house; fit out a van or fold a parachute. I didn't understand how something or someone can be around like an energy that keeps everything glowing golden, but then in an instant someone flicks the switch and the light is gone. The golden light that could be found at Velo Cafe, or on the Höhematte after landing a tandem, or in the valley, this was Adam.

Tonight we said farewell to Adam. I wasn't responsible for much because I felt I should keep my distance as a second-circle friend. His first-circle friends made an effort that would make anyone proud. I was hesitant about it, and felt like it was becoming a carnival of Adam instead of something else. But as we lit the last lanterns and his dad James gave a short speech, I realised it was a carnival: a carnival of love, of Adam's friends. It was something that created a connection from his lifestyle and friends to his family. They might not have really understood it before, but standing there on the edge of a cold lake in the middle of the Swiss Alps, they were surrounded by a community that respected their son. Loved their son.

But I don't understand death. Does it get easier as you get older? Does the frequency of it increase such that your emotions become more subdued? Adam's sister Shan wasn't subdued. She was different. She was twirling around the celebration like a whirling dervish with a firecracker inside. Drunk on sadness, but wearing the smile of her brother. She would have made Adam proud. Wherever he was, he was definitely blushing with some of the stories she was telling.

Mona wanted to give our handwritten envelope with some cash inside to Adam's parents. I didn't. There was a bucket for donations; it definitely wasn't glamorous but I was apprehensive approaching James or Dee that I might say the wrong thing and blow the lid on emotions that they'd been able to keep under control. I was wrong. We gave James the envelope and hugged tight to Dee. The connection made sense. Giving money made sense, not the amount but the formality of saying sorry for your loss. Our note explained that the money was what we should have spent having more beers, adventures or laughs with Adam, but didn't get the chance.

James's face was strong and his voice clear. His Scottish kilt proudly worn and his head high. He told us what we wanted to hear, how happy a place Interlaken was and how special it was for Adam, and now them. While I struggled to control the tears rolling from my eyes, I saw a depth in his that scared me. A depth of pain and sadness that he didn't wear on his sleeve. His glassy eyes, red and blurry made me feel a sadness that isn't just tears and crying, but a feeling of emptiness without explanation.

We had a slideshow beamed onto the wall next to the Velo Cafe. It was of Adam's life, cut together with a video of him dancing while working on an oilrig. As the images flicked past to the tune of the Arctic Monkeys, it reminded me that we weren't there to commemorate death, but to celebrate life. Adam's tragic accident showed us how to appreciate what we have. To remember that being alive is pretty awesome. And while you have the chance, celebrate being alive. All the time. And that's what Adam showed us. How to get naked; dress up; party; be part of things; build stuff; hug people. And smile.

I still don't understand death. But life? Yeah, I get it. It's wonderful.

Dedicated to Adam Macpherson, 36, who died in an accident in 2018

Haydon Gray is from Canberra, Australia. He has a degree in environmental science, and has lived in England, Ireland and Papua New Guinea. Haydon continues to fly in Interlaken.

Goal fever

Allen Weynberg

"Can we go yet?" I yell, as I lean out over the left-hand side of my harness and try to project my voice towards my nearest competitor. She looks like a mini Lady Vader, cocooned in her harness, swaddled in full-face mask and ski-goggles with her dark blade of a comp wing slicing 360s above her. I hear a dull fuzz from my radio earpiece, now flapping in the breeze below and behind my left ear. No way to make out that reply.

You'll learn as much in a week of competition as you will in a year of free flying, they say. So I carry on learning, circling, climbing and watching for a competitor to head off and show me we've started. Before launch, with help from others, I dutifully programmed the task into my flight instrument and phone app. The flight instrument now just looks the same as it does on a free-flight day. No start time countdown or turnpoints visible. I thought it might get the hint that once we took off it should provide me with directions. Why else would it think I'd spent all that time pushing its buttons? It happily chirps away telling me we're going up just fine, but stays completely mute about the task.

My phone is currently somewhere down in the depths of my pod on the end of a stretched charging cable. I take both brakes in one hand and gingerly reach down to retrieve the phone and Velcro it on the flight deck. Hooray, back in business. A little arrow points roughly in the direction I think it should. Even better, a countdown to the start! So why is everyone gliding off already? The countdown changes from two minutes to three minutes. It's not a countdown. It's a count up. Go, go, go!

How lucky is that? I'm near base with the field gliding out ahead of me. I conjure up the spirit of Russell and Robbie and Bruce, place my feet tentatively on the bar, and reach up to lay magic hands on the C risers. Does this voodoo shit work on a low-B glider? First decent bit of turbulence and I'm off the bar, on the brakes and pretending that I needed to climb again anyway. A few circles and another Jedi glide. Then the comp magic happens. "Bar-Bing!" The phone indicates that I've flown from one imaginary cylinder defined by GPS coordinates to another imaginary cylinder defined by other GPS coordinates. Never has something so arbitrary been so satisfying, and all signified by a beep from my phone. I even got here higher and faster than some other people! I fly on for another 10 seconds to make sure, and then turn like Kelly Slater off the lip to make the glider follow the little arrow again.

This is the easiest leg. Pushing along under a good cloud, watching the arrow creep closer to the circle. Vader Lady and another pilot are still ahead of me. We leave the shadow of the cloud and aim at the turnpoint located on a low ridge in full sun. "Bar-Bing!" I don't think I'll ever get used to that sound.

And then it all comes crashing in. I reached Bar-Bing but I'm now really low. The ridge is more a shallow rise, neither face steep enough to soar. Time to learn more in a week. "Be like Chrigel, change gear."

More comp magic now unfolds. Instead of my normal lonely sky, I see Lady Vader climbing, and swoop over to connect with the lift. We work away with no release and get separated. Then I hit something better and turn tighter. Now the other guy comes over and joins me. I feel like King of the World. So he fixes that by out-climbing me and disappearing off on his comp wing. I stick to it, and the faithful Buzz lifts me up until I can resume my quest to follow the arrow to the next imaginary cylinder of joy. "Bar-Bing!" This one is really fun. I don't have to turn, I can just fly through towards the end-of-speed section that marks the edge of the 3,500 airspace. I fly through like Bolt coming out of the bend on the 200.

One more low save and it's "Bar-Bing!" end-of-speed section. But it's still 3k to goal flying through the letterbox between the 3,500 airspace ceiling and the ground at about 1,500. Like Zebedee, I time it just right and step off the rising Magic Roundabout to glide towards GOAL. Before the "Bar-Bing!" I hear Lady Vader whooping and doing wingovers over a random field that is in the imaginary cylinder called GOAL. I drift over, listen to one more glorious "Bar-Bing!" and spiral down to land.

Did I learn more in the two-day comp than in two-sevenths of a year of free flying? Who cares? I learnt there were many more things I didn't know. "Bar-Bing!"

Allen Weynberg learnt to fly with friends in North Wales in 1994. He works as a high school guidance counsellor in Queensland, Australia, and is a columnist for Cross Country magazine. Allen's ambition is to fly 200km – but without making a plan.

In deep

Guy Anderson

This might hurt a bit, I thought as I looked down on my unrecoverable canopy hitting the hill directly beneath me. I'd taken a big, wild collapse while scooting low down in a windy valley, and simply had no time to even reach for the reserve before impact became inevitable.

This was the dramatic end to an otherwise untroubled World Cup for me in the spectacular and unforgettable mountains around Sun Valley in Idaho, USA. Having flown over a hundred miles (170 km) in the first task, skipping over five mountain ranges, we'd been dogged the rest of the week by windy conditions, which had stopped a few days. And while I was aware of the wind picking up during the second and last day's task, I was still unprepared for the unmanageable turbulence I found deep in Fish Creek canyon.

I thumped in pretty flat on my left side and bounced through the grass and into some scrub, coming to rest face down with my brand new sunglasses nicely embedded in my nose. Although badly winded, I remained conscious, and slowly collected myself together enough to realise that I was still alive, although in a bit of a pickle, to put it mildly.

With the blood dripping off my nose, I fished out my mobile phone and took a photo of my face to check that arguably my finest feature was still intact. Vanity restored, I felt up the rest of my limbs and was actually relieved to find that I had only broken my left arm and a few ribs front and back on the left. Although my legs seemed fine, I knew my pelvis was buggered too, and walking was going to be tricky. My radio had gone dead only an hour into the flight, and I could see that as my phone had no signal the live tracker wouldn't be much use either. I got the tracker out anyway and my spirits sank as I saw its batteries were flat, which potentially meant that nobody would have a clue where I was along the 100km course... bugger.

I'd been flying with a couple of other pilots on Niviuk Icepeaks, but we'd split up when getting low and I was pretty sure they wouldn't have seen me crash. I spent a while looking for other gliders in the sky, and then it slowly dawned on me that my long-distance vision was closing down. I had been looking at clouds and mountains on the other side of the valley, but suddenly I could only focus on the grass 100 metres away. Thirty seconds later my vision was down to the leaves on the bushes around me, and I knew I was in trouble. As I became slightly freaked at the prospect of losing my sight completely, I heard a calm voice say, "Loss of vision is a classic sign you're going into shock, what you need is some oxygen."

At the time I didn't think about it, but looking back it felt very familiar, quite like my Dad's voice; he's a bit of a know-it-all on important trivia like this. I'm sure that life-saving information like that is subconsciously logged away until needed. I never heard it again, but it spurred me on to act. Luckily, in Idaho you often fly super-high and use oxygen, so oxygen was something I had loads of. I whipped out my kit and gulped in great lungfuls for about 10 minutes, and sure enough the vision rebooted to normal.

Feeling pleased with myself, I lay back in my harness and relaxed for the first time. I'd crashed at about 3pm; it was now about 8pm and getting dark, and I knew nobody was even going to think of me as missing until at least midnight, so I made myself as comfortable as I could for the night to come. I thought about the speech that Mike Pfau, the competition organiser, had given a few days before following concerns voiced about how wild the country was that we were flying over. "Don't worry," he'd said, "if you're out there we will come and find you, we will not leave anyone on the hill". Very comforting stuff when you're totally lost in the boonies.

When I crashed I had thought: "Where the hell am I?" In every direction as far as the eye could see, there was no trace of man: no fields, no fence lines, no cables, no houses… nothing. The hills and mountains were covered with tall grass and blue/green sage scrub about a metre deep, which at that time of year was covered in yellow flowers. It was absolutely full of quails and the odd covey of ptarmigan that would explode out of the ground right under your feet. There were a few silver birch in the bottom of the valley, some of which had been blown over by the wind that must rip through. I had crashed about 200m above the floor of this V-shaped valley. 'My' hill would have been about 300m high and was more of a pimple towards the head of a valley where the sides rose to around 2,500m.

I had no map, but I did have my tablet, which I could have looked at but didn't. In the first briefing we'd been told always to head downhill, so when deciding whether or not to walk out the way down was obvious. With my pelvis in pretty poor shape, I couldn't go uphill anyway. From where I lay, I guessed that at the worst I should find something in about 15-20km max, and so as I notched off the distance by eye it seemed do-able.

I might have dozed off for a while, but I nearly shat myself when I was woken by deep growls coming from the top of the hill just above me. It sounded suspiciously like a big bear, although with my ribs broken I couldn't roll over to look up the hill. I reached into my harness and found my penknife, not very useful against a hungry grizzly, and then even more pathetically took a few pictures using the flash on my mobile hoping to scare whatever it was away. Then nothing, just silence. Looking up at the starriest sky you could imagine, I had the awful feeling that I was edible. More growling a few hours later, this time in the bushes below me, was met by more flashes from my mobile and this time some tuneless singing from me, which again seemed to do the trick. I decided that once it was light, I'd be making tracks.

I woke at about 8am deciding I needed a pee, the first I'd had since crashing 18 hours before. I wasn't ready to see the small stream of blood, as I certainly hadn't felt any pain from anywhere down below. I knew the pelvis holds a large number of important organs and blood vessels, and the blood did worry me for a while, but I remembered hearing that the bladder and kidneys could bleed if bumped, and after a bit more prodding of my guts I contented myself that I wasn't a goner quite yet.

I had about four litres of ballast, but not knowing how long I was going to be out there I wanted to find water while I was still feeling fit. So at about 10am I set off down the hill hoping to find a stream. The bottom of the valley looked to be only 200m away. My pelvis was definitely broken, so I shuffled down on my arse, all the time keeping an eye out for spotter planes or helicopters, but blissfully unaware of the mayhem I'd caused for both the organisers and my family.

A huge search and rescue operation had kicked into gear, and most involved had not got more than a wink of sleep. Perhaps one of the hardest jobs fell to Zak Hargreaves: to call my wife and daughters to say I'd been missing for over 24 hours and there was real concern for my safety. This he did with a calm and assurance that even now I can only marvel at.

Meanwhile around 75 people combed hillsides over the full 100km of the course line on foot, mountain bike, motorbike and even private light planes. And although the competition was over, lots of competitors stayed on to help in the search, captured for PWC TV by an uncharacteristically serious Philippe Broers.

Halfway down the hill, about an hour after I'd set off, it dawned on me that I had left behind my penknife, anything waterproof and the only thing I had to eat, a cheese sandwich. By then, though, there was no chance of going back up so I struggled on towards what looked like a little stream. As my luck was going, I shouldn't have been surprised to find the stream bed bone dry, but at least there seemed to be an animal track to walk along; all I needed was a crutch to walk with. As if by magic I stretched out my right hand and there was this perfectly solid-feeling stick about five feet long, complete with a notch to hang my ballast bag on. All I needed was to get on my feet and I'd be on my way. This was a good deal harder than I'd imagined, as the bones in my pelvis crunched about. Twice I slipped and fell down the bank of the stream, and it took up to an hour to get back to being upright.

Finding yourself in a position where you know that whatever movement you make is going to be accompanied by brain-numbing pain, there's a big temptation to just be still. Each time I fell, I would lie there looking up at the sage flowers and the cumulus above. Half of me just wanted to enjoy the moment of relief from what the other half was telling me I had to do. It's tremendously hard to square such opposite viewpoints going on in your own head when one side wants to stop and the other knows it has to go. A few times I did have to give myself a stern talking to: "Do you really want to die here Guy?" would generally get the right response.

I reminded myself of the conversation another pilot, Arnold Franzenburger, and I had had with a couple of jovial local farmers while we waited for the retrieve bus on the first task. The farmers were out hunting elk and were moaning about how the newly released wolves had decimated the elk population, knocking out 80% of the elk in the last five years alone. "They only released the wrong goddamn wolves!" they said. "These critters weigh 300 pounds (130kg) and would eat my auntie if they could catch her. They've already eaten half the dogs at home!" How much more motivation do you need to get to your feet and look a little less like edible road kill?

I'd look around and something would tell me that although stunningly beautiful, this was not the spot I was going to end my days in. In a situation like this, I am sure many would draw great strength from their faith but I simply don't have one. I have been brought up an atheist, so I felt no guiding hand to help me, and had no one to pray to. I knew that I alone had got myself into this, and it was possibly only me that could get myself out. I've had the odd bit of scary stuff ski-touring in the Alps, but I'd never been this lost, this alone or this injured before.

That day I managed about a mile, walking with tiny steps and making such slow progress that three huge rattlesnakes that I disturbed had plenty of time to slither away totally unbothered. Each step needed immense concentration. Perfect placement was everything to minimise pain, and I became absorbed by getting the pattern right. My left leg created less pain than the right one despite the stick being under my right arm. I started counting the steps in threes: I'd start off with the left ("one"), swing the right ("two") and then place the stick ("three") to steady myself. One, two, three. One, two, three. With this as the all-absorbing background, I'd find myself free to think about my wife and daughters a lot. We've been very happily married for 24 years, and my girls are everything. Making it home was without doubt my biggest single motivator, and once you have that at the front of your mind any discomfort from the body becomes secondary.

During the afternoon the clouds had been building quite ominously, and with nothing waterproof I knew I was going to get wet. By 8pm the thunderstorm started to dump, and I was so exhausted I just lay on the path under the only small bush I could find and got properly soaked. With a woolly ski jumper and a few layers of wool T-shirts beneath, I was hoping for a wetsuit effect to keep me warm, but by midnight I had the shakes good and proper. I slipped into a dream world where my legs and shoulder assumed human identities that I could chat to, the English legs less optimistic than my Canadian shoulder. In my strange imaginary world, there was a camping trade fair with people looking at lightweight tents and asking how they compared to my woolly jumper. Thunder and lightning would jolt me briefly back to the real world, but before long I'd slip back to my imaginary friends who all told me I'd somehow qualified for a lift back in the bus that I could see 20m away. Strange how the mind plays tricks on you.

The storm blew itself out around 3am and I woke up cold and wet, just as it got light, and decided that I would be better off walking than lying in a muddy puddle. It was now 36 hours since I had crashed. Once again just getting to my feet proved a real ordeal, and the first 100 metres were tortuous. Fifty metres further I came around a bend in the valley to see a pretty little wooden farmer's hut with a door and a window tucked in under a large willow. As I crept towards it, I couldn't believe I'd just spent an uncomfortable night in the open when I could have been tucked up in the cabin. I soldiered on thinking at least I'd be able to find a tin of beans for breakfast, only the next time I looked up the cabin had vanished like a mirage.

I think I was a bit low on blood sugar, or just going slightly mad, as at this stage I started to play games with the 20 or so flies that swarmed around the clot of blood on my nose. It was getting hot so I made a hat out of sagebrush, thinking it would deter the flies, only to find it attracted clouds of them. Of the scrum of flies only two were green, and each time I disturbed them the same two would be first to land, always in the same place. For quite a while I played "musical noses", to see if any of the others were quick enough to take the green fellers' seats. I'd shake my head, sing a little song and see who settled first. This went on for what seemed like hours without me thinking I was even remotely deranged.

A few small planes had drifted over very high that morning and I'd tried waving my red T-shirt on the end of a stick and reflecting the sun with my phone but to no avail. Now three miles (5km) away from my crash, and with the track rapidly improving to something recognisable as usable for humans, I was elated for the first time to hear a helicopter. I swung round and glimpsed a Blackhawk dipping into the valley, but from where I was looking no sooner had it arrived than it was gone. Hope of rescue was turned on its head as the noise of the engine disappeared. They obviously had missed my glider (understandable, as it's pretty much the same colour as sagebrush), ticked off my valley, and were off to search elsewhere.

I turned back to my track, cursed my continued bad luck and got back to the rhythm of the road… two steps, name of a cocktail, two more steps, cocktail. My eldest, Chloe, is in her third year at university studying languages and had just come back from a year in South America where, together with hopefully a few other things, she's learnt to make world-class caipirinhas and pisco sours. She'd written down the recipes for dozens of cocktails for me in a small book, and I mentally leafed through, each page taking me a further ten paces down the track.

In fact, aboard the Blackhawk was the ever eagle-eyed Russell Ogden, who was in charge of where the big bird hunted. In a final 20-second sweep further south than usual, Russell had spotted my canopy and had instructed the pilot to "put this baby down" (Nick Greece and Nate Scales think he's half American already). All of this happened out of my sight, so when they shut down the engines, I'd assumed they'd gone.

Russell ran down to find my harness empty and, fearing the worst, started looking for a half-eaten body nearby. Seeing the route that I'd left in the grass, he tracked me down to the stream, where he found a footprint and started to believe there might be more than a corpse to take home. A mile further on, with a more definite set of tracks to follow, he radioed the helicopter to come down and pick them up further down the valley.

Hearing the helicopter for the second time and then seeing it fly straight towards me, I was convinced I was indeed rescued. I stood on the track and waved my T-shirt to make sure, but as it slowly turned just 50m over my head I had the sickening feeling they still hadn't seen me. Imagine my despair when off it went back up the valley, around a corner… gone. So close. Shit. Surely they were coming back. Forty-five minutes went by. I sat on the road for what seemed like forever until at last I couldn't take it any longer. Time to start walking again.

Another ten very long minutes went by until finally I heard the engines and then saw the Blackhawk, this time coming straight towards me 20m off the ground. What a relief when I saw the pilot waving. I braced myself for the wash from the rotors and still nearly toppled over as they touched down 30m away. A few last hard, slow yards up to the loading bay and there was Russell's beaming smile. All the pain was gone, just elation as I gave Russell the biggest hug I could manage. It was about 3pm, about 48 hours since the crash.

Fifteen minutes later we arrived at Hailey hospital where I was patched up, before being sent by chopper to Boise hospital for surgery on my arm. The injuries included seven acutely broken ribs, one punctured lung, multiple stable fractures of the pelvis, broken humerus (I knocked the ball joint off the top of the arm), and a lacerated kidney. A lucky escape.

Perhaps the strangest story of the whole saga came two days later with a phone call from Rob Wolf, a retrieve driver whom I'd made friends with on the first day. With maps covering his kitchen table, he had the strangest trance-like experience as he watched his finger, seemingly with a mind of its own, plonk itself firmly down on the map. Amazed, he marked it with a big cross before heading off to bed for a couple of hours' sleep.

The next morning Rob was up at 6am and at the sheriff's office to explain where he was going and why. The sheriff agreed, so by 8am Rob had got to the end of a track and was faced with a three-hour hike up and over a line of hills. As he reached the crest of the mountain, he looked over to see a Blackhawk flying into the same valley from the other direction. He got his binoculars out and watched, incredulous, as the chopper landed on the spot he'd marked on his map. He saw Russell tracking me down the hill and along the valley, so he scanned ahead until he spotted me staggering along about two miles further on. He sat in shock for the next hour as the rescue unfolded until he finally saw me loaded safely into the Blackhawk. You just can't make this stuff up.

My very special thanks go to Zak Hargreaves, Nick Greece, Tony Lang, Nate Scales, Farmer, Bill Belcourt, Rob Wolf, my Blackhawk Ranger Russell Ogden, my rock Mike Pfau, all the doctors and nurses at St Alphonsus in Boise, and all those involved in my rescue.

Russell Ogden on the search:

There were over 100 of us involved in the rescue effort, but we had no idea where Guy was. My guess was that if he was going down, he would be running to the low ground to the south, but if he had had an incident up high then he would have been blown into the big stuff to the north. The only logical search pattern was to zig-zag along the 100km course line; we were probably doing 10km zigs to the north and 10km zags to the south. The helicopter pilots were brilliant, carving up and down valleys investigating anything that looked suspicious. We checked out lots of rocks and cows, we even found a small marijuana plantation! We covered every inch, I reckon I know the area better than the locals now. In the end we found him in the low ground at the very southern limit of our search pattern.

When I spotted the glider I thought he was dead. I was expecting to find a bundled wing with him wrapped inside to keep warm. Instead the wing was untouched from the moment it had hit the ground. The harness was in some bushes so I couldn't make out the body, but I feared the worst.

We landed on top of the hill a few hundred metres from his position. I immediately jumped out and started to run to the rescue and promptly went arse over tit down the slope. I had barely regained composure by the time I got to the wing and was surprised to find he was not there. His instruments and flying jacket were just lying on the ground as if he had made a hasty retreat, so my first thought was that he had crawled somewhere close-by to die. I was struggling to grasp the situation but I tracked his movements by following a trail of bent grass down the slope to a small creek at the bottom of the valley. I then followed the valley floor, and after a few hundred metres found a footprint and immediately my spirits rose. If he had got this far and he was on his feet then, surely he had to still be alive!

I continued down the valley and after a kilometre or so the helicopter came to pick me up. We found Guy after about another kilometre, heroically walking his way to safety. That was an amazing, unforgettable moment. I was completely flooded with emotion – it was pure joy to find him alive and kicking.

Guy on being prepared

As I've demonstrated, I'm no survival expert, just very, very lucky. So what would I do differently? I'd recommend using a Spot or InReach satellite tracker. Juan, a pilot who landed a couple of kilometres away from me, had a Spot and was picked up at midnight on the first night. Even if I'd been out all night, being able to send a position and an 'Injured but OK' message would have spared all the anguish at home.

And I'd pack an 'emergency kit': spare radio batteries; a powerpack to charge everything else; a little food; a lighter; a light plastic mirror for signalling; a light waterproof or even a very light tarpaulin; mosquito netting; headtorch; strong painkillers; water purification tablets (I drank from a stream but was lucky); and a whistle (I couldn't shout due to the punctured lung). And finally, to help your rescuers, if you have the strength, try to spread out your glider to make it as visible as possible, and even if you haven't deployed it, put your reserve out too. Then concentrate on saving your skin.

Guy Anderson continued to compete at the highest level in the sport, finishing second in the 2017 FAI Paragliding World Championships. He lives in Somerset, and is the director of a wine business. Russell Ogden is a professional test pilot who lives in the south of France. He won the FAI Paragliding World Championships in 2022.

MINI STORY

Paragliding and the informal economy

Andrew Craig

I climbed out of Combe Gibbet, got quickly outpaced by a Pole and a Czech, and landed in a Hampshire field 30 km away; small beer for some of those flying that day, but a delight for me.

It's a difficult hitch from Andover back to the Gibbet on country lanes. After a few minutes, two lads drove past in a tatty Vauxhall, shouting and gesticulating. I thought they might be mocking me, but just in case they were offering me a lift, I ran a hundred metres to find them waiting a bit sheepishly in a layby.

Very politely, the passenger asked me: "We wondered if you were hitching because you had no money for petrol?"

A lightbulb went on over my head.

"No," I replied, "I have got money for petrol, and I'd be very happy to give you a tenner to take me to Combe Gibbet."

"Ah," said the driver, "We know Combe Gibbet – we sometimes go shooting there."

"What do you shoot?" I asked; they didn't look like country-sports types.

"Rabbits," he said. Oh yes, I thought, and what else? But I said nothing.

I handed over my tenner and got in. We drove to a nearby petrol station, where they used my note to put in exactly ten pounds' worth of juice. As we motored along the back roads near Faccombe, a fat pheasant trotted along the tarmac ahead of us. The driver sped up, gave the pheasant a good whack and stopped, declaring: "That's my dinner – I haven't had a roast for ages."

He jumped out, but returned empty-handed. "The bugger kept running!" he complained.

A tough bird. The driver apologised for his brutality.

"No need", I said – I wouldn't do it myself, but it's certainly no worse than buying a chicken in the supermarket.

The lads were astonished to hear that I'd flown from the Gibbet nearly to Basingstoke. When we arrived, they asked lots of questions about the gliders still flying there. I made them tea in my van, and over a custard cream or two I advised them to contact the local flying school. If they said they'd retrieved a pilot and were short of funds, they might get a cheap tandem flight each. And I was pleased to have demonstrated that hitchhikers with big rucksacks might be happy to fork out.

And then a further piece of serendipity; one of Britain's top cross-country pilots, Graham Steel, arrived after flying from Selsley, much further upwind in Gloucestershire, to near the South Downs. He'd got a first ride as far as the Gibbet, but still needed a lift to Cheltenham. He had money. The lads had time, but needed more petrol. A deal was done. The wheels of the informal economy turned a few more revolutions, and everyone ended the day happy.

Andrew describes a retrieve more memorable than the flight

The way of the Samurai

Bill Belcourt

"The Way of the Samurai is found in death. Meditation on inevitable death should be performed daily. Every day when one's body and mind are at peace, one should meditate upon being ripped apart by arrows, rifles, spears and swords, being carried away by surging waves, being thrown into the midst of a great fire, being struck by lightning, being shaken to death by a great earthquake, falling from thousand-foot cliffs, dying of disease or committing seppuku at the death of one's master. And every day without fail one should consider himself as dead. This is the substance of the Way of the Samurai." Yamamoto Tsunetomo, Hagakure

I'm sure many will think the above quote is a bit extreme when put in the context of paragliding, but I don't think so. Not a flight goes by without me thinking about what it means to fly, what it means to fear flying, and how I've come to accept the inherent risk of flight. Paragliding is not natural, so it is only natural that your brain is going to perceive many things in flight as 'life and death' when they really are not. But since perception is reality to our basic instincts, we all have to figure out how to deal with fear. There is a lot we could learn about fear and mental toughness from Hagakure – The book of the Samurai.

The Samurai figured out a long time ago what mental state was necessary to achieve their best performance in life-and-death situations. Those with fear were those who had not fully accepted the reality of their chosen vocation. Those with fear could not perform at their best in battle. But those who accepted the consequences up front were the ones unburdened with what they had to lose. They were the warriors of legend.

From this, I made a conscious choice to admit every time I pulled that glider up; it could be my last time. In this state I felt relaxed, but also very focused and aware of the task at hand. And on those days, the potential of the day was the limiting factor of the flight and not my capacity for fear. The decision to confront death is one of those breakthrough moments. Also, our past successes and failures largely shape our ongoing perceptions. How we reflect on them and learn from them gives us the resolve to continue flying.

"In just refusing to retreat from something, one gains the strength of two men."
Shungaku

My first serious close call on a paraglider was in 1994. I was flying in one of Willi Muller's meets at Golden in British Colombia. Conditions were fantastic, which was rare in the Canadian Rockies, where it either rains too much or blows too hard to fly paragliders. My glider of choice back then was an Edel Rainbow, complete with trimmers that had slick webbing and lots of travel.

On the first transition I got worked and completely lost the glider behind me. Somewhere in there the trimmers released to full fast as the glider came surging asymmetrically, ugly and huge. The glider shot way off to my left with a tip stuck; the perfect recipe for the dreaded tip-stuck-spiral. This was before the days when anyone in North America knew what a tip-stuck-spiral was, let alone knowing anything about trying to get out of the trap once in.

The Gs came on like a runaway train. I was pinned to the back of the harness while the world became a blur. The risers seemed like they were 10 feet long, and I had lost all ground reference. I couldn't reach anything. The brakes were all I had, and they were completely ineffective. I was hauling as hard as I could on the opposite brake and the trailing edge felt as solid as a picnic table. Let me state for the record, I was no weakling either. At the time I was doing a lot of training for climbing, and I could do a one-arm pull-up with either hand. But I still could not deflect the trailing edge enough to escape the spiral.

My time was quickly running out, so I did what climbing taught me when I couldn't pull hard enough with one hand: use both. I let go of the inside brake, matched hands on the outside and hauled for all I was worth. If the brake line snapped, I was done, as I didn't feel like I could get to the reserve handle after all the harness adjustments had slipped open from the force of the spiral. Miraculously, it worked and the glider returned to normal flight with a small asymmetric, which I easily pumped out.

It was hard to get a sense of how much time had passed. I lost some altitude but I was, surprisingly, still in the game. I flew on to goal thinking hard about my first paragliding test of fire, shaking uncontrollably, a constant stream of blood dripping down my left arm. I had pulled so hard the brake line had cut through my leather flying glove, slicing my index finger to the bone.

I still have the scar to remind me of how close I came that day, and a few new scars since from other days with greater consequences. These tests are gems. They are the windows into the soul of what motivates you. You get to open the mind's black box and see what's inside. You get the chance to make changes for the better. You get to come to terms with what you do. You become a better pilot.

I am just as committed to flying now as I was then, even though the consequences are clearer now than they were then. It's been a long journey, mentally, and some years were better than others, but I learned from all of them.

Fly long enough and you'll have some days that will test your ability to deal with fear, and you'll still react with 'certainty'. You have a choice: bear the burden of the mantle of fear when you fly, or work to minimise it. It is no easy task and there is no permanent solution. I personally think there are two kinds of people when it comes to being scared: those who admit they're afraid, and those who lie about being afraid. There is no avoiding it.

"There is something to be learned from a rainstorm. When meeting with a sudden shower, you try not to get wet and run quickly along the road. But doing

such things as passing under the eaves of houses, you still get wet. When you are resolved from the beginning, you will not be perplexed, though you still get the same soaking. This understanding extends to everything." - Yamamoto Tsunetomo, Hagakure

Also known within the US community as 'Yoda', Bill Belcourt is a multiple winner of the US XC league. In 2022 Bill received a 'Lifetime Sender' award to acknowledge his coaching and mentoring efforts. He works in the climbing and outdoor gear industry, and lives in Salt Lake City, Utah.

One hundred miles

Chris Gibisch

Beads of sweat were developing, condensing, and running down my forehead, falling to space from my brow, only to make streaking contact across my sunglasses. I gazed across the tarmac; the tin hangar to my right, a grassy median to the left, and my good friend Jeff Shapiro positioned on the launch cart in front of me.

Heat leaving the sun-baked ground distorted the distant landscape, while behind me I could hear the engine of the dragonfly piloted by Johnny approaching. He landed to our left and came racing by, moving into position for the next tow. I could see the launch assistant connecting Jeff to the tug while exchanging a few words. With the assistant's signal, the tug's engine came to life and whisked Jeff down the tarmac and into the air. It was my turn.

My heart was pounding as I heard the tow plane return. I laid prone, put my legs in the harness, grasped the cart handles, and waited for the launch assistant to connect my shoulder bridle to the tow line. Sweat continued to pour from my brow, and my heart-rate spiked as he casually clipped the karabiner to my tow bridle, leaned over and said: "Your buddy suggested I keep an eye on you 'cause you are brand new to towing. This may be the stupidest thing I've seen but, by the end of the week you are either going to be a pro at this, or dead. You ready?" I didn't look at him, just nodded and heard the engine roar to life. The line pulled tight and I was ripped down the tarmac for my first flight in Big Spring, Texas.

It was August 2008 and I was heading south with Jeff Shapiro, picking up Jeff O'Brien along the way, en-route to Big Spring. I had been flying hang gliders for only three years, but I couldn't have been more psyched. Shapiro had taught and mentored me, and I had soaked up everything I could from him. Two weeks earlier, I had travelled to Morton, Washington, learning and earning my aerotow endorsement for this competition.

Although only my second comp, I would be teaming up with good friends who would officially form the US Worlds Team at the time. Waiting for "the Jeffs" (Shapiro and O'Brien) and me in Big Spring were the rest of the team: Dustin Martin, Zac Majors and Davis Straub, accompanied by his partner Belinda.

Big Spring is a small town in the west of Texas at the intersection of US Highway 87 and Interstate 20. With a population of 27,000, it's the largest city between Midland to the west, Abilene to the east, Lubbock to the north, and San Angelo to the south. Fairly quiet and filled with friendly folks, the surrounding landscape is roughly flat, littered with oil pumps and crisscrossed with back roads. In addition, Big Spring lies within a unique weather pattern. Strong southerly winds coming off the Gulf of Mexico bring moisture to combine with intense heat, making Big Spring a great place to fly long distances.

Registration was early on our first day, so Dustin suggested we go for a casual 50-mile (80km) out-and-back as a warm-up flight. Now mind you, up until this point in my 'flying career', the longest flight I had achieved was 19 miles, and that was downwind! "50 miles, ha!" I laughed at the thought of being able to fly that distance so casually, but if everyone else was going to, then why not try?

Speeding down the tarmac, my mind stumbled with what the launch assistant had said to me. "What a pep talk," I thought. Refocusing, I popped out of the cart doing everything I could to ensure the wing stayed level while the tug pilot eased the Dragonfly off the runway. We climbed fast together. I was in a near panic, doing everything I was taught to stay in position while being towed, but this was nothing like the nice calm mellow morning air of Morton. This was midday Texas, and dust devils were ripping off the dusty desert ground on either side of the airstrip. I knew that if I were to get out of position, Johnny would release the towline, so I worked hard to maintain composure. The tug was all over the place in the strong convective conditions, and I did my best to stay with it as it climbed violently in lift and plummeted out the back of the thermals that we were flying through.

The towline dropped below me in a huge curve of slack. I tried to stay with it, but cringed waiting for something violent to happen. The line went tight, "SNAP" and I was off tow. The weak link had broken and I was free, thank God. My heart slowed. The lift was strong and abundant, but so familiar, so I gaggled up with the guys and we headed north.

It was amazing tagging along with the country's best pilots. They were marking all the lift and helping me become a better pilot. Before I knew it, we had reached our turnaround point and were heading back to the airport. Despite the headwind, we were basically just gliding a straight line back. Lift was so abundant and strong; we were racing between the clouds, covering ground fast. Of course, with those guys being faster and more comfortable in the robust conditions, I found myself lagging behind. As we neared the airport, I spotted a large storm cell beyond the tarmac that was being discussed on the radio. Unfortunately, between that cell and us was a wall of dust, marking a defined gust front, pushing our direction.

Through the radio banter, I saw the guys diving out of the sky, racing for the ground while hoping to beat the gust front. Shapiro nearly flew his glider directly into the hangar, and Dustin snuck it in behind a barn.

That left O'Brien and me in the air. I looked down at a small pond that I was crossing over. All whitecaps, I was too late. The gust front was here and I was now in a position Shapiro had always told me not to be in; in the air, wishing I were on the ground. I had no idea how to handle the situation, so I radioed O'Brien. "Just fly the base tube into the ground like at the south side," he said, referring to the classic site Point of the Mountain in Utah. O'Brien was lower than me, so I watched him slightly to my right, as he slowly came down in front of the hangar and a handful of people grabbed him.

Now it was my turn. I eased the control frame towards myself and slowly descended straight down. I was in disbelief. I was flying such a fast glider and I had absolutely zero groundspeed. In fact, I started going backward. The entire situation was so serious and absurd that I started laughing out loud. The ground crept closer and closer. My heart was pounding faster. I kept focused on the need to fly the base tube into the ground, but just as my feet were about to touch down, I started moving forward.

Despite the strong wind, there was still a gradient and I was flying through it. A little thrown off my game, I went with it, taking a few steps and driving the base tube into the ground. As I did, in a stumbling motion, I dove for the nose wires like a linebacker trying to destroy a quarterback. Knowing those lines meant my safety, I latched on with a kung-fu grip. I quickly unclipped from the glider and a wave of relief fell over me. I was safe.

Unfortunately, I had landed in the middle of the airport so it took some time before a crew of folks could help me get the glider back to the hangar. As we entered it, my eyes adjusting to the dim lighting, Jeff Shapiro came walking towards me with a huge grin on his face, "Welcome to Texas!" he laughed.

The comp began the next day and started out great. My goal and focus were to survive the tows, and any flying was a bonus. To my surprise, not only did I manage the tows, but I even made goal a couple of the days. Triangle, lightning bolt, and dogleg routes were all new experiences, I was being challenged and pushed unlike I'd ever experienced before, and I was learning a ton.

I woke one morning excited and nervous, which had become normal. After coffee, we worked our way to the daily pilots' meeting to learn what the event organisers had deemed our flight task for the day. When I looked at the task board, it was laid out very simply. 109.9 miles with one turnpoint. A slight dogleg to the left, most of which was downwind.

I had been very happy with how I had been flying at the comp, but this was a 100-miler we were looking at. A pivotal moment in any pilot's career, I had only been flying for three years and thought, "No way I can pull this off." But I knew I wanted to try. My plan: stick to the plan, survive the tows and most importantly, have fun!

Gliders started filtering out of the hangar to establish the launch line. It was a scorcher of a day and dust devils were ripping across the tarmac. Sweat and a racing heart-rate had become a daily occurrence and expected. Race assistants were handing out water as the heat from the tarmac built, distorting the horizon. The line moved forward as one pilot after another launched into the perfect-looking sky.

Then it was my turn. I towed up, terrified, and pinned off. Despite my best effort, I bombed out, landing next to the line for another attempt. Again I launched, but this time I had forgotten to pull half-VG (standard practice while aerotowing) and once in the air, started oscillating all over the place. I quickly pinned off, banked right, and hooked around landing again next to the launch line. The stress of towing was weighing on me. I just wanted to stick to the sky so I could do what I enjoyed most – flying!

This time my tow was relatively uneventful. When we reached a nice thermal, my tug pilot Johnny signalled me to release from the tow. I pulled my release and continued to climb in the perfect lift. Because I needed three attempts at towing, the race start time had already lapsed, so I was free to go down course as I pleased. The only problem was that because everyone else was ahead, I was entirely alone. I did my best connecting the clouds, using thermals to efficiently fly down the course line until I neared the town of Post. I knew Post was the turnpoint, so I glanced at my GPS to see how close I was to the turn cylinder. To my surprise it was off. That was strange because I had installed new batteries the previous day. I tried powering it on and it came back to life. I resumed my route and raced towards the turnpoint. I heard the GPS beep indicating I reached the turn cylinder and veered left along the course line.

I radioed my position to Belinda, who was our official chase driver. I was the weak link in our group and she was incredibly patient waiting for me. She then drove a short way ahead and again waited for me to report my position. After a few thermals I referenced my GPS to ensure I was on course. Again the screen was blank! So again I turned it on and reacquired the course. I couldn't make sense of why my equipment was failing me. My flight was going well and I didn't want to be hobbled by my electronics. I continued on but finally, what I knew was likely inevitable, my GPS gave up completely. Not knowing what to do, I again radioed to Belinda my predicament and she sprang into action.

Belinda is an incredibly sweet woman with a beautiful smile and even more wonderful personality. No stranger to the southern sun, she wore a large sunhat protecting her from the harsh environment. She wasn't only a driver, but also a pilot and solid, savvy dedicated support for her partner Davis Straub, arguably one of the most experienced Texas distance pilots. She had been involved with the sport since pilots were using film cameras to prove their locations over turnpoints and helping them navigate via maps. She was an important half of the team and she knew how to play the game well.

Belinda pulled out a road map and began asking me to describe what I could see on the ground. She would align my description with the map, identify my location, and then relay to me a landmark that I should be able to make out from the air. "Up ahead you should see a major intersection with a farm on the northwest corner. I'll meet you there," she said. The day was ending, the clouds were gone, the sky was pastel blue, but I continued to work my way towards goal one mile at a time. One landmark after another she guided me towards goal. At this point I felt I was just scratching my way along. "Fall out of any one thermal and you're on the ground," I thought.

Eventually I reached a rendezvous point with Belinda where she was certain I should be able to see goal: "It's a small airport on the outskirts of Lubbock." It took a moment to zero in on it, but there it was. I was so close. Just then, Shapiro came across the radio: "Is that you constantly turning right? Dude, you got this. Just go on glide." I pulled the VG, eased the bar in and raced toward goal. In that moment, I remembered to try my GPS again in hopes of capturing the exact instant I crossed the goal line in order to be scored for the day's effort. Continually glancing down at the lame instrument, I began pleading out loud, "Please stay on long enough to capture goal." Goal, GPS, goal, GPS, please! Then, I heard the beep indicating I crossed goal. When I looked back at the GPS, it was dead for good.

I decreased my remaining altitude with a few wingovers to celebrate and came in for a safe landing. The team had been patiently waiting two hours for my arrival, and when I touched down they mobbed me. Not necessarily to celebrate, but to break down my glider and get the hell out of there. They were of course super psyched for me, but we had 109.9 miles to get home and start all over again the next day.

I've looked back on that experience many times over the years. As I've aged and matured as a pilot and person, I've come to recognise the uniqueness and brilliance of such a day. I launched into the Texas air and flew back in time. A time without so much technology or reliance on it, where communication and teamwork were necessary for success. Without all of the previous lessons learned, and of course the quick thinking and resourcefulness of Belinda that day, I would not have realised my dream to break the magical mark of 100 miles.

Chris Gibisch works part time as a respiratory therapist. This leaves him time to explore his passions for climbing, hang gliding and photography. He lives in Montana.

Who's packing?

Christina Ammon

One sunny December day in Pokhara, Nepal, I was savouring an après-flight lounge in the landing zone when my peaceful vibe was shattered. A fellow pilot stood in the centre of the LZ, holding his wing in a messy rosette, and let loose an expletive-filled rant. The issue? The rising cost of getting his glider folded and packed.

As in many countries that offer the combination of good flying and a good exchange rate, there are teams of local people in the LZ who will fold your glider for well under a dollar. It's generally a win-win situation: the locals get badly-needed jobs, and pilots get a factory-grade fold on their glider.

Fretting about such a small charge – 44 cents, 30 pence – seemed ridiculous to me (you always reserve the option to fold your own!). But this pilot's protest did make me wonder. What sort of living were these glider-packing guys making? To find out, I asked my glider guy if I could follow him home one day. "No problem," he smiled.

Sweaty curls clung to the neck of Parsu Ram Sigdel as he zipped up the last glider bag for the day. The thirty-something stuffed some bills in his pocket, took a swig of water, and smiled broadly: he'd made 500 rupees – or around $5.50. A good day.

We set off from the LZ at a quick pace. Parsu was wiry and agile – commuting on foot four miles to the LZ each morning and folding gliders all day burns a lot of calories.

He spared me the long walk, and headed for the bus stop instead. On the way, we threaded through Pokhara's tourist district, passing bars advertising mojitos for 500 rupees each. Was it annoying to see tourists downing the equivalent of his daily pay cheque from a cocktail glass?

"No," he said with his usual equanimity. "I know it can be expensive here." Having grown up in Pokhara, Parsu was long used to tourism and its accompanying two-tiered economy; the same cup of chai that costs him ten rupees can cost a tourist five times as much.

We boarded a local bus, and rumbled off through what felt like a parallel universe – lurching along streets that I'd never been down. Instead of the standard-issue dance bars and shops selling embroidered T-shirts and overpriced prayer flags, the shop stalls that lined these streets sold more pragmatic wares: plastic buckets, mops, potatoes. Fifteen minutes later we arrived in Parsu's neighbourhood and walked toward his house through fields planted with plump cabbages.

The streets were clean and peaceful; the neighbours waved. When we arrived at his cement-block house, his children ran out and enthusiastically pulled me inside.

Parsu's place was one dingy room that tripled as a bedroom, living room and kitchen. We sat on the bed (which now functioned as a dining room table) and ate biscuits with milky tea while his sister-in-law squatted on the floor and stone-ground ginger for the evening dal bhat.

Although Parsu didn't consider himself poor, the 500 rupees that he earned each day was just enough to cover vegetables, books, pencils, and clothing. When health problems cropped up, he relied on the neighbourhood's informal insurance system. If one person gets sick, everyone rallies together to cover costs.

Working in the landing zone clearly wasn't making Parsu rich, but was a comparatively romantic job considering his previous ones: for seven months he stuffed pillows in a foam factory in Punjab, India. He also spent a year in Dubai, toiling with heavy marble for 14 hours a day and sharing a small room with ten other guys. Most of the money he made that year went to cover the cost of his passage there. "They treated me like an animal," he recalls.

His prospects are better now. Like many glider-packers, he harbours ideas of becoming a tandem pilot and earning up to €100 a day. But he is careful to gird his aspirations. The cost of lessons and a glider are prohibitively high for someone earning less than US$1,500 a year. When we talk about it, he chews his biscuit thoughtfully and gets a far-off look. He has a five-year plan in mind. "First, I'll need to start a goat and chicken farm."

His son, however, leaps at the idea of working in the LZ and becoming a pilot. The ten-year-old has been on a couple of tandem flights and, unburdened by adult considerations, is less restrained with his dreams. He jumps on the bed like it's Christmas morning.

It's understandable; glider-folding can be the on-ramp to a pretty good lifestyle for a Nepalese kid. The wage is often higher than the local restaurant staff earn, and the packers learn English – a skill that can take them far. But there are problems as well. Parsu has seen first-hand the issues that can arise when kids work in the landing zone.

"They sometimes start skipping school and can end up going down the wrong road," he explains. "It can damage their life."

To counter this, some pilots opt to hire only older guys to fold their gliders. Parsu doesn't want his son to miss out on a well-rounded education. He reaches over and calms him: "First he has to go to school," he explains.

I left Parsu's house and walked back to the bus, which shuttled me back to the other world that was the Lakeside district, the touristy La-La land where I would fly, drink, and never complain about paying Parsu 40 rupees to have my glider folded.

Christina Ammon grew up in Nebraska, on the Great Plains of the USA. She's spent much of her life travelling the world in a van.

MINI STORY

Fat cats don't hunt

Ed Ewing

"What is wrong with you?" I asked the cat. It was sitting in its garden chair half asleep. "A couple of years ago you would have chased that squirrel out of the garden and up a tree."

The squirrel was busy eating its way through the sunflower seeds while the cat sat and looked on through half-shut eyes.

"I'm tired this morning," the cat replied, surprising me. "How about you? I bet you're disappointed after yesterday."

"Don't talk to me about yesterday," I said. "It was a disaster. I was at the wrong site, it was boiling hot and I was on that hill for four hours, bottom-landed twice, top-landed once and the highest I got was 60m above launch all day."

"Brutal," purred the cat, who knows nothing about flying. "Why did you go there?"

"Well, I thought it would be tricky, but difficult is OK. And it's quite close. I usually get away."

"What did other pilots do yesterday?" said the cat, zeroing in on the main issue.

"Loads were out west, flying big triangles for five, six hours. It's amazing conditions."

"Why didn't you go out there with them?"

"It's a long drive, it's a pain."

"So you'd rather spend four hours waiting and not fly than spend three or four hours travelling and fly?"

I shrugged. It yawned.

"It sounds to me like you need to do better planning." It stretched, and extended its claws. "I don't fly but if I did I reckon I'd give it the space it deserves, enjoy it. Not try to fit it in."

"I've crossed countries, even continents to go flying, to go where the conditions are best. I remember that time…"

"Isn't it time for breakfast?" the cat interrupted, rolling onto its back. "Also, I have these terrible tangles in my tail which need seeing to."

"You just want everything served up on a plate, don't you?" I said. "You're not prepared to do any work to get it, you don't catch mice or chase squirrels anymore. Just, 'breakfast time!' every morning. Well, let me tell you, life isn't like that. You have to put in the effort, you've got to 'do the work'."

The cat opened its eyes wide and stared at me unblinkingly, daring me to carry on.

"Fat cats don't hunt," it said, "only the hungry ones do."

And I don't think he was talking about himself.

Ed on the dilemma of investing time and effort in flying

Storm over the Mediterranean

Andi Seibenhofer

December 23 2004: almost everything appeared to be perfect. 20-40km/h of wind from the northwest forecast for the entire journey, and just a slight chance of storms, 250km away, around Crete was forecast. I made my move.

I had two aims in setting off across the Mediterranean: to protest against the re-election of President George W Bush and to set a new world record for the longest non-stop paramotor flight, from Greece to the pyramids in Egypt.

Crowds of curious onlookers watched my arrival at the airport in Kalamata. It was well known that my previous attempt had ended in the water. Just after 2pm I launched My U-Turn U2 tandem glider into a clear sky and began to make quick progress. My cruising speed with my Fresh Breeze Proto Paraplane motor was very good, often more than 70km/h, and I was soon out over the sea, where I tried hard to switch off my mind to the worries of the flight.

Two and a half hours into the flight, I saw the first flashes of lightning out to the east close to Crete. A huge storm was brewing over the island. By the time I reached Crete, there were dark clouds building around me, so I accelerated the engine to pass between two tall cloud towers at 2,500m. I thought about landing on the island, but I could see blue skies ahead and three independent meteorological stations had given reports of better conditions after Crete, so I continued. I passed Crete just before 5pm; not long after, it got dark and I entered one of the longest nights of my life. I was already numb with the cold.

At 8 o'clock I saw more lightning flashes just east of my course. From my position it was impossible to guess how far away it was, so I calmed myself down, telling myself that the storms would be moving away from me towards the east. Ahead, everything looked calm. I assured myself that the weather would improve soon. But then events started to get out of control very quickly!

A dense cloud cover formed over the sea below me, forcing me higher and higher till I was flying at about 1,700m. More lightning to the west. I started to feel really uncomfortable. Keep going, keep going! In an hour's time I'd be 80km further on and things would be different, I assured myself.

Suddenly there was a flash of lightning right below my feet; I was only flying about 100m above the cloud tops. When the second flash came a few seconds later, I decided to climb higher, but the clouds seemed to keep following me. It was freezing cold now, far below freezing, and my fingers and legs were numb. Then I saw them, momentarily illuminated by a flash of lightning, two towering cumulus clouds. They were right in my line of flight, and had already begun to join forces and connect at the bottom to form a single U-shaped cloud. The only way through was to climb over the col that was their now-connected bases, and hope to squeeze through the gap between the two towers.

With my heart pounding, I squeezed full throttle and climbed to 3,400m, where I could just creep over the lowest point in the col. Either side of me lightning crackled and flashed inside the towering clouds. I silently thanked God that at this moment at least I was watching it from outside the cloud. I focused hard on the route ahead, and prayed that beyond the col would be clearer weather.

As I crossed the highest point, my eyes straining in the direction of my course. A flash of lightning lit the scene ahead, and my blood curdled. Eerily lit by the flashes and forks of lightning, I saw very clearly a solid wall of cloud. The towers had united. No! At that moment I knew I'd blown it. I looked around for a way out, but every direction was the same: a mass of billowing, flashing cloud. A panicked glance to the GPS told me the next solid ground was Africa, over 300km away!

I didn't freeze up or pray for help. Instead, I just felt absolutely lost and lonely. Any moment now I would be engulfed in the clouds. I tried to map out a strategy, accepting the inevitable as best I could. Surely things could only get better? Reaching for the radio, I tried to raise contact with any aircraft in the vicinity. I tried to transmit my position, height, course, speed and the probability of an emergency landing in the sea. No one answered. I was totally alone. Suddenly I was desperate to relieve myself, the last thing I wanted to do right now, but without hesitation I peed in the neoprene suit and felt the warmth I had been missing for nearly nine hours. The urine escaped very slowly; it was like a gift. The warmth encouraged me and actually gave me back some self-confidence and faith.

Two minutes later all hell broke loose. The glider took a huge collapse and a wall of freezing hail and rain hit me. In seconds, everything around me was iced up. I couldn't see a thing through my ski goggles, so I tore them off but the hailstones battered my eyes with such force that all my reflexes screamed at me to shut them. I forced them open, knowing without sight I had no chance. Quickly the glider began to fill with hailstones, and within minutes there was about 50cm of hailstones in the trailing edge.

My eyes were in agony. It was like going to the dentist and having root treatment without anaesthetic. Looking at the speedometer scared me even more! One moment I was hurtling along at 140km/h, the next moment it felt like someone had hit the glider with an oversized hammer and I'd be back at 40km/h or even less. Keeping track was critical, and looking away from the instruments for even a second saw me careering all over the place. Amazingly the U2 worked wonders, and somehow kept on flying in air that was so violent it seemed impossible a paraglider could survive in it. More and more I learnt to entrust my fate to the glider.

At over 4,000m I began to feel the effects of hypoxia, so I decided to memorise my course of 134°. Losing my course and flying around aimlessly, or even in the opposite direction, would mean my fuel wouldn't last. If I was to have any chance of survival I had to get out of here as quickly as possible. 134°, 134°, 134°. Again and again I repeated it to myself whilst the visibility steadily deteriorated; deep in the middle of this hail storm, I could hardly read my course on the GPS.

There was a big flash right next to me that actually made my cold feet prickle and then, a moment later, the engine started vibrating so violently it made my seat shake! Worse still following the shaking… was silence. The engine had cut! I turned around and looked at the engine for the first time in the two and a half hours. The whole machine, even the hot parts of the engine, was covered in a thick layer of ice.

I was in deep, deep trouble! 4,000m below me, churned by the storm, the waves could be up to eight metres high, and the winds could easily be over 100km/h. The year before I'd struggled to make it in daylight and 30cm waves! With one hand I started to pack up and prepare for an emergency water landing, whilst the other hand flew the glider through the turbulence. When the glider folded in, I didn't interfere too much, I just placed all my faith in the U2. For the first time I was really afraid. I sent another blind message by radio but got nothing back. I was going down alone. Then at around 2,500m I completely lost control and began to plummet like a stone towards the sea. I didn't think I'd ever get control back. My descent rate was up to 49m/s! Then suddenly there was a shock like a hammer and I was flying again.

I still had 1,000m over the water and, as I had already completed all the preparations for the water landing, I tried to start the engine once more. The same again: vibrations as if the engine was actually falling apart. I gave it one more try, and suddenly the engine spluttered back into life. I couldn't believe it. It was coughing and choking a lot, but with some playing with the gas I got it running enough to limp on.

80km away from the coast, after more than three hours deep in the cloud, I dropped back down to 1,000m and finally saw lights from Africa. Unbelievable. I began to have a vague hope of surviving this. In the meantime, I still had to coax my ailing aircraft towards dry land and safety, whilst the engine stalled another 20 to 30 times and each time I worried that that was it; the battery would be dead, and I'd be going down in the sea.

At 2am on Christmas Eve, after eleven and a half hours airborne and 871.6 km, I finally came over dry ground. But my troubles weren't quite over. Below me, the stormy weather continued and a dangerous landing in wind and rain beckoned. Squinting through the mist and rain I spotted an illuminated strip close to some buildings where I managed to bring my aircraft down safely. The moment I touched down I jumped out and cut down the glider. Then I broke down and cried. I could hardly see a thing; the hailstones had damaged my retinas, and I could only identify dark and bright. After a couple of minutes, I heard men calling. They were soldiers.

I was held and questioned for five days. Every paper and document was examined in great depth. It turned out I had landed in a minefield 200m from Mersah Matruh, the military headquarters of Northern Egypt!

Andi Seibenhofer first achieved notoriety by landing his paramotor in St Peter's Square in the Vatican on 28 March 2003. He was arrested, but released the next day. Now a gyrocopter and helicopter pilot, in 2009 he established The 7 Group, which trains helicopter pilots in Iraqi Kurdistan

Lifting the veil

Nick Greece

For two years, the names Mohammad Razeghi and Soheil Barikani have appeared on my computer screen. We've exchanged posts on Facebook and developed an online relationship, leaving each other comments of mutual admiration. I've tagged them at scenic paragliding locales here in the United States. In return, they've tagged me at even better sites in their home of Iran. As my new Iranian friends' photos continued to appear on my Facebook feed, I became deeply interested in visiting a country I knew very little about.

During my lifetime, Iran has been alternately vilified and ignored by the Western media. It's become the proverbial Ivan Drago from Rocky IV, a manifestation of every stereotype that triggers America's exacerbated fear of foreign superpowers.

A year before I would get to go to Iran, my mother sent me an article about several pilots who'd been forcibly admitted into an institution with arguably the highest concentration of foreigners in the country – the infamous Evin Prison in Tehran. Because these adventure tourists had unwittingly landed inside a nuclear facility's sensitive zone, they were held, along with their Iranian host-pilot, for nearly four months.

Once I'd made up my mind to go to Iran, everyone I talked to about my visit predicted a similar outcome for me. "You'll end up in jail," they said. "The Ayatollahs will keep you," they warned. "You're gonna film and fly paragliders? You're crazy!" To which I'd jokingly respond, "It won't be so bad. Maybe I'll come out twenty pounds lighter and with a book deal." This usually eased the paranoia in the conversation, which would shift to the other, less harrowing aspects of a trip to Persia.

I wanted both to see what lay behind Iran's cultural veil and to disprove the barrage of extremist stereotypes forced down our throats by the mainstream media. With Homeland, Madame Secretary, and Fox News relentlessly perpetuating the stereotype of Iranians as turban-wearing, bomb-wielding zealots, I saw it as my duty as a sportsman to get a glimpse of the real Iran and report what I experienced.

My timing was fortunate. As the USA and Iran began talking under the guidance of President Obama and Iran's new president Hassan Rouhani, who'd been elected with the hope of reducing cultural and political isolation, I became the first American paraglider pilot to go on a flying road trip throughout Iran. No handlers, no government sycophants – just pilots on the road.

Some points to clear up right away: Iran is thriving, even in the face of crippling United Nations and US sanctions. Selfie-sticks and rhinoplasty are popular and Facebook is accessible through VPNs, though Tinder, well, not so much. No alcohol is readily available in public venues, but the Iranians have turned concocting non-alcoholic libations into an art form all its own. Religion is at once all-governing and quietly subdued. The food is outrageously good and plentiful. Ironically, or perhaps not, younger locals prefer fast food like fried chicken, pizza, or a lesser quality rice and meat option to their delicious national cuisine. Last, and most important, Iran's people, as a rule rather than an exception, are among the most welcoming, considerate, kind, and generous that I've encountered in my years travelling all around the globe.

Getting into Iran wasn't easy. After being told every month it was "imminent", it actually took two years to get a visa reference number. In 2014, a team of US pilots were all set to go and assured everything was in order. But when our day of departure arrived, the visas did not, and so our trip was abruptly cancelled.

Officials informed me that timelines for sporting visas for US citizens are difficult to predict, and mine was no exception. By September 2015,

I'd resigned myself to never seeing Iran. As often happens in life, just as I gave up, my reference number finally arrived. I received my permit late on a Sunday night. On Monday, I packed and wrapped up as much work as I could. Tuesday I flew to Washington, so I could apply for my visa in person on Wednesday and depart that same evening.

The embassy was filled with soon-to-be travellers. A gentleman next to me, curious about what appeared to be the only non-Iranian in the room, quietly inquired: "You go to Iran?"

"Yes, sir," I responded.

"Aren't you afraid of the danger?"

To be honest, up until that point, I hadn't been. I struggled for a reply.

"It's perception versus reality, isn't it?" I asked hopefully.

I'd started strong, but the second those words came out of my mouth I began to falter. Yet when I got to the window, I submitted my documents and secured my returned passport and visa. By 10.30pm I was on a plane headed to Iran.

I arrived in Tehran late the next night after three airports and 17 hours. The Iranian admission process was easy, even friendly. Soheil Barikani, Iran's number-one pilot, was on hand to pick me up and ushered me to the luxurious Hotel Evin. Ironically, this is also the name of the famous gulag where political prisoners and foreign nationals are held.

Soheil had given up a solid job as a mechanical engineer in order to dedicate his life to paragliding and, after six years in the air, had won several World Cup tasks. He confessed he'd become obsessed with racing paragliders, often paying for his frequent travel by selling the prizes he won, importing flying gear, and teaching SIV courses. To obtain a visa, Iranian pilots often have to travel to Turkey or Dubai just to visit the embassies of the countries they wish to visit, as there are very few diplomatic operations in Iran.

Over the next two days, Soheil and I spent a lot of time together, crawling through Tehran's traffic sharing a prodigious amount of knowledge about our esoteric adventure sport – from reserve tosses to comparing sport-defining wings ranging from the Avax RSE to the Mantra 10.2. We could nerd-out for hours.

When I exited the car to take photos for the first time of the Azadi Tower in Freedom Square, truth be told, I was deeply intimidated. The vilifying rhetoric ground into me back home had taken root, even though I prided myself on being an open-minded individual.

That evening we met Lilly, a pilot who lives in Tehran with a second home in Tabriz, where she imports auto parts from Turkey. Slim and blonde, she was dressed as if she'd just finished a yoga class. Lilly, who's been flying for a few years, greeted us with a smile and beverages. She's been fighting both publicly and privately to live the lifestyle she desires under a relatively all-encompassing system of government control. A young woman living on her own in Tehran, business owner, crusader against the chador (the clothing worn by Muslim women that covers everything but their faces), and paraglider pilot are just a few of this remarkably strong woman's defining characteristics.

The next day, I met Mohammad Razeghi, the contact who'd secured my visa. He was headed to Turkey for an APPI training course and said Soheil would take good care of me. After a long conversation and a delicious meal, Mohammad escorted me to a hasty roadside hand-off to Soheil, where a photographer for the Iranian Paragliding Association's magazine snapped a photo of all of us. It was late, we were on a dark road with cars whizzing by, and, much to my surprise, my caretakers started screaming at each other in Farsi, as the photographer and I shared an awkward desire to be anywhere but there.

I learned later that Soheil was angry at our late arrival for the arranged meeting with him. He'd been waiting for hours and felt resentful about having to begin our five-hour drive to Esfahan. Soheil is a pilot's pilot, and could not believe that we'd jeopardised getting to launch the next day for a meal, and since he had planned for us to fly the Rokh, the crown jewel of big-air flying in Iran, early the next morning, we had to get on the road. Even more infuriating was the fact that Mohammad did not have my flying permit from the National Association to send with me, which I would be required to present to the police if I landed anywhere but in official landing areas. Not having the permit presented a problem for Soheil, as his liberty was directly tied to mine as my new guide.

We drove through the night, arriving in Esfahan at 1am. Every town we passed through was adorned with the faces of soldiers, celebrated for their ultimate service, who perished in the no-holds-barred Iran-Iraq war (1980-1988) that claimed more than 500,000 lives. This seemed to be not only an honouring of fallen soldiers, but also a constant reminder that all Iranian citizens may be called upon again to repel invaders at any cost necessary.

Soheil debated whether to stay with a local pilot or check into a hotel so my passport would be registered at a lodging, giving the officials the ability to track me. We took a chance and stayed with Mohammed Miralei, who epitomised Persian hospitality. Mohammed provided not only an amazing array of teas but also a lovely guest room, consisting of a large common sitting parlour with a kitchen, and showed me around the amazing city of Esfahan. Blankets were brought forth and unfurled over ornate Esfahan rugs to make our beds. We set our alarms for an early start, and I fell asleep to the rhythmic pattern of Soheil's snoring.

On the way to launch the next morning, we met Fateme Eftekhari, Mohamad Semnani, who holds numerous distance records at the Rokh, and four other eager pilots. The Rokh is one of the most famous places to fly in Iran and, in fact, the reason Iran popped onto my big-flight radar, after Oriol Fernandez and Mohamad Semnani put up numerous 200km flights on Xcontest.org. The Rokh is on the eastern side of the Central Zagros mountain chain. As the biggest-air site in Iran, a decent number of pilots fly 200km flights every year, and base can be at 6,500m. However, it sits near a military installation.

Rokh is also the site where the group of Slovakians and their Iranian host had inadvertently become entangled with the government in 2014, landing them in jail for more than three months. One of the pilots had set down inside the military installation, another turned out to be a nuclear scientist, and other members of the group were flying with large digital cameras as well as contraband. The incident became a debacle, and a huge weight for Soheil when we flew there, as the previous group's host had also served the same amount of time in prison.

Accompanying an American without a flying permit in hand, and only the second foreigner to fly the site since the Slovakian incarceration, Soheil was stressed. I was told not to bring the DSLR camera on this flight, to which I happily agreed, and to land in the designated landing zone. If I didn't, there was a strong chance I (and probably he) would be detained.

The weather looked ideal, and I thought it would be reasonable to go anywhere I liked, and more importantly, return, for a few hours, assuming there was no catastrophic failure. Competitions and all the flying I'd done over the last 15 years gave me confidence I could reach any landing zone, if necessary. And in Iran, I knew I had to.

We took off and, after a little struggle, climbed, but when the inversion popped, I climbed to 4,570m, adopting a conservative flying style. I wanted to be sure I returned to the exact spot where I had been told to land after our short 40km cross-country or, at the minimum, to land alongside my local guides.

After working for two years to get to Iran, flying the Rokh and climbing to the clouds with a gaggle of desert eagles, and very skilled and enthusiastic Iranian pilots, was wonderful. Soheil Barikani, Mohammed Miralei, Mohamad Semnani, and Iran's best female pilot, Fateme Eftekhari, among others, made for exceptional company. And as I hypoxically glided along, I marvelled at how fast the team charged downrange. These pilots rocked.

Some say nothing good happens easily; in this case, they were correct. I carefully flew after my friends, made sure to top-out every climb, and celebrated every glide in ecstasy. I had a GoPro on board, stabilised by a gimbal attached to my karabiner. GoPro had expressed interest in doing a piece on the trip, and I thought it would be an honour to present Iran and its amazing flying community to the world. As I went on glide, I did check-ins with the camera, full of jubilation, turned it around to perform follow-cam with my new friends, or just filmed the cloud streets that we moved under.

After an hour of flying, we turned around, due to a tricky-looking transition and changing atmospheric conditions. While thermalling on the way back, I heard an odd metallic noise and watched in horror as my GoPro contraption spiralled down away from me, plummeting 15,000ft towards very remote mountainous terrain. I stared, petrified, after it. A million thoughts flooded my oxygen and sleep-deprived mind. What if it hits someone? Or kills livestock? What if the authorities find it, and I'm arrested for espionage? Would I be put in jail for using a GoPro, while making a GoPro video? It took a while to shake the feeling. Luckily, I was deep over uninhabited terrain at 5,000m when it fell. I never heard about the camera again, but occasionally wondered if an authority would show up with hard questions over the next few days.

The sky began to turn nasty as the clouds grew and blocked various corridors around us. We flew back toward launch and landed directly below, about an hour before the entire sky overdeveloped and a gust front ripped through the landing zone. We shared high fives and tales of eagles screaming past us in strong climbs. The only difference from a normal day at my local big-air site was the absence of a cooler in a truck in the LZ.

Packed up, we headed into Esfahan to eat lunch and admire the sites. While walking through a maze of covered-market stalls touting their wares, we spotted both locals and a steady trickle of tourists, who were cautiously returning to Iran after President Hassan Rouhani put in a significant effort to reconnect the country with the outside world.

We continued to wander through the souk, eventually popping out onto a breathtaking plaza, which the group of pilots proudly identified as a Unesco World Heritage site and one of the largest plazas in the world – Imam Square. Local clowns put on shows for Iranians and their children who laughed and ran throughout the square as their parents conversed. Persians use any opportunity to collect and enjoy the company of others, even though they also, like Americans, are obsessed with their cell phones.

As we were travelling, Soheil was supposed to report to Mohammad, who was supposed to report to the Ministry of Sport, who was supposed to report to the 'government' the details of where I was, what I was doing, and where I was staying, every few hours. This became a very laidback procedure, without any significant oversight. Most evenings Mohammad texted Soheil for updates, and Soheil commented: "If he were with us, he would know where you are." It was entertaining but a bit unsettling at the same time, like having parents embroiled in a battle.

We rallied back to Tehran to catch a domestic flight from Mehrabad Airport to Shiraz on a completely full flight. After checking in, I sat across from a mullah with a black headwrap, signifying that he was a direct descendant of the Prophet Muhammad. He was on his iPad, and I on my iPhone downloading the most current This American Life episode. A team of bulging weightlifters wandered around waiting for a flight. Soheil recruited his best friend, Sadr Barikani (no relation to Soheil), to accompany us. I could tell Soheil was elated to talk with a countryman in his native tongue, after spending 15 hours over two days driving with an English-only speaker.

We arrived in Shiraz, a proud, historic, bustling city filled with both high-end hotels and sites of antiquity. Shiraz hosts throngs of tourists poised to explore two epic and important Persian sites – the Tomb of Darius the Great and Persepolis.

Because I mentioned I lived in Salt Lake City, Utah, my guides took me out early to the Maharlo Salt Flats. We arrived to a full-on American West experience, replete with burning two-stroke oil wafting through the air as dirt bikes, paramotors, trikes, and tents popped up all around us. I'm not sure how you say "redneck" in Farsi, but after many years living in the Rocky Mountain West, I felt right at home.

A father-and-son tandem trike outfit, the Asadi family, pulled up in a new Toyota Hilux loaded with a beautiful trike and new paramotor, wearing the huge smiles of a team that is about to have a ball at work. We helped them unload and, as we were just about finished, a father of one of the pilots invited us for a delicious breakfast of porridge and homemade bread. Through gestures he made me feel completely at home and welcome.

Because an official from the local airport was on the scene, everyone decided it would be better if Soheil flew and I took photos from the tandem trike, piloted by the young Asadi. This was the only location where I got an uptight feeling. It was great for me to be on the front of a trike with cameras in hand piloted by a phenomenal pilot. We took a magnificent tour of epic algae formations and colours, stirring thousands of flamingos that call it home, and returned to the camp so the duo could continue working, flying tandems for cash.

The next day we returned to Tehran, where we planned to fly Damavand with the legendary Paragliding World Cup pilot Alireza Esna Ashari. Alireza bailed out of a successful family business to build an A-frame at the base of one of the most consistent and epic flying sites in Iran, just one hour from Tehran. His relocation was just like 95 percent of my friends in the US who headed west to make their own way in the mountains, and his carefree attitude immediately set me at ease. Under Alireza's care I had two of the best flights of my trip – one a 50km cross-country in front of a 5,600m volcano, and the other, a lovely glass-off session with 25 other pilots. In between, we were treated to one of the finest meals I have ever eaten, full of berry, nut, saffron and lamb flavours.

The Iranian flying community and pilots are some of the most welcoming, skilled, passionate, and driven in the world. Being part of a global community is the greatest weapon we have for breaking down illogical stereotypes. During these troubling times, it makes me a little more comfortable knowing that political demagogues will come and go, but like-minded people on both sides of the fence will remain the same.

Nick Greece is a multiple US paragliding champion, and a former editor of USHPA's national magazine. He has served on the board of the Cloudbase Foundation. When not at home with his young family in Truckee, California, Nick continues to compete and coach other pilots.

This is not a drill

Jorge Atramiz

It was another beautiful morning in Hawaii. I woke to a crisp blue sky and a gentle and cold northerly flow that predicted a perfect flying day. While sipping my morning tea, a digital sound broke the peace of my Saturday morning, but it was too early to be connected. I ignored it and continued to enjoy my herbal drink by the kitchen window while looking out to the Koolau Range.

A minute passed, then gradually the sounds of the early birds were completely overtaken by a noisy chaos: people running desperately in the street, my neighbours yelling on the phone, ambulance and police sirens all over. I finally picked up my phone and saw a bright message in full capital letters on the screen: "BALLISTIC MISSILE THREAT INBOUND TO HAWAII. SEEK IMMEDIATE SHELTER. THIS IS NOT A DRILL."

Before I had the chance to slap myself on the face to wake up from this bad dream, the phone rang again. It was my better half.

"Man, we had to cancel the trail running race! You got the alert?" Yes I did. "We're running to the basement of a building nearby now! Look for a good shelter. I hope to talk to you soon."

In the end, I wasn't dreaming.

I looked at the alert time 8.10 am. It was now 8.14 am. I might have eight more minutes to look for a safe place before the missile impacted us.

I ran out into the street looking for a concrete shelter, but we don't have that kind of thing in Hawaii. Instead, I witnessed a surreal scene, a man desperately trying to open a manhole cover to access, with his little kid, the sewer system.

I got back home and checked the time again, 8.18 am. We should have four minutes left or so. Not much to do. I decided to check the wind readings and pretend that nothing was happening. A beautiful graphic showed perfect conditions filling into the north face of the island and, if I was right, there was one guy who wouldn't miss an instant of this flying opportunity. I made a second call.

"Hello Alex, where are you brother?"

"Dude, I'm at the bottom of Dillingham trail about to hike, it's perfect!"

"I know, but did you get the alert message?"

"No, what alert m.... Hold it... yes I can see an alert here... WT..."

"No worries man, it's already kinda late, start the hike and if the missile decides to hit somewhere else I'll catch up with you shortly."

We laughed nervously and said goodbye.

It was 8.22am, and the chaos continued. I kept looking through my window, and at times I forgot about our possible future and switched my focus to the perfect conditions out there.

At 8.48 am we received a new message: "There is no missile threat danger to the State of Hawaii. Repeat. False Alarm." I loaded my car and immediately drove to the North Shore. A good part of the Hawaiian Armada was already charging, soaring along the face of the Waianae Range, the eroded remains of an ancient shield volcano that comprises the western half of the Hawaiian Island of Oahu, while a massive swell hit the shore.

Once in the air, the movie memories and the shaky feeling from the early morning were replaced by the salty air from the Pacific.

Jorge Atramiz is a surfer, paraglider pilot, filmmaker, photographer and writer. A pilot in Sean White's 2004 film Never Ending Thermal, Jorge's work appears regularly in Cross Country magazine. He lives on Oahu.

Entering the kingdom

Ed Ewing

500km from launch, Nevil flew over the grass-roofed huts of a small village called Habojo. A red and white marquee was set out for a wedding.

"I let out a whoop of joy as I flew over, enjoying the amazement in the upturned faces of the wedding guests," he remembers.

Nevil had crossed the border from South Africa into Lesotho, a small kingdom of barely two million people. He landed smoothly, with normal forward speed, 10 minutes before sunset, and let out a shout "that echoed into the mountains".

He'd done it: 502.6 km. Now all he had to do was get home.

Ed Ewing on Nevil Hulett's 2008 world record

The Monarca expedition

Ben Jordan

A butterfly blows past my window. It seems no more than a tiny moment of beauty, and no part of me thinks: "There goes my teacher". Where is it going anyway? Is it flying around aimlessly, or is it on a cross-country mission so great that it would make even the most ambitious of pilots green with envy?

It's 1 November and Mexicans are celebrating the Day of the Dead. From the sky I see families gathered, eating, lighting fireworks. I figure as long as I fly high, I'm safe. But as I near the Nevado de Toluca, a 4,680m volcano 60km east of Valle de Bravo in Mexico, a band of overdeveloping cloud seals my fate, forcing me to land in a shady meadow, about 3,000m ASL. Strange; rather than the usual mob of kids, I'm swarmed by a sea of butterflies.

I pack quickly and follow them into the nearby forest. The further I walk into the trees, the denser they become, until the sound of rustling leaves is drowned out by the beating of millions of tiny orange and black wings. I stand like a kindergartener on their first day of school. I look around and feel that I'm surrounded by teachers; the butterflies that will change my life forever.

The Day of the Dead is a holiday when Mexicans honour the lives of their ancestors. In the Sierra Madre mountains, it's also a time to celebrate the return of the Monarch butterflies. Over the next few weeks, millions more complete their long, arduous journey from Canada. Beginning from a band of lakes thousands of kilometres wide, they flock to one of the few, small mountain tops in this region of Mexico where they will land on the exact same trees where their ancestors overwintered the previous year.

How can a life form with what seems like the piloting skills of a post-it note find its way across North America to a destination no larger than a school playground – which neither it, nor its parents, nor its grandparents have ever seen before? It's a mystery that baffles scientists to this very day. What do these tiny pilots understand that we cannot? What does their journey entail, and what wisdom have they found along the way? There's only one way to find out.

Borderlands

The tall, thick fence stretches across Southern Arizona like an infinite series of rusted metal spikes from medieval times. I reach out to touch it and, almost instantly, a white SUV appears over the horizon, kicking up the desert dust, speeding towards me. It's the US Border Patrol. They exit their vehicle, hands on guns, and ask me what the hell I'm doing here.

I struggle to find the words. Though I'd written a sea of sponsorship proposals, this was the first time I had to say it out loud, and my elevator pitch needed work.

"I'm a paraglider pilot. I'm going to fly all the way across the United States!" I say quickly. "All the way to the Canadian border."

"You can do that with one of those things?" The guard asks. The scope of this expedition hits me like a tsunami.

"Yes", I respond hesitatingly. "In theory," I add.

"Well, good luck," he offers, before continuing his patrol of the infamous fence line.

Leaving the fence is harder than I could have imagined. Taking this first step means committing to a journey that I fear I may be physically unable to complete – while simultaneously I know that, once begun, I can't allow myself to fail. I step away from the fence.

The Arizona desert

WSW at 35km/h, WNW 40, NW 36. This is the wind forecast for the next few weeks. As if the razor-sharp cactus and sagebrush landing options aren't enough, the intimidation I feel at the thought of sketchy, blown-out thermals is a reality that I'll just have to suck up.

This morning I'm relieved by the relatively light wind and, after a restless grounded week, I know that if I don't make distance today, I'll be sitting out at least three more before being granted another chance. I close my eyes and count to three. With a subtle tug of my A-lines, my factory-folded Alpina 3 pops up, a strong cycle lifting my body before I have a chance to turn around. War drums in my head beat with conviction. There will be no metres lost, no thermal spared. I'm one with nature, and the only difference between myself and the monarch butterflies is the combination of peanut butter and Nutella that has somehow become one with my facial hair.

Gaining only 0.1m/s on average, I turn patiently, each centimetre gained lessening the anxiety brought on by the cactus fields below. An hour passes. I'm only 200m over launch, too low to go anywhere yet just high enough to realise that every creek bed within 10km is bone dry.

I close my eyes, trying to feel the air. The smell of peanuts is overwhelming, and BOOM! My climb accelerates to a heart pounding 10m/s almost instantly. Quickly reaching 3,000m ASL, I plan my first move as the climb continues to a whopping 5,200m, higher than I've ever been in my life. Cactus or crocodiles, drought or drenched, this is an entirely new kind of flying and any move is now a good move. I'm a freaking astronaut!

I skip along northbound as my luck continues. High above the desert floor, I can see mines, aqueducts and distant mountain ranges, and the sprawling city of Tucson is no larger than my boot. With days like this, I'll get to Canada in a week! Mildly hypoxic, I land somewhere outside of the ruins of Winkelman, a small mining town that was washed away by a 1993 flash flood. The lowest point (600m ASL) on my 2,800km route, the desert heat sinks into the ghost town as if it were the bottom of a drain.

My improvised launch, a 300m ridgetop above the old copper refinery, is a painstakingly cleared dirt-patch amidst a cactus salad and hot rocks.

I carry 10 extra litres of water up the hill now, 13 in total, to avoid dehydration, spend the night and then launch from my precarious perch day after day.

Four stable days have passed, and I can't pretend to understand the conditions. It's sunny, the wind is reasonable, but it takes a total of seven days for me to realise that I've never actually flown in the desert. Too proud to ask the local Facebook group, my afternoons are spent playing my travel banjo in the shade of an old mineshaft. My sad songs exude the regret of a gold digger that showed up about 100 years too late.

It's 15 May. Though I've already used up 25% of my expedition season, I've covered not even 10% of my route. Unless something changes, I'm not going to complete this journey. I search for wisdom amidst the 200-year-old cactus, the dry river beds and tumbleweeds blowing between them, and realise that the only thing that will ever change out here, is me.

This first step is the hardest. Not because the 60km of flat pavement will become painful blisters nor because of the diminishing heckles from Arizona-licensed pickups. It's hard because on some level, this feels like giving in. I don't want to walk, that's not what I do. More bruised than my feet is my ego. Instead of proving itself in these states of miraculously-long XC flights, today it's trying to swallow the reality that I'm way out of my league and that the only miracle that I might find on this expedition is the finish line.

After three long days I arrive east of Phoenix. Despite their imposing spires and name, the Superstition Mountains instil a familiar confidence. Glider, check, harness, check, cameras hanging from everywhere, check, check, and I'm airborne. Petty grievances and fragile ego give way to giant red rocks and dagger-like grey spires. They shape-shift, moving through the parallax below, reminding me of my great purpose. Desert lakes and cityscapes become my focus as the rough air carries me to elevations that play games with my depth perception. Peering down just long enough to witness a stealthy jumbo jet coming in to land, I realise that I probably shouldn't be here, jump on bar, and push in to the northern unknown.

Never have I felt so great while simultaneously recognising my minuscule existence. Though void of trees, the rough, cactus-laden desert screams "Fly or Die!" So fly I do, forgetting what I think I know, absorbing what lessons the desert has to offer. With some hesitation, I skip low over the Apache Lake canyon and soar my way to the top of Brown's Peak (2,334m), the highest mountain on my journey thus far. The sweet aromas of progress blow in from the south, pushing me along. The terrain, though foreign to me, produces climbs fair enough to allow my game of desert leapfrog to continue. I hop north and cloudbase rises, as does the valley floor. Below me is a pencil-thin topographical line where the cactus gives way to trees and streams rich with water. As if I'd flown into some parallel universe, the air, once hot and dry, is now filled with the crisp scent of pine, and before me stands the great Mogollon Rim. This 300km escarpment cuts across the north of Arizona, marking the southern edge of the Colorado Plateau.

Patience pays off and my luck continues, making quick work of northern Arizona in the coming week. From the great Rim to Sedona to the high city of Flagstaff and an epic flight north, along the eastern edge of the Grand Canyon. Though I'm legally required to walk across national parks and monuments, Utah, after all this time, is just a stone's throw away.

The mountains of Utah

The sun rises, and from the 3,400m summit of Monroe Peak, Utah, I exit my tent and stretch my arms out with confidence and pride. After two months of negotiating short ranges, flats and odd bumps, I'm standing at the south end of a series of expansive, tall mountain ranges, and the birthplace of some of the longest flights in the US. Unlike my improvised launches in Arizona, there are actually other pilots on launch, and a healthy sense of competition fills the air. With the first cycles, some locals launch, making it clear that today will be windy but from the south: perfect.

I wait half an hour for base to rise, but on my first transition, just one other pilot dares join this one-way journey north. Both on EN-C wings, we leapfrog forward in the heavy drift of the 25km/h southerly. Sometimes I find the climb, other times it's his turn. Now 40km north, the features become much lower but, with plenty of height, I lead the charge with a new found sense of confidence.

Another five kilometres pass and I glance back to see my wingman coring a steady climb about 2km behind me. I turn back quickly, only to realise that the 30km/h southerly gusts have other plans for me. I revert back north and fly like a banshee but the low, wind-swept ridges suck me in like a butterfly in a wind tunnel. My groundspeed clocking minus 10km/h, I touch down in a canyon east of the town of Salinas, covering about 50km in all.

I pack up, find water and walk west to exit the canyon that same evening, regrettably checking XContest.org to see if my fellow pilot made it much further. The gentleman had flown a whopping 160km and not landed for another three hours! While until now, I had always justified my shorter flights by telling myself that I'd flown the maximum potential of a given day, objectively witnessing another pilot clobber my distance sends my psyche into a tailspin. Do I walk back 50km and try to do better, or do I walk to the next launchable terrain, 50km north and affirm my position as a lesser pilot? I toss and turn all night, weighing the pros and cons of each, ultimately realising that no matter which I choose, I lose. In one case, I can't hold my own with the Utah pilots. In the other, I do something outrageous out of a desperate need to prove myself to them. In shame, and only marginally decided, I roll up my tent and shuffle north.

Three days have gone by. Two days of highway blisters, being honked at randomly and trying to convince myself of my half-hearted choice, and another day bushwhacking 1,300m up the west face of a mountain, 15km south of Utah's legendary Wasatch range. Nursing my feet and licking my emotional wounds atop, my pride can't stand to take another step.

A fresh sun brings strong thermals and, while the overnight wind hasn't died down, I launch into the void with the humility of a junior attending his first day of high school. Whack, I lose 40% of my left wing. Please be kind. Swoosh, there goes the right. From the scene of my impromptu SIV, I fly out, realising that I'd be content with a sledder at this point. My confidence shot and ego deflated, I'm no longer full of the kind of hot air that's been carrying me north, and I don't know what to do.

Beep-beep, goes my vario, now far from the hill and 1,000m above its foothills. Beep-beep, I turn. Beep-beep, this continues for another 1,000m. I can visualise my momentous glide to the Wasatch. Further north, I become a bystander as the flight begins to direct itself. Not the way I had imagined – scratching the towering ranges and specking out above them. Instead, the wind, wing and thermals dance in a conservative manner, keeping largely over the smaller foothills and a respectful distance from the turbulence-inducing terrain.

At 90km north, my zen flight ends in the unexpected thermal-block brought on by Provo lake breeze. Undeterred, I climb back up the Wasatch and make the most of each day, day after day, 21 days in a row. While many five-hour flights have only 50km to show for them, the daily routine of making coffee, flying to the best of my ability and finding a new place to launch before pitching tent is the meditation I've long searched for. I learn here in Utah that this expedition isn't about pushing the limits of a sport and being the Best, but rather about finding the edges of myself, ultimately discovering my Best.

The Idaho express

Wind rips fiercely across the face of Number Hill. Aptly named by the Arco locals for all of the numbers painted on its face, these digits signify the graduating year of each high school class since the early 1920s. Above the potato fields below, I gain the decorated 400m ridgeline with a lighter than average pack. With rather low expectations of the day to come, I imagine bombing out and have chosen not to restock my food in the town below. But if you've read this far, you know by now that I'm almost always wrong.

Three-two-one, and I'm off on an express train to the rapidly growing cloudbase. Climbing so fast that I can't even swallow my own saliva, I'm now 500m up after just 30 seconds of flight. Damn Idaho, today is full of potential for both distance, and the other reality that I'm trying hard to neglect: massive overdevelopment.

But unstable days like this are like finding a needle in a haystack. Having suffered through three months of stable conditions across Arizona and Utah, if I sit this out, I'll surely die of regret. North I go, spinning around the summits of the famous flying site of King Mountain and his friends in the great Lost River Range. Unstoppable, I relish in delight, witnessing small planes and cars passing far below my feet, oblivious to the increasing wind or clouds closing in all around me.

CRACK goes the first roll of thunder. Following the flash by only four seconds, I do the math and realise I am just 1km from becoming a flying shish kebab. Still 3,000m above the valley floor, the wind and lift have both increased significantly and, shy of stalling my wing, I have no way to get down within the next 30 minutes.

CRACK goes a second charge, this time right in front of me. Without thought, I turn southeast, using the tailwind to run as far as I can. Water pours down in every direction and the spot of blue above me is closing in quick. Darting along at 70km/h, I'm sinking fast and taking collapses in the rotor that trails behind the peaks that I skirt around. Now, somewhere deep in the Lemhi Range, I turn back into the wind and, moments later, touch down, not in the valley, but rather atop a massive ridge that I could not commit to flying over, because I could not see beyond. This 3,233m mountain, I would later learn, is named Junction Peak.

Flashes of lightning burst outside the walls of my ultralight tent. A torrential downpour washes away any hopes of flying on the next day. Suddenly, my choice to fly lighter and not load up on food in Arco turns my stomach with regret. Regret transforms into hunger as I reach into my food bag to find only one day's ration remaining. Damn.

Rain continues through the morning and early afternoon. Lying in my tent, trying not to burn calories, I play banjo as insanity consumes me. Alpine mice scurry around my shelter, keen on the smell of my dwindling peanut butter ration. Guarded, it doesn't leave my right pocket save for mealtime, and my Ramen noodles are safely stashed in the left.

I fall in and out of sleep, my stomach grumbling with hunger, and hope for anything but rain tomorrow.

Stuffy air overwhelms me mid-slumber. A feeling that I haven't known in days and one that can only be caused by direct sunlight warming the inside of my tent. The sun! Desperate to get my head straight, I build a fire, boil snow, pound a coffee and consume my final pack of noodles. It's 9am and cumulus clouds take shape like popcorn all around me. It's not a good sign, but I'll try to remain positive.

Though my return to safety involves crossing a giant, remote mountain range, the next civilised valley is only 15km away. Just one climb should do. Cu's grow all around me. Spots of blue now scarce, I clip in with a sense that this is all or nothing. Do or die; the Rambo within me has been summoned, and my Hollywood sequel now hangs in the balance of my unlikely success.

I wait here for the south face's cycles to begin, but a gust emerges from the north, blowing my glider downhill, towards me. With only a cliff and canyon to the north, this south face, my only out, is beginning to feel more like an emergency exit that's about to slam shut. "PLEASE!!!" I scream to any of the mountains and towering clouds that can hear me; a tiny, insignificant speck of life, clipped into a wad of nylon in the middle of nowhere. Again, from the north. Again and again I reset my glider, resolving that my only path is to run with the tailwind and pray.

Like a Hail Mary pass in the final seconds of a college football game, I charge like the running back, head first, arms out, straight down the rocky slope. One yard, two yards up, my legs still spinning circles like a cartoon running off a cliff unknowingly. At 60km/h, my mostly inflated glider takes flight, and only then do I gain context of where I am. Tree-lined canyon walls surround me with only white water rushing some 500m below. I'm sinking fast while trying to wrap around the east end of the ridge, praying for the lee-side climb that's nowhere to be found.

At 250m above the river, I fly forcefully into the awkward ridge lift produced on the pointed spires half-way up the north side. From dagger to dagger I soar figure eights, saying thank you for each metre they offer until reaching the top, where, like a rocket of gratitude, the south-most spire sends me skyward like the last kernel to join the infinite bucket of popcorn above.

At 700m over my hazardous launch, I look down at the vast wilderness below. Though I had hoped to fly north, survival instincts force me eastward, dashing through turbulent airways, as fast as I can from the brewing storm. With an epic 30km tailwind glide, I reach the town of Lemhi, and while only just soaring the bump above town, I feel the profound emotion of a dream come true. Though just a foothill, I have now come upon North America's Continental Divide; the rocky, red carpet to Canada.

From the front hills I bench up to the back, then finally over the main spine of the Great Dividing Range. Momentous peak after peak, I'm gaining the kind of ground I'd longed for since day one. The smell of gratitude inoculates the sweet, thin air as I drift from Idaho into Montana and back. I soar over old towns and bundle up, clapping my frozen hands on transitions to help restore blood flow. Along the divide I go, pushing stubbornly into the increasing north wind, making up for all the hardship I have faced over months of challenging terrain and conditions. Still frozen and tired from six incredible hours in the elements, I touch down in North Fork, Idaho only to be greeted by a landowner and his son, each toting the largest assault rifles my tender Canadian eyes have ever seen.

"What the hell are you doing here?" the younger one asks. "Thank you, wow, amazing, thank you!!!" I cry out, my elevator pitch now just a ranting deluge of gratitude, stoke and love. As if I'd said the magic words that I had been missing all along, the pair lowered their guns and gave in to my barrage of laughter and enthusiasm as well.

Made in Montana

More than 2,000km along, and with so much of this great country in my rear view, the cactus, the Grand Canyon, the Great Salt Lake, and even the unassumingly badass state of Idaho. A journey that once seemed too great to tackle is three-quarters complete and with only the cherry on top left to consume, or so I thought.

Familiar to me, Montana's Rockies remind me of those I've cut my teeth on back home. From here on out, it's no longer a question of how to fly, but only a matter of when. But the sky is becoming dark, not with cloud but instead, a blanket of smoke. Though 3,000km away, California's wildfire exhaust has made its way northeast, shading the sun, causing mind-numbing waits of five days or more.

Stubbornly refusing to walk any of this Rocky Mountain landscape, I sit for days now, only to pull off a 20-30km flight north then climb back up to my next camp. Food rations dwindling, my diet shifts to blueberries, which grow abundantly here. Despite being antioxidised as all hell, I'm also experiencing mild hallucinations. The berries, the smoke, the banjo, the loneliness, this is my life, though somehow, I can live with that.

Day 150. I awake from a berry-induced coma, exit my tent and feel that old, nagging northwest across my face. At least it's clear, I think to myself, having lowered my bar for conditions to pretty much any day I can breathe. I clip effortlessly into my harness and wing, my uniform now, launch amidst the sharp rocks, break a stabilo line, assess the risk, and plug on to the north.

Like I am watching myself from above; this man and his psyche have become more devoted to this one goal than I've ever been able to commit to anything in my life. For he has surrendered his heart and soul so completely to the dream, that he has relinquished any last shred of personal identity and now he, himself, has become the dream.

2,815km along, I see now that the dream is not a world record but a record of lessons learned along the way. While Arizona teaches patience and one's place in the world, Utah preaches humility, reminding us that one's greatness can only be measured against itself. Idaho, on the other hand, reminds me not to judge books by their covers, and illuminates that gratitude unlocks the solution to any problem unsolved.

And it is right here and now that Montana unveils her wisdom. A rugged, no-bullshit landscape built up by seismic activity, chiselled away by mineral and gas exploration yet still thriving with an abundance of nature and beauty that leaves the most cynical in awe. Montana teaches surrender; the art of allowing Mother Nature to govern our experience as she always has, and always will.

Low, just 50m above a gravel pit and still 20km from Canada, I prepare to land, overwhelmed by gratitude for this final flight and good things to come. Beep, beep, I give it a whirl. The warm breeze continues and, despite drifting away from my safe landing area, I lean to my left and turn circles out of sheer habit. I gain 50m, doubling my clearance above ground.

My eyes closed, I ascend another 400m and at 1,000m, it clicks. This final climb was born in a moment of patience, unconditional gratitude and surrender to the world as it is, free of judgement of the unfavourable conditions or my worn-out self. It serves as a reminder that miracles aren't just arriving at the finish line but rather the infinite number of tiny circumstances, good or bad, that got us here.

Now just 1km away from the razor-thin line marking Canada's southern border, the true success of this journey will be measured by those who imagine a tiny butterfly attempting the same feat. With ninja-like skill, these vulnerable warriors defy the limits of the known universe and remind us that, on a global scale, we humans are just as small, and better yet, just as capable.

From setting up a paragliding school in Malawi to crossing most of North America's Continental Divide and paramotoring 10,000km across Canada, Ben Jordan has had many adventures in the air. He lives in Nelson, Canada, with his wife and daughter, and continues to fly.

Karakoram express

Damien Lacaze

July 24th 2018, midday, 6,500m. It's been 30 hours since we were confined to our tent by bad weather, waiting patiently on the high plateau that stretches below the summit of Spantik (7,027m), which we tried to climb the day before. Ever since we set up camp, in a hurry and under the storm, we haven't moved, numbed by the early symptoms of AMS (Acute Mountain Sickness).

We know we have to descend fast, especially Antoine, who is doing worse than I am. He can barely get up and he has slept 25 of the last 30 hours. I lie on my glider, listening to the snow lashing the tent, and I let my mind rave. Time doesn't matter anymore, and I go over the dream that started 20 days before.

Antoine and I travelled to Pakistan to combine bivouac flying and mountaineering in an ambitious project: start from Skardu in the Karakoram to fly across the massif to the west by vol-bivouac, and then go back towards the northeast and stop off in Karimabad after 1,000km of wandering.

Then we would try to climb a 7,000m mountain, Spantik, using an ultra-fast technique of approaching and descending with our gliders. Finally, we would close the loop to Skardu. It would be 1,500km of bivvy flying going through the Baltoro Glacier and its famous 8,000m summits.

For us, bivouac flying is paragliding in its most pure and committing form. Add huge mountains like those in Pakistan (the Karakoram, Hindu Kush, and Himalaya massifs), the almost non-existent rescue services in case of an accident, and you get the perfect cocktail to put to the test your mind, your endurance, and your will to get out of your comfort zone.

Skardu, 7 July. The start of the trip was hard. We're carrying 15 days' worth of food and six litres of water, and our bags weigh a huge 37kg. It took us two days to get to our first take-off, at 4,100m.

What followed could be almost summarised in one phrase and some adjectives. That's how easy and perfect it was: stunning flights and bivouacs, huge mountains, crazy encounters, and incredible cloudbase! Should I tell you about it? No? Come on, I'm gonna tell you everything! From the first day, the skies lined up for us. We hadn't acclimatised well enough yet, so we were a bit frightened when we saw clouds forming above 6,000m. The first thermal catapulted us to 6,200m, breathless. It was impossible to speak normally, and we were forced to breathe between each word. But we were so happy to have such a great day that we weren't going to waste it.

We headed straight to the west on a raging airmass filled with perfect cumuli. In the distance, a huge white mass emerged over the clouds: Nanga Parbat (8,126m). It was still 80km away, but it was already drawing us to it. It served as our compass and it overwhelmed us. We kept heading west. Our lighthouse, the Nanga, kept getting bigger, overwhelming us. I never felt anything like it before. It was still 40km away, but it's so isolated from the other high mountains that it's the only thing you can see. We felt pathetic, foolish with our pieces of fabric.

This first flight knocked down many of my prejudices. Yes, we can fly far on a glider way over the top of the weight range. Yes, we can climb at 10m/s and not be too scared. Yes, we can go up to 6,200m the first day and not die (but you'll get a headache). Yes, we can scrape the foothills of a monster like Nanga Parbat after flying 100km, ridge soar over its seracs and say hi to the multicoloured tents at base camp 2,000m below, and finally, keep flying 50km, cross the immense Indus Valley and land on a paradisiac pass at 4,300m with water, cows, and a view of Nanga Parbat at sunset that makes you want to die there.

I'll add something on behalf of Antoine: Yes, you can tear your ankle's ligament on the first landing and add some excitement to the rest of the adventure! Because, undoubtedly, it was inconceivable for him to quit this adventure that started so well. "We just won't walk," that's what he said. Luckily, we had already planned not to walk so much!

Things went well from there on. Days followed on. Cloudbase and thermals were still amazing, but at that point we weren't fainting anymore whenever we saw a 6 or a 7 in front of the altitude, or when the vario showed two-digit climb rates.

Our procession towards the west would end close to Booni, 40km before the Afghan border, after crossing wild massifs, each different from the last. Naked mountains, others covered with bus-sized granite blocks, where it was impossible to take off. Or others that looked more alpine: green, with amazing high lakes, life at the bottom of the valleys, bucolic streams, or rough torrents. And finally, real Himalayan mountains: high, cold, dry, where no one has ever even set foot.

Bivouacs followed on wonderfully and a gentle routine settled over the days. Each afternoon at about 4.30pm we started looking for a ridge or a col with the right orientation to land and take off the next day. We woke up with the first light of the day, we charged our instruments with our solar panels, we collected some water, and waited for thermals.

Sometimes, shepherds would come and keep us company, take our photo, and watch us launch, amazed. Sometimes, a glacier that was a bit more deceitful attempted to destroy our nice routine by surprising us with katabatic winds. We were able to enjoy some real thrashing and backward flying in undesirable conditions. Here, some of the glaciers have their own climate, and I must say that they're not suitable for free flying.

7,961m

The days kept getting better. Our altimeters were shouting figures close to 7,300m up until 16 July. That day, we knew the first part of the adventure was coming to an end, and we had around 250km to go to Karimabad.

When we launched at 10am, we saw that the day was extraordinary. Thermals were stronger than ever, cloudbase was about 6,600m in the morning. Our varios wouldn't stop beeping, first at 11m/s before ending at the wisps of a cloud above 7,500m. Later, at the end of a glide, a monster caught us. This thermal was incredibly wide. When we found the core, the cry of our varios mixed with our voices that were screaming in unison to whoever could hear us, saying that we were having one of the most amazing times of our lives, in the middle of the Karakoram, on a wonderful 13m/s elevator that didn't seem to want to stop. If it had told us it was taking us to the moon, we wouldn't refuse.

I wasn't exaggerating when I said the moon. Once we left this missile, 50m under the wispies, we didn't know it yet but we had become the second and third people on Earth to fly the highest on a paraglider (Antoine was the first when he flew over Broad Peak at 8,157m in 2016). That night, when we were going over that unreal 170km flight, we couldn't resist looking at the flight log in our instruments. The verdict left us speechless for a few seconds: GPS altitude: 7,961m. We exploded with joy that night, during our bivouac, lost on a glacier at 6,100m. We should have taken another turn!

Climbing Spantik

We rested for a few days in Karimabad. We left for Spantik (7,024m) on the first window of good weather. We were in ultralight flying mode. We took our cross-country gliders, string harnesses without reserves, mountaineering equipment, and three days' worth of food.

Believe me, those 40km to get to the plateau where we planned to land put us in a cold sweat. But it was amazing to be there, at 6,200m facing Spantik, the Golden Peak, after two hours in the air, when it usually takes a two-week expedition to get here. After turning in cloud to climb the extra 100m we needed, we crashed into the soft snow of the plateau at 6,300m. After a few euphoric moments, we got going. All we had left to do was to find a place to camp, spend the night, and climb early in the morning the 700m that separated us from the summit, where we hoped to launch.

We camped at 6,500m. When we woke up, at 3am, the weather had changed: it was snowing, the wind was blowing strong... shit! We left for the summit anyway, and we were moving at a pace I never would've thought possible, even at this altitude. We barely went faster than 100m per hour. The weather kept getting worse, as well as our health. The ascent wasn't that technical, but it was hard due to the deep and crusted snow. Antoine was doing particularly badly; he hadn't taken the relay in an hour to break trail.

When we were at 6,900m, we stopped. It was 7am. This time the storm hit and at 100m from the summit we had no choice but to turn around. We made it back to the plateau in a deplorable state, we set up camp as fast as we could and collapsed. We waited for 30 hours in the fog, snow, and wind.

Antoine kept getting worse; he would sleep all the time. We needed to fly. We knew we couldn't leave by foot through the face we came in. It got dark again and we didn't have sleeping bags, but our gliders worked just fine.

At the end of the following morning, some gusts different from the usual brought me out of my thoughts. The wind had changed: and despite the snow and the fog, there was some hope for taking off. We preferred taking off in the fog to dying there.

We packed our gear and, after a few attempts, we dragged ourselves from our misery and flew deep inside the clouds. We got out 5km later thanks to our GPS, relieved to have escaped that nightmare. What followed was just a long glide of almost 40km and 4,000m difference in altitude that took us to the nearest town and spared us another week of walking through tortuous glaciers. Paragliding is an amazing tool that allows us to accomplish things that only our minds can limit.

We went back to Karimabad to rest.

Closing the loop

It was on 2 August that we tried to "close the loop". For the next flight, we needed a cloudbase of 6,500m to jump over the Spantik plateau, where we'd been the previous week, and continue to the southeast towards the Baltoro Glacier, K2, and Broad Peak.

I remember the excitement made my throat constrict with fear. My eyes looked for our traces, erased by the storm, and they would see a crevasse here and a serac there. Cloudbase allowed us to fly to the other face of Spantik, to follow the very long ridge of the normal route, and to fly over some mountaineers walking on deep snow. We were excited and relieved to leave Spantik, the hardest part of the flight.

What followed was even wilder. We flew down a glacier for 30km, jumped over a massif at 6,000m, turned to the left and voilà! We landed on a slope at 5,200m above the town of Askole, at the entrance of the Baltoro Glacier, after a 130km flight.

There we were! The grand finale of our expedition! Trying to fly high above the 8,000m peaks of Baltoro, flying over the Trango Towers, trying to do what takes 15 days by foot in just one flight. That had been our dream for a year!

The Baltoro Glacier is 60km long, and the last town, Askole, is eight days by foot from Broad Peak (8,047m) base camp. We couldn't land — first of all because Antoine couldn't walk, and also because flying over the Baltoro area is forbidden without a permit. The night went by; in the morning the thermals started right on time. There was no turning back. Let's go for the flight of my life!

The day was beautiful; there were cumulus clouds everywhere. We made good progress, we flew over the Biafo Glacier and we went straight to the point. I could clearly see the moraine and the beginning of the Baltoro. The summit of Masherbrum (7,821m) set the tone: it's high!

Flying to this glacier is logical, almost textbook. Beautiful south faces for 40km with relatively short glides between them. But these "beautiful" south faces are called Trango Towers, Paiju Peak, and also Muztagh Tower, among so many summits of over 6,000m and among so many names that resound in the minds of mountaineers as well as mine like inaccessible myths. Add a valley whose bottom is filled with ice and littered with bus-sized blocks as far as the eye can see, and you'll understand that the "aerologic" textbook case becomes a torture for the mind.

We were fully committed. With every glide we flew further away from "the exit". We needed to fly back the same way we came to stay on schedule. There we were, above the last relief before Broad Peak, over Concordia, this famous confluence of two mighty glaciers in the heart of the Karakoram surrounded by 8,000m mountains. We could see different base camps sprinkled on the foot of the mountains, tiny. Cloudbase was below 6,500m, not high enough to fly to Broad Peak and back. We chose, wisely, to turn around and try again the next day.

Broad Peak

We found a place to camp at 4,700m at the entrance of the glacier. The following day, conditions were different: a lot drier and stable. We were pushed by a marked south-westerly wind. We knew it would be harder to get out of the glacier because we would be flying against the wind. But once again we flew the same summits.

Even if I was less intimidated because I knew the route, this second flight over the Baltoro was mentally more demanding. I knew the difficulties, the commitment, that landing was forbidden, and I also knew that the flight back would be complicated. Bearing all that in mind, I forced myself to commit.

There we were again at Concordia. A wisp was forming over Broad Peak, at over 7,000m. It was decided, we're going! Crossing Concordia, with K2 (8,611m), the second highest mountain in the world, to the left, and Gasherbrum 4 (7,925m) to the right, was a great moment. We climbed the beautiful south ridge of Broad Peak on horrible thermals, broken by the southwest wind that was still strong.

The day was not exceptional and it was too windy. But patiently, we managed to climb to the wisps at 7,700m. The wind was blowing everything out aloft. It was 3.30pm, our deadline to turn around. The flight back was long, the slopes face to the southeast, and if we took too long, we wouldn't make it out of the glacier.

We fought for each thermal as we patiently waited for cycles; what mattered was not to land. We finally made it out of the glacier, gliding at

6:1 towards our campsite from the previous day. We thought it would be easy. But all of a sudden we found ourselves in a downslope breeze and we flew down the side of the mountain.

We didn't have much time to think because it was forbidden to land in the valley. We found a steep slope where we "crashed" at 3,500m. It was the last landable slope before countless cliffs and fallen rock until the bottom. Whew!

We enjoyed our last night among the stars that looked closer in this clean high-altitude air. The flight back to Skardu was just a formality, despite a 5,700m col we had to cross, because we only had one chance as we knew the weather would deteriorate the next day.

Pakistan offered exceptional conditions at the beginning of the trip. You can't have everything at once. It would have been too easy to fly to 8,000m over Broad Peak on the same trip. You have to deserve that flight. Some pilots have come for almost 10 years without even getting higher than 7,700m. We're happy that we thermalled the faces of this giant and achieved an incredible height after a pioneering vol-bivouac. We will have to come back to fly over the summit!

Damien Lacaze is a paragliding instructor, alpinist and rock climber. He has competed in the Red Bull X-Alps and won the Bornes to Fly race twice. Alongside other acheivements, Damien has crossed the Atlas Mountains by vol-bivouac.

Tumble in the Owens

Bruce Goldsmith

On the first day of the 1993 World Hang Gliding Championships in Owens Valley, I tumbled my glider in extreme turbulence over White Mountains Peak. I will now describe what happened, and then analyse why it happened and what I will do to avoid this ever happening to me again.

I climbed to 14,000ft (4,300m) on a spine that protrudes west from the peak of White Mountain. The lift was beginning to weaken so I set off on a glide, exiting the thermal at about 30mph (48km/h). I flew for approximately 200m with Peter Harvey and Drew Cooper immediately behind me. Suddenly the nose dropped and I was pointing vertically at the ground. I held the bar tightly to my chest to maintain my 30mph flying speed. I felt my legs drop back behind me and touch the keel, and at this moment the glider tucked and I fell into the sail. A fraction of a second after this, the left outer leading edge broke and the glider started to spin quickly.

The instant I saw the glider was broken I pulled my reserve, which was surprisingly easy, and it was very reassuring to see it open a couple of seconds later. I was 2,000ft (600m) above the spine that I had been flying over, and I quickly descended towards the jagged crags of rock. I was face down underneath my broken glider, pinned in this position by the bridle of my reserve. All my strength was not enough to get out of this dangerous position and I hit the ground face first covering my face with my arms. Very luckily, I hit a small patch of snow, and I was almost totally unhurt.

My reserve did not then collapse, but started to pull both me and my wrecked hang glider back up the mountainside. I unzipped myself from my harness and slipped out of it, which released my glider to fly away in the same 2,000fpm (10m/s) climb that I had been in five minutes earlier. The glider flew up the mountain 200ft before smashing into the rocks and getting caught on the top of the spine.

It took me a couple of hours to climb up and recover what was left of my equipment. My radio was smashed, and I could not communicate with the rescue services. A small plane flew up to me and saw I was okay, and at 7pm I started to walk down the mountain, having left a note for any rescue party telling them what I was doing.

I decided to get lower down the mountain before dark because it was very cold and I was having trouble breathing without my oxygen. I did use some of my oxygen at the time when climbing at high altitude. I walked down until 9pm, when it got dark. Then I slept, as it was too dangerous to walk in the dark. I was at 10,000ft (3,000m) and I slept in my flying suit and harness to keep me warm. I laid my reserve out on a nearby rock as a signal to any rescue party to show them my position.

At dawn I continued my descent, carefully rationing my isotonic drink. I reached the main road at 4,000ft (1,200m) in the valley after another five hours of walking, just as I finished my last mouthful of liquid. I reached the town of Bishop just in time to borrow a glider and go up the mountain to launch in the second task. I continued to fly the rest of the competition, but I was not flying on form and did not make the cut.

After the tumble, many people told me they thought I had been flying too slowly, and this is why I had tumbled. I am sure this is not the reason, because at the time of the incident I was on glide at 30mph at least. I know that I did hit a strong downdraught close to the thermal, and I am sure that anyone would have gone upside down in the same situation.

I believe my only possible mistake is what I did during the tumble. What I did was hold the central bar to my chest to maintain my 30mph airspeed. This allowed my legs to fall over behind my head and hit the keel, perhaps causing the glider to tuck. Instead of holding the bar to my chest, I should have pulled the bar to my knees. With all the weight of the pilot forward, he is going to stop the glider from tumbling.

Imagine if you could put the pilot right at the nose of the glider; the glider would never tumble, but would simply dive vertically down at very high speed. This is a position which is much easier to recover from than a tuck, and this must be the key to avoiding tumbles in similar situations.

I have certainly learnt a lot from this incident and I hope that passing my experiences on will help other pilots avoid such dangerous experiences.

Bruce Goldsmith enjoyed a competition career in hang gliding and paragliding that spanned over two decades. This incident saw him move more wholeheartedly into paragliding. Bruce went on to win the Paragliding World Championships in 2007. Cross Country's longest-serving columnist, Bruce continues to live and fly in France, where he heads up BGD.

MINI STORY

Harrold

Ed Ewing

Yesterday I flew 124km.
From Golden Ball in Wiltshire to a village called Harrold.
"You're in Bedfordshire!" the man shouted from his garden when I asked.

Ed on landing in unknown territory

The Naked Mountain

John Silvester

Tarashing, 28 October, 2005. The cold night is broken by the sun rising through the Kashmiri mountains. It wakes me, shining through the east-facing curtainless window of our ice-cold room. I turn over, still content to snuggle deeper under the mountain of quilts until the sun begins to melt the frozen condensation on the ceiling. The icy drips on my face shock away the sleep of the night.

Soon the cook arrives with an armful of kindling for the stove, and serves us morning tea. Just five kilometres away the summit of Nanga Parbat shines in the sunlight and begins to shed last night's snow.

Olivier and I have only been here three days. We've positioned ourselves on the southeast side of the massif to get the best chance of an early start to follow the sun around the mountain through the day. Already we've found a perfect take-off, pioneered a successful first glide across the first big glacier, and climbed up on to the immense Rupal face. It's a first, but crucial, step on the tour, but now we only have two days left to realise our dream: to fly up to the head of the Rupal valley to the 5,400m Mazeno pass, and cross through the gateway to the grand tour of Nanga Parbat.

From the first climb above take-off, it's obvious that there is a moderate northwest wind at altitude. It's putting the southeast face that we're flying on in the lee. It's going to make finding the crucial second climb difficult. Cloudbase is looking ugly too; the clouds are overdeveloping and depositing light snow into the already freezing air. When I finally reach base, I run out through the wispies to the edge of the lift high over the Rupal valley, then follow its edge up towards the pass. Olivier, wary of the growing development and terrain ahead, turns back to Tarashing.

Now alone, out over the ice, cloudbase begins to rise, so I keep pushing on up the centre of the glacier, into the meteo wind, until the lift fails. Looking back towards Tarashing and the way I have come, the whole valley is obscured by overdeveloped cloud. Caution says I should glide home while I still have the height, but first I have to take a quick look close to the Rupal face, just to see if it's lifting. Somehow it works, there's lift, and soon I'm dolphining along in the lee, sheltered from the wind by the huge massif of Nanga with snow flurries bouncing off my Icaro visor.

My gamble's paid off, and soon I've escaped the big lee-side cumulus. A couple of quick climbs have magically put me at 6,300m above the Mazeno pass, where a whole new blue world opens up on the remote west side. I can see down into the barren brown Indus river valley 40km away, and then on northwards to Rakaposhi and K2, more than 100km off. More importantly, the air is much better, with only the smallest milkiest cumulus occasionally marking the sky. The tour is on!

Almost without considering it, I'm off on the glide into 50km of utter boonies on the back side of an 8,000m mountain. The first big obstacle I have to cross is the huge Diamir glacier. With thoughts of Reinhold Messner stumbling down it exhausted and alone, having lost his brother after the summit, I cut the glide as close to the serac-threatened face as possible. Now it's a competition, a race against time and commitment rather than caution to clear the wilderness before I lose the power of the sun. The penalty for failure will be a painfully long walk. I obsessively watch the massive ridge on the far side of the Diamir glacier, calculating my glide angle against the height of the ridgeline, my potential prison wall. I'm not going to make it. I'm not going to clear the ridge, so I focus all my attention on hitting it at just the right point, where any thermals would be tracking up a weak gully line. Down below is just ice. This steep 1,500m wall of rock is the only chance.

And then I see it. The smallest whisper of milky air above where I'm heading, negating that horrible sinking feeling as I power on, stiff legged, towards the rock face, my tiny little Mamboo dwarfed by the enormity of this arena of rock and ice. The sink gives way to turbulence, then lift, and soon the wing is stood on a tip amongst a blurred kaleidoscope of ice, rock and snow, spiralling upwards into the welcoming sky.

Next it's the big Raikot glacier, with the Fairy Meadows, a trekker's paradise, out of sight in the distance. Then the Bulder glacier, which is crossed after half a climb, because time is running out rapidly. I'm hurrying along the northwest face as quick as I can, but the shadows are still getting longer, running up the valley walls, and announcing that the end of the day is close.

I turn the corner on to the northern flanks of the mountain and finally glide back into the Astor valley and civilisation. Crossing the lower gorges, I'm limping home on a helping valley wind, but as I get lower and lower it's obvious that the wind is too strong in this tight V-valley. The fairytale ending back at Tarashing is not to be, so I land high up with no one to welcome me.

Happy to be on the ground, happy to be able to walk off alone, I've geographically closed the circle but it was really more of a spiral, because I'm still 9km from home. By the time I reach a house it's dark, and everyone is preparing to eat. It's Ramadan and no one has eaten since dawn, so I'm ushered in to sit cross-legged on the floor and break the fast with the family, before they kindly find me a jeep ride home. The perfect end to a day's wilderness journey... Maybe only in Pakistan.

The next day, our last, is absolutely amazing. It's post cold frontal, but I last only an hour in the air, before the extreme sub-zero temperature of this winter air removes any pleasure. Olivier, duvet jacket bulging with a massive digital camera, is annoyed at his lack of foolishness in not following me into the ominous conditions of the day before. He makes the second flight over the Mazeno pass, before giving in to frostbite and making it an out and return. His frozen enthusiasm on the Tarashing landing field said it all. He had made the hardest crossing without even managing to take out his camera. He'll be back for more!

John Silvester was a top-class climber before taking up paragliding in 1988. He broke the European distance record in 1994, and was British paragliding champion in 1995. In between extraordinary paragliding adventures – one of which is described by Bob Drury elsewhere in this book – he lived in North Wales. John Silvester died in 2021, aged 60.

Finding Kiwi

Andy Pag

The Nevada desert downwind of Spanish Peak (3,012m) is nicknamed Nevadastan by the pilots who fly there. It's not just because of the remoteness of the dusty, roadless terrain, but also for the unforgiving aerial assault of brutal 10m/s thermals that whip up into the thin air over the scrubby 12,000ft peaks. Dodging summer dust-devils can make this place as inhospitable as paraglider flying gets, but Nevadastan can also deliver 5,000m cloudbase, big triangles and 200km flights. For James 'Kiwi' Johnston, on 22 August 2020, it tragically delivered his final flight.

Three hours after launching, Kiwi's Garmin inReach satellite tracker posted a position 1,670m (5,500ft) over Nine Mile Peak (3,072m) in Nye County, southwest of the small town of Eureka (population 480), and 115km from take-off. Then it stopped transmitting, and to the outside world, Kiwi vanished. The mystery of what happened to him would taunt his friends and family for the next month, and bring them together to search for him in death.

Originally from New Zealand, 53-year-old Kiwi started flying in the US in the late 1980s, and was among the pioneering Jackson Hole pilots who first left the ridge to find thermals. The risks were high, and the equipment and the techniques were new and unproven, but that was all part of the attraction. His interest in flying had grown out of skiing, and he lived a ski-bum lifestyle, cherishing the identity of being part of the extreme sports community.

In the years that followed Kiwi carried that search for the extreme and his love for the alternative into other parts of his life, becoming an acknowledged expert on psychedelics and a key member of the Burning Man community, an annual festival in the Black Rock Desert, also in Nevada.

He wrote three books about his experience with psychedelics, most successfully The Tryptamine Palace, about his life-changing experience with 5-MeO-DMT, a drug found in the secretions of Sonoran Desert toads and in some plants. The almost literally mind-blowing experiences that it invokes when inhaled as smoke can deeply affect its users – former heavyweight boxing world champion Mike Tyson said it changed his life. Clearly not for the merely curious, with the resurgence of interest in using psychedelics to treat mental health it's being investigated for use in patients with treatment-resistant depression.

Rob Whittall, the 1991 Paragliding World Champion, was one of Kiwi's closest friends. The pair met in 1993 "over a bong", as Whittall tells it. "He had an incredible exploratory and vast mind. Whether weed or psychedelics, he was very happy to bend and twist reality into what he wanted it to be. He had so much up top you couldn't cloud it with anything."

As a celebrity psychedelics author, Kiwi was known by his nom-de-plume James Oroc, and introduced on the speaking circuit as "his generation's premier psychedelic philosopher". His books, talks and stories could have profound impacts on his readers. One fan, Nicole Christianson, said that in the wake of his disappearance: "James's writings helped me a lot. I have found much peace through them. I feel blessed and honoured to have found them."

Kiwi's wing sported the number 420, a coded reference to cannabis, but among the flying community he played down his association with psychedelics, perhaps fatigued by the need to demystify their use, or perhaps fearful of the stigma that might come from a community so understandably safety-conscious and conservative.

"This incident has nothing to do with psychedelics," said Rob Whittall, who strongly defends Kiwi from any suggestion that he may have been impaired while flying. "He was flying in Nevada knowing it's extreme, and using an inReach and oxygen. He might have had a puff on take-off, but that's not the anomaly for him. He wasn't reckless with it. He was very studied with what he did and what he knew."

A large gregarious man and a joyous raconteur, Kiwi lit up friendships around the world. He was occasionally accused of talking up his own self-image, and his brusque, self-confident ego could sometimes leave him with bridges to mend, but he grew to value the friendships from each of his three different identities deeply. By the mid 2000s, Kiwi had seen so many fatal accidents in the sport that he parked his glider and focused on kitesurfing. By then he'd moved to New Orleans to be closer to the psychedelic community, but following his divorce a few years later he got back into the sky.

Interviewed by Gavin McClurg for the Cloudbase Mayhem podcast, Kiwi reflected on how the risk levels had changed over his 30 years of flying: "In my twenties, it was the absolute perfect sport. We were lunatic 20-year-olds. And now in my fifties, it's the perfect sport. It's been progressing with me."

"Kiwi was a fixture for years," recalled Bill Belcourt, a longtime US pilot who was a key figure in the search to find him. "We'd camp together at comps. He was one of the core guys in the community since the early days.

"We didn't see each other a lot, but we've seen each other regularly for 25 years. I'm not a Burner, or psychedelic journeyer, but he was a good solid pilot, a good guy to hang out with and fly with. One of the brothers."

A few years ago, his fellow New Zealander Matt Senior suggested that Kiwi should try to qualify for one of the small number of spots on their national team, and the idea seemed to have lit a fire in him. Close friend and neighbour Jenny Blow found among his possessions a list Kiwi had handwritten entitled "Life Goals Left". "Represent NZ @ Worlds" was at number six, with "Fly Karakoram" at number one.

In his last three years Kiwi had travelled to flying competitions around the world, flown at altitude around Keylong in the Indian Himalaya, chased distance in Brazil, and spent months at a time living and flying in Colombia and Mexico. Along the way he clocked up a couple of reserve throws and some minor injuries. By February 2020, he'd already racked up a respectable score of 789 points on XContest from four flights in Colombia, always flying his trusted Ozone Zeno (EN D).

"He wasn't flying a wing above his ability," said Robbie about Kiwi's last flight. "In terms of ability, he had the right to be where he was. He was a very proficient flyer. But he wasn't a natural. He had to learn how to do these things, and sometimes in the more aggressive moments of flying, being a natural can be the difference between a good outcome and bad outcome."

In the Cloudbase Mayhem interview Kiwi acknowledged this. "I'm flying more due to good luck than good management. And I've watched a lot of great pilots not be as lucky. So I feel really fortunate about that." Eventually, that luck ran out, and people from all his tribes came to look for him.

The Burners are said to have sourced information from military insiders, using secret satellite technology to locate Kiwi's non-responsive inReach. As many as 35 remote viewers, savants who claim to use psychic powers to see a target, provided hints to his whereabouts.

Without knowing Kiwi, one of the remote viewers mentioned a frog and other details that implied a connection to him. He also provided Kiwi's neighbour Jenny Blow with a location name: 'Steak Pass'. A google search revealed a Beef Pass on his expected flight path.

Nervous about leaving any stone unturned, Jenny's husband drove by it to look around and eliminate it from their list. The military satellite scan didn't lead to the discovery of his tracker either, but in a way these unorthodox attempts reflected Kiwi's persona.

IT programmers meanwhile created a website that allowed an army of 500 online volunteers to compare old and new satellite imagery of the area, methodically searching for white shapes that might be wings. Countless square miles were scoured, generating leads.

On the ground those leads were followed up by 30 volunteers who appeared at the scene within a day of the alarm being raised. Mostly US pilots, equipped with an understanding of the terrain, the possibilities, and the odds, they brought with them eight planes, a helicopter, drones, 4x4s and hiking boots. $97,000 was crowdfunded to pay for the search, and the family posted a $10,000 reward.

Co-operating with the local sheriff and state search and rescue teams, Reavis Sutphin-Gray, who had been flying with Kiwi on the day he went missing and raised the initial alarm, and Bill Belcourt co-ordinated the air and ground search teams. They prioritised and deployed resources to different areas and eliminated promising leads as they were checked.

As an author, Kiwi liked to draw comparisons with Hunter S Thompson, the creator of Gonzo journalism, who believed in living a more interesting life than the subjects he wrote about. Many searching for Kiwi harboured the hope he would soon turn up with a smile on his face and an amazing yarn to explain away all the anxiety over his disappearance. Bill Belcourt admitted there were frustrations when assessing which leads to prioritise, and anxiety about making the wrong choices, knowing Kiwi could be counting on them for rescue. "Rocks, sand, Winnebagos, farm equipment. We investigated so many white things," he said.

But as the days passed and the window of survivability closed, the search morphed into an opportunity to process and accept the loss of their friend. Individuals had their own lingering threads of hope, and even if they seemed strange to the others, they needed to be eliminated to allow grieving.

After a week the sheriff's office stepped down its active search. Seventeen days after his disappearance, over 100 volunteers had taken part in the search, but reluctantly they packed up, leaving contact details with the local hunting community. Meanwhile Kiwi remained hidden, invisible under a tree about 15km from his last known location.

Kiwi's sister Kim Johnston and Rob Whittall left the search site to begin the solemn process of sorting through his home and possessions in New Orleans before preparing to return to New Zealand.

"In the last few years he'd become more open and communicative with the family," Kim said. "He appreciated our parents are ageing, and he'd gotten a lot closer. He'd been over for a Christmas at home.

"It was amazing to meet all his friends, they filled in a lot of gaps, and told me about the trips and adventures that he'd had. Lots of war stories come out with emotion."

Rob said, "I was struggling massively with the open-endedness. How can it finish there? There was nothing. When there is no clue, it's hard to do anything other than thinking and worrying."

When all the foot teams, helicopters, military satellites and psychics had moved on, all that was left were paper posters taped to Stop signs that flapped patiently in the same desert breeze that blew over Kiwi's body. Then, on Wednesday 16 September, one of the posters caught the eye of a couple of local mine-workers, and prompted them to think back to the billowing fabric they'd seen earlier in the day.

When their shift finished, they drove back to find it. Sure enough it was Kiwi's wing. It was just 15 metres from a track that the search teams had driven along multiple times, but without the right breeze it was obscured from view by vegetation. Rob Whittall and Bill Belcourt had flown over the spot in a helicopter at least twice, scanning the ground for exactly this needle in the haystack of landscape, but it hadn't revealed itself.

Two days later, on Friday 18 September, a small team including the local sheriff and Bill Belcourt found Kiwi about 2km from where his wing had been found. His body had come to rest under a tree; his harness was intact, and no attempt had been made to deploy the reserve. In a reserve deployment test done at the scene, the packed parachute pulled out normally.

The following Monday, the Eureka County Sheriff's Office stated the cause of death as "multiple blunt force trauma due to high elevation fall."

"It's a personal loss for us here," Ozone test pilot Russell Ogden said in the immediate aftermath. Kiwi had been part of the scene when Ozone was founded. "He was like a brother, part of the family."

Russell led the investigation looking at Kiwi's wing and equipment, including tracklogs. In early December a 12-page report was released. It made for sobering reading, not least because it revealed that pilot error had, as so often, played its part. Emails showed that Kiwi had re-lined his glider himself in February 2019. In doing so he had used a basic lark's foot to attach many of the lines. No professional glider service centre would have made this mistake – larksfooting any rope or line degrades its breaking strength, as a rule of thumb by 30%. For maximum strength the loop of the line must be rolled back over the tab and seated properly, so the pull is directional, without bending back over itself.

Kiwi was also overweight on the glider. The maximum load of a large Ozone Zeno, the biggest size, is 125kg. Dressed for high-altitude flying and loaded with water and oxygen equipment, he was flying at an all-up weight of 130-140kg. It means he would have been flying fast, and any blowouts would be powerful.

Three hours into his flight, with a 25km/h WSW wind, at 2.27pm – the strongest part of the day – at high altitude (4,230m) and 2,200m above the ground, Kiwi hit a climb that averaged 5.4m/s over 20 seconds. A recorded peak of 13m/s suggests he hit a strong gust immediately before the incident.

Whether it was a collapse or a spin that followed, 11 seconds later the glider entered a spiral dive, "probably close to a SAT in character" according to the report. The spiral averaged -12m/s and accelerated to a peak of -23m/s. After 300m, the lines failed catastrophically and Kiwi went into freefall. The report suggests that given the steepness of the spiral, the high G involved, and the fact he did not deploy his reserve, Kiwi was probably already unconscious when the lines failed.

Further analysis of the wing showed that the left riser lines were damaged, probably through friction caused by a twist. It's thought one of those lines went first, two others followed, and then the glider unzipped.

It's easy for pilots to think "couldn't happen to me" when reading the report, because the headline-grabbers are the incorrectly lined wing and the fact he was overloaded. But the truth is more prosaic. Among the nine recommendations in the report (service your glider regularly, don't overload, be aware when flying at high altitude), the main one is aimed directly at experienced pilots. "Never allow an incident to progress to an out-of-control situation, especially on a high performance EN D or competition wing. G-forces build fast and can quickly result in a loss of consciousness.

"If you are in a situation where an unwanted spiral is developing, your first course of action, within 180 degrees of the start of the turn, should be to control/reduce/stop the rotation. This has to take priority over anything else. If you are twisted, get directional control before attempting to untwist. If necessary stall the wing, the aim is to kill the energy and associated G-forces whilst you still have the ability to do so."

It adds: "If you are unable to regain directional control and the G-forces are mounting, throw your reserve parachute immediately. This reminder is especially pertinent for experienced pilots – it is easy to believe that when high, it is possible to recover from any situation. [This incident] clearly illustrates that this is not always the case."

The impact disabled the inReach satellite tracker, giving Kiwi four weeks to lie in peace before he'd be found. Working back from the estimated drift of the falling glider, it didn't take long for the Sheriff, Bill Belcourt and a smaller search team of eight to locate Kiwi, who was just two kilometres away. The discovery extinguished any last embers of hope that he might be alive, but removed any fear that he'd suffered while he waited for rescue.

In the days following the find, both Reavis Sutphin-Gray and Bill Belcourt were exhausted. Speaking softly and occasionally faltering, Belcourt said, "I feel worked. I haven't been sleeping very good since I went out there [to recover the body]. I'm hoping to get back to normal at some point. It's just a lot to process. It comes out of your sleep." It was a hard scene to witness for all the team, even for Belcourt, who had recovered friends' bodies from the mountain before.

Both he and Reavis have been feted as heroes for the selfless effort they invested in organising the search. They both recoil from the moniker and quickly divert praise to the more than 100 volunteers that gave their time.

"I was just lucky enough to have skills that were helpful and didn't need to be back at work or looking after kids," said Reavis modestly.

"The last big thing you can do for a friend is to help their family close," said Bill. "This is our lifestyle, these are our choices, this is not the family's work. But they're forced into it when it goes tragically wrong. This is our job, we have to do this for the family."

The endeavour was appreciated. "After living with it for four weeks, it was a feeling of relief," said Kim Johnston about the discovery. "It has been a roller-coaster, up and down, but now we can stop worrying about him. I didn't want to go home without him and it's such a relief to be able to take him home." She flew back to New Zealand with her brother's cremated remains a few days later.

'He died doing what he loved' is an easy trope, often uttered to families and friends outside adventure sports in the hope that they will forgive the unexpectedly early loss of their loved one over what can seem in these moments like selfish thrill-seeking. Undoubtedly, Kiwi understood the risk of flying and the consequences of accidents better than most. In three decades of flying he was involved in searches for missing pilots and saw several friends die, so he also would have known that it's his family and his tribes of friends that carry the pain. Before flying home, Kim said, "There's always going to be a part of regret. You never want anyone to leave you. We definitely want more time with him, but I know he was loved, and loved what he was doing.

"His way of life was doing what he wanted to. He was never going to be in a retirement home. Living and loving his life. To have gone fast, and not have to suffer, you can't ask for more than that."

Andy Pag is an eco-adventurer and former BBC investigative journalist who spent two years driving around the world in an old school bus powered by cooking oil. A paraglider pilot, he worked for several seasons flying tandems in Nepal, before heading off to sail around the world.

The greatest day

Ed Ewing

In June 2012, distance-hungry pilots gathered in Zapata, Texas, as they had every summer for years, aiming to beat Manfred Ruhmer's decade-old world record. And on 4 July, long-time friends Jonny Durand and Dustin Martin did it. They raced each other wingtip to wingtip for over 11 hours, and just as the sun started to set, Dustin slipped just ahead of Jonny to claim the new world record.

Jonny came on the radio: "We just need fifty more of those and we're set!"

He and fellow pilot Dustin had just taken their first "true" 1,000ft-a-minute thermal (5m/s) to base. Jonny was right – another 50 thermals was "exactly" what they needed, Dustin said. "We did about 90 thermals the whole flight."

The two pilots were halfway through setting a new open distance hang gliding world record. It happened on 4 July 2012, a day the hang gliding world stopped and stared at a Spot track online as they watched the two pilots cover more than 700km in 11 hours. Jonny flew 759km, while Dustin managed a crucial extra few kilometres to set a new world record of 764km, the longest hang glider or paraglider flight ever.

The hang gliding open distance world record had stood for over a decade. Manfred Ruhmer set it when he flew 700.6km from Zapata, Texas in 2001. A year later Mike Barber flew 703km (438 miles) from the same place. But Mike was denied an official world record because his flight hadn't broken the previous record by 1% or more, as the world record rules dictated.

Both pilots flew during the World Record Encampment, a tow meet held each year in Zapata, Texas, and established by Gary Osaba in 2000. Gary, a pilot and meteorologist, had identified Zapata as the place in the USA to go for big distance cross country, and had put the call out for pilots every year since.

To fly here is by all accounts no small undertaking. The first 100km is across mesquite-covered desert, with locked gates and tortuous retrieves. Further north there is airspace around the town of Laredo, the 'bombout paddock' for pilots who decide the day isn't quite world record enough. After that, you have to race hard all day to have any chance.

In 2012, the forecast looked good, the best for years. Andre Wolf flew in from Brazil, Jonny Durand from Australia, and Dustin Martin from, well, Dustin drove down from Montana. It had been a while since he'd last flown in Zapata, he said when we rang him at his workshop a few weeks after the record flight. "My batteries have only been re-charging for four years, I wasn't quite ready to go back," he joked.

However, with Wills Wing keen for him to go (they covered his costs), plus a 'come fly' phone call from Jonny, he checked the forecast, in particular the wind. "And it looked amazing," he said. "Pretty much within 24 hours I was on my way."

Dustin first went to Zapata in 2000 and had done "four, maybe five," separate trips since. In 2001 he flew 200 miles (320km), but with no driver got stranded in Rocksprings. He spent the night sleeping in his harness in an abandoned storefront and later that day, "Manfred flew over my head."

That, he said, "pissed me off."

"I remember having a conversation with Manfred a few days later … and he said, 'Well, you know, with your experience and how long you've been flying, I think you're probably capable of 200, 250 max.'"

The dry humour rankled.

"I was like, man, I'll show you!"

"But I didn't show him, I think I ended up at 200 again, with no driver. And that's been my legacy every year going there."

In July 2008, though, he set a new personal best and completed the sixth longest flight ever flown, with a 410 mile (660km) monster. It wasn't good enough though: Bronze to Olympic Gold. "I was a little disappointed," he said, "considering how close I was."

After that, "the weather fell apart like it usually does after a big day, and I didn't get to go again."

That flight, his 410-miler, had been the last flight he'd done in Zapata.

'Today's a good day'

The forecast was good for Monday through to Wednesday. Dustin showed up Sunday night and set up his glider. "I'd already had a few test flights, so everything was straight." Sure enough, the next day already looked "amazing" at 8am.

Flying in Zapata involves towing up early and releasing above the clouds. Pilots then glide downwind and come in at base, and start to use the weak lift. They then work it slowly, drifting north with the wind, across the mesquite bush, past the locked gates, over the oil fields towards the more agricultural land and later, better conditions further north.

But nobody flew Monday. "It was doable, but strong. Probably 20mph to 25mph on the ground. Kind of breezy," said Dustin.

With base at only 1,000ft (300m) early on it was "just a little intimidating".

The next day, after much discussion about the day that might have been – it had been good, but had rained to the north – he was in his harness and ready to go first. Gary Osaba had briefed on the weather by group text message.

"Basically he texts things like 'Today's a good day', 'Get there in good time'."

Gary had also been up in a sailplane early. "He told us it was working." He'd also told the pilots that it looked like it might be good east of Big Spring later in the day, where convergence might set up. And indeed, "that's how it kind of turned out."

"I took off just before 10am, and released seven or eight minutes after that," Dustin said. Cloudbase was already high, at 850m (2,700ft). In the tow they passed one cloud street, levelled off and headed to the next street. He released about 50m above base.

"As soon as you release you're on your way," he said.

The first task is to drift downwind towards a road 15km away. "If you don't make that road, that retrieve will take most of the day."

After that road, there's another one 25km further on. Retrieve between these two roads "is a nightmare" but the day was working. "It wasn't really easy to get to base for that first 50km," said Dustin, "but around Laredo, at 70km, things turned on pretty well."

Base had risen rapidly and was at around 2,000m, with a "strangely consistent" tailwind already well established. That wind averaged 35km/h in the climbs and about 50km/h in the glides all day.

Dustin said. "It was definitely showing that difference – where the drift of the thermals is a little lower than the wind between the thermals."

He averaged 75km/h for the first two hours. "The day wasn't amazing up to that point," said Dustin, "but it was definitely on."

Where's Jonny?

Behind Dustin, with only one tug and a 15-minute turnaround time, Jonny had taken off second. By the time he was in the air Dustin was 10km downwind. "It took me 180km to catch up to him," Jonny said.

They had been talking over the radio and arranged to meet above an airfield approaching the 200km mark, where they found a climb. Dustin was "sort of relieved," when Jonny arrived. "I didn't want to be pushing out and taking chances."

Both pilots knew it was in their interests to stay together – but they also knew they couldn't let the other get ahead. In the thermal they took a breather. "We had something to eat, talked about what we were going to do," said Dustin.

From there, "It was just like any race ... we were wingtip to wingtip 70 to 80% of the time."

Jonny agreed: "It was just like racing ... like a competition task but you're doing it for 11 hours."

For pilots in Zapata, the Texas Hill Country is notorious. It's a remote, rugged landscape that stretches from the Mexican border into central Texas. When Will Gadd set the paragliding world record here in 2002 he described it "as though God had rumpled up the landscape like a carpet". If you landed out here, he said, "You could seriously die of heat exhaustion and dehydration."

Here, at around 300km, just past where Manfred had flown over his head 11 years before, Dustin got low. They had shared a rough thermal together and Dustin "jumped the gun" and left early. "I just got hammered. Hammered all the way down to two grand. And that's where I stayed."

He was at 700m above the ground, "but it felt like I was on the deck." It wasn't too much of a surprise, he explained. "I always get low there, in the hill country. I just can't figure it out."

He tracked 30km across the hill country, drifting in zeroes, before he could make a move. "Jonny was at base to my left a few miles away. I definitely had to calm down and find a climb." He wasn't panicking too much though. "You know, we're at 200 miles (320km) and there's no way he's going 300 more on his own. We need to work together. I figured at some point alone he would make a mistake and I would catch up."

"Six to eight thermals" later, according to Jonny, Dustin had caught up. From there, the day really switched on, with 1,000ft a minute (5m/s) thermals the order of the day.

Racing hard

The aim of both pilots was to smash the record, not just break it. Both wanted to fly 500 miles – 800km. Jonny, said Dustin, was flying "a smarter, higher line" than he was. "He wasn't hanging back, but he would stop in a thermal I would pass through. He would take a 400 or a 500ft a minute (2 or 3m/s)."

The topping-up technique worked. "You know, Jonny's a great pilot, he pretty much knows what's happening ahead with just a glance," Dustin said. "I'd go ahead because it looked better. And then I'd get low and he'd be on top of me, and I'd be asking 'How'd that happen?'"

Dustin was racing Jonny as much as flying with him. "It was pretty involved having Jonny right there and racing so hard. I think I glanced at my GPS knowing that we'd passed 300 miles, I glanced at it again knowing we'd passed 400. That was pretty cool."

Just before that 400 mile (640km) mark, the pair had to cross to the west "pretty hard". With the sun low at 7pm an "amazing" convergence line was throwing shade across their path to the right for tens of miles. "We were nervous about that, but I dove over there at 50mph," said Dustin. "It worked out for me. I rocked into a 900-up all the way to base, kind of unexpected." By the time Jonny came over he was 300m lower. "That's where we started our separation," Dustin said.

"We'd been together, and we just went to one cloud and he went one side and I went the other," said Jonny. "He caught a particularly good climb and that allowed him to get away from me a little bit … he had three good climbs in a row."

Dustin pushed ahead by about 12km. "I was getting 900 after 900 to base at over 10,000ft. So that street was worthwhile," Dustin recalled. Meanwhile, Jonny, "didn't think I'd see him again, to be honest."

As Dustin made his way 30km or so down the street, everything to either side was drying up. "Only this street that we were on was surviving, all the way to 500 miles. We had literally crossed streets 10 or 15 times during the day and we ended up on this one."

This was the convergence cloud Gary Osaba had predicted would be there, about 50km east of Big Spring. How on earth had he known that?

"I think he got lucky!" Dustin laughed. "He's usually pretty good but it seems impossible to predict where a 9pm cloud street is going to be."

Either way, the development was east of Big Spring, Dustin and Jonny were there and "it was perfect", Dustin said.

However, it was getting late.

"At 435 miles I knew that Mike Barber's record was going down, and I was high, so I was watching my GPS to see it click over," said Dustin.

He had last seen Jonny about half an hour before and he didn't expect to see him again.

"I just couldn't imagine him putting all that together that late in the day. I just imagined he was low, scratching and was going to be on the ground. That I was going to have the record."

He allowed himself a tiny moment of celebration. "I was going to break the record, it was going to be me."

Then: "Sonofabitch, I circled a couple of times, and glanced at my instrument to see the miles and there on the horizon, coming right at me, I saw a hang glider."

Here's Jonny

During the flight Jonny's mic had stopped working. He could hear but couldn't transmit.

"Dustin was getting confused with what the driver was telling him," Jonny said, "thinking that the driver's position was my position. So he thought I was 25 miles behind him, when in fact I wasn't that far. He just didn't realise that."

However, Jonny was still surprised to see Dustin. "I think we surprised each other," he said. "I was on glide and the next thing I know he popped up right in front of me on the horizon."

Dustin "just couldn't believe that he'd made it," he said. In fact he thought for a moment it must be another pilot, perhaps flying from Big Spring.

Jonny got to Dustin's thermal almost at the moment that they both crossed the line to break Mike Barber's unofficial world record. "We were wingtip to wingtip, right next to each other, again, at exactly 438 miles," Dustin said. He literally hung his head. "I was a little bit beat at that point. Mentally beat that he had caught up so quickly."

The pair had flown for 10 hours, "And now we're starting from scratch again, head to head."

From there it was a matter of "circling, circling, circling" as the pair covered 30km over the next 45 minutes, waiting for a weak climb to improve. "But it just turned into zeros," Dustin said, "once in a while 50ft at the most."

Dustin, who said he was "as fresh as I was when I took off," said he thought Jonny was tired. "He was rocking up, stretching his back out." He didn't give it much thought at the time. All he was thinking was, "How am I going to beat this guy?"

Jonny, Dustin said, is "pretty amazing" at getting above you. It seemed "almost inevitable" that at some point, he'd get above Dustin. But instead, the pair glided from zero to zero "at least half a dozen times", each time thinking "This is it."

But the final climb didn't exist. "It was just a string of lift." Dustin said, "For 99% of that time we were right in each other's faces," at exactly the same altitude.

And then it happened, the final, crucial breakaway. On the second to last zero Jonny "got a little anxious" and left slightly early, Dustin said. "I think I did another 270-degree turn before I went after him. I was just slightly to his left and ten seconds after I went on glide I hit something. And it actually was something – it was 100ft a minute, 0.5m/s."

Dustin couldn't believe it. "I looked at him and I thought hell no, he's felt it or he'll come back. And I did a 360, then two or three 360s before you could see he was thinking 'Shit, I've got to go back.' And that was the separation. I think 300ft."

That was it. "I remember thinking, 'I am never going to be in this position again in my life. I'm going to take it for everything it's worth, every single possible circle I can take.'"

They went on glide, Dustin parked "shamelessly" 100m (300ft) above Jonny's wing. "Directly over the top of him."

Jonny, Dustin said, played the game, flying slowly, forcing Dustin to glide out front. There was a cliff ahead, their last chance for any sort of lift. Dustin got there first and flew over it at 500m. Nothing. He watched as Jonny arrived at 400m. Also nothing.

Jonny meanwhile, "was ready to land" and not playing any game, he said.

"I guess I wasn't really thinking. I thought, well, we've broken the record now, just go and land. So I kept pushing to go on final glide and he kept following me."

Jonny was also filming. "And on the last glide he stopped behind me and started circling and I didn't realise because I was trying to get video ... And I turned around and went back to him and the height that I lost doing that was what it took to get 300ft."

Dustin committed to his final glide, straight downwind. "I wanted to make sure I went as far as I possibly could before I turned around. And that's what I did."

From the air he saw Jonny land, his strobe – attached to both gliders to allow legal sunset flying – flashing on the ground. Dustin landed a few minutes later. "I took it down a little bit below a power line before I turned it around. Just to make sure I got everything I could."

The landing question

Halfway through the flight Jonny had agreed to share his retrieve driver with Dustin, and Dustin's ad-hoc retrieve, a local pilot who lives in Texas, was told to stand down. Tim Etteridge picked up Jonny first and 35 minutes later they picked up Dustin. They drove to the nearest town, Lubbock, stopped at a liquor store and then found a hotel.

"Jonny was a super good sport about it," said Dustin. "I would have been super bummed if someone had just flown over my head. It puts the whole flight into a different perspective."

For Jonny, there would be no world record. But the game wasn't over. The psychology continued for the next 24 hours as Jonny wound up Dustin over the Laredo airspace – "Jonny was sure I was a mile in" – and where both pilots had released from tow. Neither were concerns: the tracks would confirm that Dustin flew up to airspace but avoided it, and had released on tow 500m before Jonny.

But there was a "genuine question" over why Dustin hadn't landed with Jonny. After such a long flight had Jonny expected both pilots to land in the same field?

"I did, yeah," he said. "I wasn't really thinking too much about that at the end of the day. After all, he had no driver, he only had my driver, so yeah."

For Dustin however, that was "absolutely not an option." The only question in his mind "was whether I was going to pile in downwind or actually turn around. That was really the only option." It came back to his original thought – that he would never be in this position again.

Jonny conceded. "To be honest," he said with a pause, "if I was in his position I would have done the same thing."

Besides, both pilots knew that even if they had landed together there would still have been a question about who had flown furthest.

"Had we taken off at the same point, landing together might have been one thing," Jonny said. "But the fact that we were getting towed and we were releasing and that's where our flight starts, the odds are even if we landed together one was going to beat the other person anyway."

Dustin had already figured that out: "Just because you land together doesn't mean anything."

The ride home the next day took 15 minutes longer than the flight. "We drove hard!" Dustin said. Zapata stalwart Pete Lehmann checked the tracklogs and all was in order. The flights were filed with the FAI, the World Air Sports Federation and the official keeper of records.

Jonny stayed on to try again. But 800km was not to be. Two weeks later, however, he bagged the Distance to Goal record, at 521km. "If I wasn't stupid and forgot to put batteries in my instruments, I would have had a crack at taking the world record again," he said. Flying 800km, he added, "is very possible."

Compared with Dustin, Jonny's three-week trip cost him a lot of money and time. But he remained positive about flying 760km while missing out on the world record by a whisker.

"My goal was to go there and break the old world record and that's what I did, so definitely no complaints," he reflected.

Dustin meanwhile did only the one flight, then called it a day. "When I arrived I knew if I got past the record I was going to pack up in a leisurely manner, go back to my hotel, get my stuff and leave the next day. And that's what I did."

As he left the talk was of the forecast, the cloudbase, the weather, perhaps another record.

"They were talking about this day and that day and all that stuff," he said, "and I was like, 'Well, keep me informed!'"

Ed Ewing is the editor of Cross Country magazine. At the time of writing, no-one has yet come close to beating Dustin and Martin's distances.

Harvest

Hugh Miller

Five pm. An inky sky seeps through the blinds, pressing in against the living room walls. The world outside is a howling madness of low pressure systems flung relentlessly across the Atlantic; furious westerly winds blast my house's brickwork, and rain pellets penetrate the cracked paint. Summer seems long gone. The only tiny reminders of the flying season are the antics of the gulls that soar the hurricane winds as I walk home from work. Before dusk, they streak across the apartment blocks, tight white bodies with hunched wings that barrel about the sky, revelling in its mad energy.

It's a far cry from the summer of 2004, which has to go down as one of the best seasons ever for the UK's small crew of XC pilots. Cold fronts continued to sweep in, coating the country with dry, cold airmasses that – with a little help from a building ridge of high pressure – kept the promise of huge distances alive.

It was to be the year that Steve Ham's UK paragliding distance record of 175km would finally fall. Steve's record had stood untested for nine years, and was in danger of being perceived as an immortal, untouchable achievement. But in June, Nigel Prior launched from Bradwell Edge, crossed the Midlands and continued into Cambridgeshire, setting a new British record of 186km. His flight track mirrored that of Richard Carter and Matt Cook, who flew the first 160km flights from the same

Derbyshire site ten years ago. But Nigel's record was short-lived. Three weeks later Kai Coleman launched from the Long Mynd and raised the bar to an incredible 190.8km.

All in all, 29 flights of over 100km were logged by pilots competing in the UK's XC League, and the consensus is there were at least fifteen truly exceptional XC days. Although not logged in such concrete figures, it is safe to say that this summer more pilots' relationships broke down and more jobs were lost than in any other year, as flyers sacrificed whatever it took to be on the right hill at the right time.

This is a story about two such days toward the end of the season. It's an unashamed, hand-on-heart tribute to British cross-country flying, and I hope it reflects a little of what's so special about flying in England, that land of tea, chips and grim weather.

August 7. Something's not quite right. It's 6.30am and I'm picking up Jérôme Maupoint from London's Gatwick airport – and he's got his glider and cameras with him. People don't come to the British Isles for flying trips, let alone legendary lensmen who require a very particular mix of blue skies, light winds and consistent flying sites in order to ply their trade. Nevertheless, as scores of British pilots flock across the English Channel for their summer flying fixes in the French Alps, Jérôme Maupoint is indeed bundling his bag into the boot of my car and we're setting off round the M25, destination Wiltshire. Jérôme adjusts his spectacles, examines the astonishingly clear skies, and passes a quizzical look across at me. "Eh, Hugh, you are sure this is England?"

We cane it down to arrive at Marlborough by 10.00, the first cumulus puffing tentatively into the endless blue above us before dissipating under the heat of the sun. We're due to meet Jim Mallinson at Milk Hill, a 300ft-high bowl facing southwest. Jim is his usual relaxed and refined self, a picture of calm in contrast to Jérôme's and my own manic excitement at the promise of today.

Bags out, boots on, squash in sandwiches, tie laces, jump fence, run up hill, throw out glider, check wind, feel sweat drip down my back under the suffocation of my jacket, take off jacket, breeze tickles the glider's leading edge open, pull risers, turn, negotiate thistles, jump cow pat, thud thud thud, lean back … and I'm airborne, scratching along to the white horse so Jérôme can snap us over the chalk mystery, flying through lumps of temptation, waiting for a bubble to come and pick us out of this tiny ridge on the English countryside.

Out west a swathe of stratus is crawling towards us. The cold air pushing in under it triggers a change: the sun's warmth makes the slope so much warmer than the air out west that suddenly it bursts into life and we're booted up 1,000ft over the hill. Things go quiet again, then we find a small thermal, and start our slow circle around our quarry, trying to pin down the core, like we're trying to push an ill-fitting key in a lock, tweaking it gently, using patience not force, our gliders slicing past each other like knives as we 360. The lift's so weak I can hear the creak of my harness, the beep of Jim's vario, the subtle shifts in wind noise as the lift changes… all the time willing the thermic equivalent of a cartoon-style jet of oil to spring up from beneath and ping us skywards.

I remember – I always do, don't know why – a line of advice etched in my mind from a technique article that Patrick Laverty wrote for Skywings magazine back in 1989: "If it's a two-up, stick with it and cut your anchor with the hill." Flatland flying in the UK is all about getting away – clearing that mental attachment to the ridge, and putting your full faith in the snotty, weak-as-shit thermal you've committed to as you drift downwind.

It takes 30 minutes of delicate and determined flying before we're finally up among the curtains of cloudbase. The sky opens up downwind: a simple reward for the work invested in climbing. Below us, the Marlborough downs extend out to the east, and Marlborough and Savernake Forest beckon downwind. The air is as clear as a bell.

Conditions slowly improve. 30km out a squadron of sailplanes whistles past, all white sunhats, waves and civilised smiles. Cloudbase has risen as we've ridden a tight corridor between the blanket of cloud encroaching from the south-west and the open blue out to the east.

50 kilometres later, and we're out somewhere over Oxfordshire at 5,500ft, trailing a blaze across the flatlands. The green pastures of Wiltshire have turned to the yellows and browns of yet-to-be-harvested crop fields, and the sky's energy has progressively improved, from Governador-style weak stuff through to Piedrahita-strength rockets that have us pinning out our bars and yahooing all the way to the next climb.

Just as I'm settling into the boom-and-zoom routine of climbing and gliding, we reach the end of the active sky. Mid-glide, Jérôme pulls alongside. He calls out: "Eh Hugh, time for the pub, no?"

Good lord! The Frenchman has been in England all of eight hours, has witnessed the best XC conditions England ever experiences, and thinks he can choose to land whenever and wherever he wants? As it happens, my arms are burnt pink and we don't encounter another blip of lift. Minutes later, we're back in the summer heat, overgrown grass up to our knees, our ears ringing from the pressure change, manic grins spread across our faces. I'm ecstatic, not just from the adrenaline coursing through my veins – but also from the pleasure of sharing one of the best days my home country has yet offered to me with Jérôme, a friend who's lucky enough to live in the Alpine paradise of Annecy. After lots of back-slapping, we ball up our gliders and stumble to the road.

"What's a paraglider then, that's like a sawn-off parachute, innit?" A community bus chugs around the corner and rescues us from an afternoon of hitch-hiking. As Jocky Sanderson says, landing after an XC is like being dropped deep behind enemy lines, and the day takes on a whole new dimension as you embark on the adventure of getting home. The driver's innocent bank-robber/aviation analogy has us in stitches, and we do the rounds of hospitals and community centres before finally getting dropped off at Newbury railway station. We eventually arrive back at the car still buzzing and in disbelief. As the sun casts a glow over the wheatfields, we drive to Jim's house for the night.

August 8. Jim lives with his wife Claudia in rustic tranquillity in a beautiful old farmhouse, Rawlings Farm. Outside, a garden table and bench sit green and warped in the grass, and vegetables grow in tilled soil. Piles of books, threadbare cushions, statues of Buddha and Indian ornaments soften the corners of rooms, and the fragrance of cumin and coriander permeates the air, a residue from the curries that are cooked nightly for visiting friends. The sun is blazing this morning. We all pile down to the river to swim and allow the cold water to shock the stony fug of last night's drinking from our minds. It's another beautiful day, but the wind's looking light.

At noon we set off back to the hill, still feeling smug inside from yesterday's success. When we arrive we find five pilots sat in stifling heat.

Small hills and nil wind is always a frustrating combination. At 200ft, you'd be lucky to get a 15-second ride before hitting the cornfields below, and the hill is less an access point into the sky, rather a small ramp to help the thermic bubbles release. But the sky is looking truly epic – white cumulus is polarised against a deep blue sky, stretched tantalisingly to the horizon.

A few sweaty walks later and yesterday is well and truly forgotten. Even a 500ft climb above the ridge would work for us now. It's a case of hunting up and down the ridge for any small hook that might lift us above the hilltop, and then hoping that the bubble might build over the ground behind take-off.

Adrian Thomas finds something, and Jérôme and I latch on tightly. We rotate skywards like a three-blade propeller. It's a five-up. At 3,000ft, Jérôme breaks away, lowers his camera, and starts flying off-set spirals, bleeding off precious altitude as he presses his shutter release. I wonder what Adrian, one of the UK's most efficient and skilled XC pilots, must think he's up to. He hitches a lift back up with Jim, who's found himself a climb, and soon we're back together and gliding north towards Avebury stone circle.

Usually, British XC flying involves a generous tailwind that allows you to drift downwind, each 360 helping you make distance. Today is different. There's almost no tailwind, and we're working for every inch of distance. RAF Lyneham looms, and with it the challenge of negotiating its airspace. We stay high above its MATZ, and concentrate on maintaining altitude until we reach Swindon, then it's game-on again. Over the next four hours I lose myself in thought as we push slowly north-west. For me, the challenge of XC flying lies as much in controlling wildly shifting emotional states as it does making good tactical decisions or keeping alert to changing conditions.

At times you're clinging onto a low save, a rock climber mid-move, dusty fingers slipping on a shallowly angled hand hold, the end of your flight perilously close, while your friends circle effortlessly miles above you. The transactional bustle of modern life – computer traumas, is-he-going-to-stiff-me paranoias, all is left behind as the mind sharpens its focus on the task at hand: staying in the sky.

Then there are those utterly blissful moments when things go way better than you'd ever imagine. You've reached base perhaps, and can't resist scooting to its side, and find a gentle 2-up that feels rougher than it actually is, because the cloud is pitching all around you, and you're feeling slightly motion-sick. Soon you're a couple of hundred feet up its side, gripped by a mix of paranoia and elation. The cloud has turned into a Jekyll and Hyde character. At times it's an innocuous, white, fluffy playfriend, then suddenly it switches, sending cold rushes of panic up your spine as it swallows you, cloaking you in its suffocating grey fog, leaving you groping for light and hope. As the greys subside and the mist clears, you can look back at the Brocken Spectre rainbow shadow behind you, and you feel so utterly alive that you shout with joy. As you pierce out into the blue, the cloud around you is like dry ice in a nightclub, your sensation of movement wildly accelerated by its proximity: ground-rush at 5,000ft.

Then there are times when you blast off at cloudbase, stamping on the bar, embarking with absolute certainty for that juicy cu over that hill downwind, almost hearing your vario's squeals before you reach it, a smug grin spreading over your face as you anticipate your utter control over your destiny.

There's the horror of arriving under the cloud and finding nothing but zeros – pushing on under its shadow with rising dread, like a cat venturing out into the garden at night, cautious of what lurks beyond. You bite your tongue, summon your inner will, and push deeper, and deeper, and still the jackpot eludes you… all the while casting one eye back at your friend who's just started to 360 off to your left… but is it good enough?

At other times you're like a dandelion blowing in the wind, sitting back, absorbed by the swirling toyscape beneath you, zoned out of anything purposeful, just drifting seemingly unseen over towns, rivers, meadows and motorways, wondering "what would life be like down there, right now?" as if you've never actually lived down there, until some stimulus – a rustle of glider fabric, a piece of straw or plastic blowing up past you – pulls your mind back to the present.

After 115km, the magic finally ends. Our flight has taken us over some of the most picturesque villages in the Cotswolds, across the sprawling estates of Gloucester, over pilots soaring the Malverns, and allowed us a peek at the rolling wilds of Wales that lie beyond. We set out on final glide towards Tenbury Wells, and land with the satisfaction of knowing that the fuel we have just harvested will last us through the winter nights to come.

Hugh started flying in 1992, and continues to have his head very much in the clouds

The LA-X

Logan Walters

It's the winter solstice. Not exactly the best time of year to go flying in the USA. We're looking out over the Los Angeles Basin. Not exactly the best place to go for a three-day vol-biv trip.

To my left is Cedar Wright, well known for his climbing and personality but totally obsessed with paragliding, and on my right is Mitch Riley, a legend in the sport and a great friend and mentor to Cedar and me.

"This is totally going to work," Mitch says, as light cycles meander up the mountain, just barely encouraged by the low winter sun. I can't help but wonder, while looking out over the urban sprawl that is Los Angeles, whether Mitch's enthusiasm is misplaced?

Is a vol-biv of the LA Basin on the shortest day of the year stupid or genius?

I launch first, holding above the terrain while waiting for my friends to come and possibly bomb out with me. There are so many question marks on this adventure. In the air we head out to the house thermal and start climbing. I'm on top with Cedar just below and Mitch 100m below him. It's up to Mitch, as the lowest pilot, to decide when to transition, and he starts his move to the east. His inner voice screams: "Turn around, you're too low!" and we all head back to the house thermal with our tails between our legs. Our vol-biv is off to a less than auspicious start; none of us want to hike the highway for three days. We are very aware that if we can't leave launch, this vol-biv might be over before it begins – stupid?

We bail back to launch and climb back up. Now Cedar is at the bottom of the gaggle, so it's his turn to lead. We aren't getting any higher than the first attempt, so we might as well try and go low. It honestly doesn't look promising, but Cedar mashes bar across a large valley towards his only hope of a climb. We follow in tight formation, sampling for the most lifty line and aiming for the base of the spine in front of us. About 5km from launch, and we are in full survival mode.

Luckily, Cedar has been training and chasing XC paragliding hard for the last six years, and in 2020 placed an impressive sixth in the US XContest – no small feat here in the USA, where we enjoy some of the most remote and rowdy flying in the world. Cedar is going to need every ounce of that experience to find the next climb, and as he begins to turn to the glorious sounds of his vario, we all exhale some relief. Mitch and I are with him before he completes his first 360, and together we crank around in unison climbing the spine an earshot away from each other. This is going to work!

We make fast moves the next few kilometres staying close. The team is flying well thanks to some team flying rules that Mitch laid down before starting the trip:

- Join each other in lift
- Work together to climb. The goal is not to out-climb your team, but to climb together, always searching for the best piece of air
- If someone opens up to search, let them back in
- When joining a thermal make sure not to affect the pilot already mapping it
- Don't out-climb your friend too much. More than 100m above your buddy helps you but won't help your team
- The lowest pilot decides when to leave and where to go
- Spread out on glide, but not more than 50m so that no one gets full 360s before you can all join
- Since it's vol-biv and it's supposed to be fun, you launch together and land together; distance doesn't matter nearly as much as the team. Adventure is better when you share it with your friends.

Mitch is our sensei. After years of racing paragliders and chasing distance records, Mitch has all the tools. When I was learning how to paraglide, Mitch was off competing in the Red Bull X-Alps, and since he returned he's been with me every step of the way, always willing to share his knowledge and push me to be better. Finally, after years of training, Cedar and I are actually able to hang with our mentor. We are no longer just tagging along holding up the rear. We are adding to the efficiency.

As the team member with the least number of years, I really don't want to be the one that lands first, forcing us all to hike. I keep my shit together as Mitch starts his trend of leaving lower and pushing harder than us. We are hauling ass, staying pulley-to-pulley as the sun stretches the shadows of the skyscrapers in the distance. Here, in the huge foothills that surround the LA Basin, it is surprisingly wild and scenic and I take a moment to enjoy the fact that this beautiful place is actually working.

Mitch makes a final transition, and scratches up to a fire-road on the ridge to top-land. Cedar and I fly two kilometres up the ridge to a larger spot and set it down about 50km and two hours from launch. We discuss our next steps. Cedar advocates hiking all night as high as we can.

"I'm ready for a sufferfest!", he says.

Mitch, however, makes it clear it doesn't always have to be about the distance, and in fact, hiking higher might actually be slower in the long run, since we have no idea if there's launchable terrain above us. We compromise on: "Let's hike for a while with no clear plan and find a nice place to camp." The adventure is as easy as getting started. Less stupid, more genius.

We hadn't said much in the air and opted not to bring radios, as we have all the information we need flying side by side. Hiking now with a running commentary, it seems like there is always something to talk about. I can't help but laugh as Cedar and Mitch argue about whether or not LA is one of the most densely populated cities in the USA. While we watch the sunset I'm enjoying the bickering.

Stepping off the dirt road to a crowded highway, people from all over the LA area are in the hills to watch the conjunction of Jupiter and Saturn, an event that hasn't happened since the year 1226. A family in a van offer us a look through their telescope and even with all our confidence combined we can't figure out how to use it. Time to walk.

"So what's our plan?" I ask, sure someone has an idea of where we are going.

"Hey Mitch, you want a weed gummy? It's good for hiking!" Cedar chimes in.

"Sweet," says Mitch, washing it down with a shot of whisky he'd ferreted away in his lightweight harness. Are these guys stupid or genius?

Cedar proposes we summit Mount San Antonio (1,897m), but with the limited service we have for checking on the weather, it's clear it might not be launchable with tomorrow's winds. The conversation continues as the fast and the furious road-racers of LA zoom by, and we dive into the bushes to avoid getting hit.

A couple hours later, the road summits and instead of walking downhill towards San Antonio, we walk around a gate on a fire-road to camp. The lights in LA are bright and beautiful, and after hours of paragliding and life talk it's time to call it a night. We really have no idea where we are, but we'll find a place to launch in the morning.

It's a leisurely morning and we decide to keep heading towards Marshall, the premier paragliding site in this area. The next step is to find a morning launch – after a couple cups of coffee of course. After less than 20 minutes of hiking we find a perfect launch. Well, it's perfect as in no bushes and the wind is blowing in, but it's facing north and we want to launch south. Plus there aren't any landing options that don't involve poison oak and eight hours plus of bushwhacking.

Cedar voices his concerns.

"If I was alone, I'd keep walking down looking for a launch because you know, I'm afraid of dying. But I'm not by myself, I'm with Mr X-Alps over here, so…" he says to Mitch, who is already unpacking his glider.

Cedar has a point. We are looking at a long glide out of deep canyons with thick brush and no trails. Mitch looks up from his glider. "Yeah, no, this looks fine." In fact, Mitch is looking deeper. He doesn't want to glide out of the canyons but instead enter its depths, heading to even more inhospitable terrain; a deep line and potential short cut, away from the subjective safety of the LA streets.

So as good teammates we agree: "Cedar, you're up."

And with his belief in us, Cedar half jokes: "Well at least I'll crash in the bushes first."

Cedar launches nervously and wraps around to the south side. Expecting to chase him down and land, I turn the corner and find Cedar 100m above launch and climbing. WTF! It's 9am and Cedar found the only thermal in California.

We climb up together feeling better about our location, and with Mitch at the bottom again we prepare for our nice glide out. But Mitch has other plans. As he goes deeper, almost 100m below us, Cedar and I can feel confident we can at least land in the bushes next to each other. Genius or stupid?

The next spine doesn't look like a sure thing, and it doesn't seem any better as we glide towards it. But Mitch is lower and he makes the call. We hold our breath as Mitch, chill as a cucumber, clears the ridge with less than 10m. We quickly realise the other side of the ridge doesn't offer any safety, only more rocks, trees, rattlesnakes, and mountain lions! He can't hold the ridge and starts his glide out the canyon, finessing his inputs to extend his glide as I tuck my legs under me to watch.

He squeaks out of the canyon, but it's not over yet. Power lines and trees everywhere, he presses the speed bar toward the other side of the canyon at a small hiking trail. Off the speed bar and a big flare Mitch executes a perfect side hill landing. Damn, he's good. I'm almost jealous of the opportunity he has to use his skills, which I have been training hard for, but at the same time I'm relieved as Cedar and I set up to land in a much less stressful flat area just past Mitch. Mitch teaches us another lesson about optimism.

Somehow, everywhere we have landed seems to have a trail going uphill. Maybe LA is a great place for vol-biv. Mitch has hooked us up with a good start, but the days are short, and so we pack up quickly and hike at a less than conversational pace to the next 'launch'. Some 700m of elevation later we reach the top of the bushy mountain, but no good launch is to be found.

Option number one is a road leaning the wrong way and a small game trail to possibly run down. Cedar opts to keep looking. He finds launch number two, which has less runway but maybe if you nail the cycle you won't swing through the manzanita too bad.

"Whatever you guys think, I'll follow," I say.

I find that for difficult launches it's best to have the person who has the clearest idea of how to execute go first and show us how it's done. After a minute of looking at Cedar's option we collectively decide to go back to the first spot. We watch with bated breath as Mitch sets his wing below him to try and forward off the winding game trail between a maze of bushes. With a deep exhale, he rocks back and powers forward like the rugby player he is and the wing inflates beautifully above his head. Two more steps and from nearly flat ground he is magically airborne.

"Well, that worked well, just do that," he says.

Cedar nails his as well and now I'm all alone watching my teammates thermal out. I give it my all as the Zeno rises above me. The left side doesn't inflate as it's behind the bushes, and it takes all my skill to keep it driving down the faint trail. I dive head first, arms stretched behind, over a pokey bush that wants to grab and stab me as the ground gets farther away. I expend a little luck! That was close but straight up and away we go.

We make quick work of the next 40km, flying together better than ever. Mitch spots a mountain lion as we chase birds towards Marshall. In a particularly rowdy thermal, Cedar shouts: "We should definitely land next to tacos!" While Europe might have manicured green landing fields, trains, and fancy espresso, here on the LA-X we have the promise of a smoggy freeway and tacos everywhere.

The final crux is the Cajon Pass that is sucking air into the desert to our north. We will need to slow down and try to get some lift off the flats. With the low sun angle in the middle of winter, that's a lot to ask, and we turn in zeros, milking the light lift. For the first time this trip Mitch is on top and before he loses it all goes on glide. I follow but Cedar is lower. We expect this is the final glide, and even if Mitch and I find something we will opt to land to hike with Cedar on the streets.

I clear the Interstate looking at the truck drivers' faces as they blast their air horns and set it down next to Mitch to wait for Cedar. Miraculously, Cedar is only a mile away on the train tracks, and as he hustles to catch us he is hard to hear over the sound of traffic, but suddenly Cedar is screaming

"NO AHHHHH" as a pitbull goes in for the attack. He goes into warrior mode, scaring off the beast with his strength and good looks.

Reunited, we walk to a cheap taco shop to load up before our hike through the city. The LA-X, as we came to call it, is turning into an all-time adventure. Rolling into the Marshall LZ at sunset, we jump in the pond to rinse off the LA grime. One more push to the campsite and possible launch in the morning. The forecast doesn't look good, lots of north wind is coming our way, but that's tomorrow, and so far optimism has been a pretty effective tool, so, tonight we set up camp as the lights turn back on in the city and our voices fill the air with stories.

At around 5am I'm pelted with small and then increasingly larger rocks blowing down the mountain in the treacherous Santa Ana winds. I roll to my side just in time to watch Cedar bolt upright awakened by the gale-force gust, and in an instant his shoes and jacket that he was using for a pillow are airborne! The LA-X might be done.

I'm stuck lying on my wing as it's my sleeping pad that I can't afford to let blow away, as Cedar limps around barefoot looking for his shoes and jacket down the mountain. I can't help but laugh in the 100km/h winds. "I found one shoe," Cedar screams. A minute later Mitch climbs up the hill holding his wing like a hurt puppy. The brutal gale ripped his wing from his rucksack and hucked and thrashed it in the bushes, leaving it torn up and unflyable. Cedar shouts as he comes up the hill with his shoes and jacket, "This is f**ked!" And just like that, the LA-X is over.

Stupid or genius? I'd say the LA-X was a little of both, which is surely true of any great adventure.

Logan Walters grew up spending more time surfing, climbing, and running around California than in school. At 16 he started flying planes and helicopters from grass strips with a lifelong pursuit of all things aviation. As the most pure form of flight, hike-and-fly paragliding has recently captured his entire attention.

MINI STORY

You will reach your destination after sunset

Andrew Craig

You will reach your destination after sunset
Dew spattering your toecaps in a distant field
As the day's last rabbit scurries to the hedgerow
You'll peer into the gloom, hoping to spot
A friendly farmer, a bus stop at least
You'll see nothing but a darkening lane
But you won't care; if you walk all night
Under the moon you'll still smile at yourself
Still circling under the clouds.

The first line of this poem was composed by Luke Nicol's instrument when he made a late start to a competition task. Andrew completed it.

Thank You

Thank you to all the writers who have generously allowed their work to be included. We acknowledge that this collection represents a fraction of the incredible stories out there, but hope they reflect some of the breadth of experience we enjoy as pilots.

Most of all, thank you to all the pioneers who have allowed us to pursue our dreams. From David Barish to Francis Rogallo, the bare-footed Californians of the 70s to the parachute-launching French alpinists of the 80s, it has taken a huge collective amount of courage, inspiration, imagination and ingenuity for us to get to where we are today. And at times, a stick-it-to-the man attitude has been required for us to gain these freedoms. We shouldn't forget that free flying owes a lot to the countercultural revolutionary thinking of the 1960s. And as increasing airspace restrictions, local political frameworks and litigation threats continue to try and ground us, we'll need to keep working hard as a community to keep the dream of flying alive for generations to come.

Stay free,
The Cross Country team

Glossary

360: a 360-degree turn, or flying in a circle. A series of 360s is the best way of keeping your glider inside the rising air of a thermal. Birds do the same.
ACPUL: a system of certifying paragliders, no longer used.
Acro: extreme manoeuvres on paragliders.
Aerofoil: a wing shaped to produce lift.
AGL: above ground level.
Airspace: areas from which free flyers are banned or restricted.
Airspeed: the speed of an aircraft relative to the air through which it is moving
Altimeter: a device to show how high an aircraft is.
Aspect ratio: how long and thin a wing is, or how short and stubby. Wings with higher aspect ratios tend to have higher performance, but can be harder to control.
Atos: a rigid-winged high-performance hang glider.
Auto-rotation: an unwanted spiral dive that can be hard to recover from.
B-stall, B-line stall: pulling one pair of a paraglider's risers to deform it and descend fast.
Bank: when an aircraft leans to one side, usually in order to turn.
Bise: a cold north-easterly wind blowing through the Swiss Alps.
Bomb out: to land earlier than you'd hoped.
Brakes: the control lines that slow down a paraglider, or steer it when one is pulled more than the other.

GLOSSARY

Canopy: the fabric part of a paraglider or parachute.

Cloudbase, cloud base: the level at which the moisture in a thermal condenses to form a cloud. Typically the maximum altitude reached on a cross-country flight.

Collapse: when a paraglider is partially or fully deflated, often by turbulence.

Comp wing: a high-performance paraglider outside the usual A to D classes. Difficult to fly.

Convection: the movement of warm air upwards in thermals.

Convergence: when two masses of air hit each other, and are forced upwards, as they have nowhere else to go.

Core: the strongest part of a thermal. As a verb, to find and stay in the core.

Crab: short for carabiner or karabiner (qv).

Cumulonimbus: a thunder cloud, often containing very fast-rising and turbulent air.

Cumulus: the white, fluffy clouds that often appear on sunny days that are good for flying. Moving under one can be a way of finding rising air.

Cravat: when a paraglider's wingtip gets stuck in its lines.

Cross-country (XC) flying: flying away from launch using thermals, usually downwind, but sometimes away from your launch site and then back to it.

Cycles: the pattern of thermals forming and moving upwards at a launch site, often accompanied by the wind strengthening and weakening regularly.

Deflation: same as a collapse.

Downwind: moving in the same direction as the wind; or a location further from you in that direction.

Drag: the aerodynamic force resisting an aircraft's forward movement.

Dust devil: a strong and turbulent thermal starting at ground level, dangerous to paragliders and hang gliders laid out on launch.

EN classes: categories of paraglider, with A suitable for beginners and D only for very skilled pilots.

End-of-speed section: the point in a competition racing task after which speed is no longer measured. After reaching it, you still have to land, at your own pace, in the goal field.

Final glide: a glide towards a competition task's goal field, or to any planned landing site.

Flatland: terrain in which there are no mountains or big hills to affect the air's movement.

Föhn: a strong and turbulent wind flowing across the Alps or another mountain range.

Frontal: a collapse of the leading edge (qv) of a paraglider.

G-force: the gravity-like sensation that affects a wing and pilot accelerating upwards, downwards or in a turn.

Glide: flying in a straight line between thermals, or in still air.

Glider bag: the large backpack that a paraglider and harness can be packed into for easy transport.

Goal: the end of a task in a competition. The aim is to land there after completing the course.

GPS: Global Positioning System, a satellite navigation system found in many free-flight instruments.

Groundspeed: an aircraft's speed relative to the ground; it may not be the same as speed relative to the air that it's flying in.

Gust front: air pushed rapidly forward by an approaching storm.

Hang glider: a usually unpowered metal-framed aircraft launched on foot. The pilot typically lies prone in a harness under it.

Harness: The fabric and webbing seat in which a paraglider pilot hangs under a wing; or the tube in which a hang glider pilot lies under a wing.

Headwind: A wind blowing against an aircraft's direction of travel, so slowing its progress over the ground.

High pressure: atmospheric condition in which the air mass over an area is descending. It often produces dry, sunny weather with light winds.

Infinite tumble: an acro (qv) manoeuvre in which a pilot repeatedly swings right over the top of his or her wing.

Inversion: when cold air is trapped under a warmer layer. This can restrict thermals.

Karabiners, carabiners: metal clips which attach a harness to a hang glider or paraglider.

Katabatic wind: the flow of air down the slope of a hill. Common at the end of a day as the terrain cools.

GLOSSARY

Kite: to kite or groundhandle a paraglider is to stand on the ground using the wind to keep it over your head. Good practice for flying.
Leading edge: the front of a wing. On a paraglider, it's where the air intakes are positioned.
Lee, leeside: the area downwind of a hill. The air there can be disturbed by its passage over the hill.
Lenticular: a flying-saucer-shaped cloud seen on windy days.
Low pressure: atmospheric condition in which the air above an area is rising. It can encourage thermals, but can also produce storms, especially in mountains.
Low save: when a glider pilot is nearly forced to land, but finds a thermal near the ground and gets high again.
LZ: landing zone.
Maximum glide: the setting of the controls at which a glider will move as far as possible forwards for each unit of height lost.
MATZ: Military Air Traffic Zone, which free flyers sometimes have to stay clear of.
Minimum sink: the setting of the controls at which a glider will descend as slowly as possible. Not necessarily the same as maximum glide (qv).
Mini-wing: a small paraglider, designed to soar in strong wind or descend from a mountain quickly.
Open class: uncertified paragliders, typically used in high-level competitions.
Overdevelopment: when cumulus clouds grow big enough to threaten rain or thunder; alternatively, when they spread out to block the sun and stop thermals.
Paraglider: a usually unpowered aircraft made of cloth and string that has no frame. It's kept inflated by the air flowing into the holes at its leading edge as it moves forwards.
Paramotor: a paraglider powered by an engine and propeller fitted behind the pilot's back.
Pimping: on a cross-country flight, hanging back to see where other pilots ahead of you find thermals. Considered unsporting, especially in competitions!
Pitch: the motion of a glider's nose up or down.

PLF: parachute landing fall, a technique for dissipating the energy of a hard landing under a parachute or sometimes a paraglider. Not needed in a normal landing.

Release: to disconnect the tow line, and start a free flight.

Retrieve: the process of getting home or back to launch after a cross-country flight. Sometimes organised in advance, but more often by hitchhiking or public transport.

Reserve parachute: a parachute carried by most hang glider and paraglider pilots to use in an emergency when control of the aircraft is lost and can't be recovered.

Restitution: the gentle, widespread lifting air sometimes found at the end of the day, especially over valleys and forests.

Ridge soaring: flying, usually to only a modest height and distance, in air that's forced up as it hits a hillside.

Risers: the webbing that connects a paraglider's lines to the karabiners and the harness. Sometimes pulled to control the wing.

Roll: the movement up and down of an aircraft's right and left wings.

Sail: the fabric stretched over a hang glider's framework; sometimes used of a paraglider's canopy.

Sailplane: an unpowered but conventionally shaped aircraft, with wings, fuselage and tail. The pilot sits inside. Often tow-launched behind a powered aircraft.

Scratching: flying low above the ground, often while searching for a thermal to climb high in.

Sea breeze: cool, moist air that flows from the sea to the land on sunny, thermic days. It often stops thermals and ends cross-country flights – although it can produce useful convergence (qv).

Sink: the descending air that free-flyers usually try to avoid.

SIV: Simulation d'Incidents en Vol, the French name for training in dealing with departures from normal flight. Usually done over water with a rescue boat standing by.

Speed bar, bar: a bar or webbing pushed with the feet that speeds up a paraglider, at the cost of faster descent.

Spin, negative spin: when only one wing of an aircraft remains flying, producing a rapid turn. Can be dangerous, but occasionally done deliberately to turn tightly.

GLOSSARY

Spiral, spiral dive: a manoeuvre used to descend rapidly. Produces very high G-force.

Stable air: air that, because of atmospheric conditions, tends to stay still rather than rising in thermals.

Stall: when a wing stops producing lift, leading to sudden and rapid descent. Can be dangerous, but can be done deliberately to clear a cravat (qv) from a paraglider.

Tandem: a paraglider or hang glider designed to carry two people. In paragliding, the passenger sits in front of the pilot. In hang gliding, the passenger and pilot lie side by side.

Task: the cross-country route set on each day of a competition. May be downwind, or in the form of a cat's cradle.

Thermal: a column of air that rises because it's been heated more than the air surrounding it. Used by all types of glider to get high and fly cross-country.

Top-landing: landing a foot-launched aircraft back on the hill from which it took off, or on other high ground.

Tow: A method of launching a glider from flat ground, using a powered winch. Sailplanes and hang gliders can also be launched behind a powered tug aircraft.

Trailing edge: the rear edge of a wing. On a paraglider, it's where the brake lines are attached.

Trike: a three-wheeled buggy slung underneath a powered hang glider or paraglider. It can make launching and landing easier.

Trimmers: devices that shorten or lengthen a paraglider's risers to change its flying characteristics. Often found on tandems or powered paragliders, where a foot-operated speed bar would be impractical.

Tumble: when a hang glider suddenly pitches down too far, so that the air presses on its top surface rather than supporting the wing. Can break the glider.

Turnpoint: one of a series of points on a competition task which each pilot must reach in the specified order. Or a corner of a triangular cross-country flight.

Tracker: a device which communicates a pilot's position, using a mobile phone network or satellites.

Trim speed: the speed at which a paraglider or hang glider will fly with no control input.

Valley wind: the breeze which typically flows up valleys into mountainous areas on sunny days.

Vario, variometer: a device which beeps in different tones to indicate how fast it's ascending or descending.

VG: variable geometry, a way of adjusting a hang glider to fly faster or slower.

Vol-biv: Using a paraglider (or rarely a hang glider) on a multi-day trip, camping in between flights. Usually done in remote or mountainous areas.

Weak link: a section on a tow line designed to break if the tension on the line gets dangerously high.

Weightshift: leaning one way or the other to help steer a paraglider or hang glider.

Windsock: a tube of light fabric hung on a pole to indicate the strength and direction of the wind.

Wingover: a manoeuvre in which an aircraft does a series of sharp turns in opposite directions. Can be used to lose height.

XC: cross country.

Yaw: the movement of an aircraft's nose and tail left and right in relation to its direction of travel.

Zero: a weak thermal, strong enough only to keep a glider at the same altitude.

Publication Credits

The stories in Head in the Clouds have been edited from original articles first published in the following publications

1973: A leap of faith, Ground Skimmer magazine, 1973

Across India, Cross Country issues 52 and 53, Aug and Oct 1997

Dreamcatcher, Cross Country issue 194, Oct 2018

The Croatian survivor, Cross Country issue 60, Dec 1998

Hard day at the office, Cross Country issue 199, May 2019

The longest day, Cross Country issue 25, Feb 1993

Big Southern Butte, Ground Skimmer magazine, 1974

Between heaven and hell, Cross Country issue 216, Jan 2021

Wake up, Cross Country issue 72, Nov 2008

Ninth life, Cross Country issue 60, Dec 1999

Blue sky blues, Cross Country issue 36, Dec 1994

Into the vortex, Cross Country issues 184 and 185, Oct and Nov 2017

On paragliding and certainty, Cross Country issue 185, Nov 2017

Breaking three hundred miles, Cross Country issue 11, Autumn 1990

The King's Trail, Cross Country issue 201, Jul 2019

The ballad of Robb and Joe, Cross Country issue 176, Jan 2017

Stewart's story, Cross Country issue 178, Apr 2017

Dosti, Cross Country issue 124, July 2009

Je suis un test pilote, Skywings magazine, 1996

Chasing the dragon, Cross Country issue 216, Jan 2021

Dust devil, Cross Country issue 198, Apr 2019

Out of practice, Cross Country issue 107, Sep 2006

Girl gone wild, Cross Country issue 190, Jun 2018

Kilimanjaro, Wings! magazine issue 4, 1979

Celebrate being alive, Cross Country issue 197, Feb 2019

Goal fever, Cross Country issue 179, May 2017

In deep, Cross Country issue 144, Nov 2012

The way of the Samurai, Cross Country issue 112, Jul 2007

One hundred miles, Cross Country issue 229, May 2022

Who's packing? Cross Country issue 150, Nov 2013

Storm over the Mediterranean, Cross Country issue 99, May 2005

Lifting the veil, Cross Country issue 178, Apr 2017

This is not a drill, Cross Country issue 189, May 2018

The Monarca expedition, Cross Country issue 218, Apr 2021

Karakoram express, Cross Country issue 197, Feb 2019

Tumble in the Owens, Cross Country issue 28, Aug 1993

The naked mountain, Cross Country issue 105, May 2006

Finding Kiwi, Cross Country issue 207, Feb 2020

The greatest day, Cross Country issue 143, Sep 2012

Harvest, Cross Country issue 96, Nov 2004

The LA-X, Cross Country issue 221, Jul 2021